Fieldwork

An Expeditionary Learning Outward Bound Reader

Volume I

Edited by
Emily Cousins
Melissa Rodgers

KENDALL/HUNT PUBLISHING COMPANY
4050 Westmark Drive Dubuque, Iowa 52002

Cover photograph: Rafael Hernandez Bilingual School (Boston) teacher Arlene Agosto de Kane works with fourth grader Washington Chang during the school's learning expedition on pond life.
Photograph by Brian Smith/NASDC.

Expeditionary Learning℠ is a Service Mark of Outward Bound, Inc.
Outward Bound® is a Registered Trademark of Outward Bound, Inc.

Copyright © 1995 by New American Schools Development Corporation (NASDC), A Virginia nonprofit corporation.

ISBN 0-7872-0229-0

Library of Congress Catalog Card Number: 94-79896

All rights reserved. No part of this publication may be reproduced, stored in a retrieval system, or transmitted, in any form or by any means, electronic, mechanical, photocopying, recording, or otherwise, without the prior written permission of the copyright owner.

Printed in the United States of America

10 9 8 7 6 5 4 3 2 1

Contents

Foreword   vii

Acknowledgments   ix

Introduction
Expeditionary Learning: A Design   xi

Part One

A Design, Not a Program   1

Building an Expeditionary Learning School Culture   3
by Emily Cousins

What We Are Learning about Learning Expeditions   7
by Leah Rugen and Scott Hartl

Expeditionary Learning in the Classroom: One Teacher's View   12
An Interview with Ron Berger
by Emily Cousins

Outward Bound Enters the Classroom   20
by Thomas Duffy

Expeditionary Learning: A Design for New American Schools   22

1. Introduction 22
2. Design Principles 25
3. Our Key Concept: Expeditionary Learning 30
4. Why Teachers Are Key to Expeditionary Learning 36
5. Role of Family and Community 42
6. World-Class Standards and Assessment and National Education Goals 44
7. How a School Becomes a Center of Expeditionary Learning 50
8. Our Structure 51
9. Evaluation and Self-Assessment 51
    Bibliography 52

Part Two

Self-Discovery   55

The Only Mountain Worth Climbing
An Historical and Philosophical Exploration of Outward Bound and Its Link to Education   57
by Thomas James

Having Wonderful Ideas
An Interview with Eleanor Duckworth   71
Conducted by Mieko Kamii

Teaching Discovery   74
by Nan Welch

School Matters: Free Your Hands
Learning Is Doing at These Schools   76
by Diane Loupe

A Willingness to Learn   78
by Meg Campbell

Walking Fine Lines   80
by Tammy Duehr and Nora Gill

Outside-the-Classroom Experiment
A School Weaves Ideas from Outward Bound into Lessons   84
by Lynda Richardson

Part Three

Educators as Learners   89

Professional Development through Planning and Design
The Mini-Sabbatical and Summer Institute   91
by Leah Rugen

Dubuque Teachers Map a New Course   98
by Mike Krapfl

A River, a Raft, and a Summit   100
by Melissa Rodgers

Northbound on an Expedition 103
by Mike Krapfl

School Visits 107
by Meg Campbell

A Principal Reflects on the First Semester 108
by David Olson

A Conversation with Expeditionary Learning Principals 110

Part Four

The School Community 115

Student Agreement for Participation in the Rocky Mountain School of Expeditionary Learning 117

Circles
"Where Everyone Knows You Really Well" 120
by Meg Campbell

The One-Day Community Exploration
An Expeditionary Learning Professional Development Experience 122
by Leah Rugen

Service: Crew, Not Passengers 126
by Emily Cousins

Students Open Shop to Keep Broken-Down Bicycles on the Road 130
by Edie Lau

A Letter in Praise of a Fourth-Grade Condor Expert 132
by Walter Peterson

What's New in the Wires
A Closer Look at Electronic Mail 133
by Melissa Rodgers

Respecting Parents 137
by Emily Cousins

School Opens Bid for New Learning Paths 141
by Janet Bingham

Part Five

Rethinking Time 143

Slaying the Time Giant
A Discussion with Harold Howe II 145
by Emily Cousins and Melissa Rodgers

Inventing New Wheels
Redesigning School Schedules for Expeditionary Learning 148
by Emily Cousins

"My January Happens in October"
A Look at Multi-Year Teaching 151
by Meg Campbell and Emily Cousins

Part Six

Standards and Assessment 155

Beginning the Conversation
Assessment in Learning Expeditions 157
by Mieko Kamii and Marie Keem

No More Mysteries 162
by Mieko Kamii and Marie Keem

Opportunity Favors the Prepared Mind
Integrating Assessment and Curriculum 166
by Mieko Kamii

Outward Bound Resources 169

Dedicated to the memory of Paul Norman Ylvisaker, former dean of the Harvard Graduate School of Education, who encouraged us all and lent us a measure of his grace and vision.

Foreword

We have said from the beginning that we are on an expedition ourselves. From the start, we pledged ourselves to living up to what we had proposed to the New American Schools Development Corporation when we submitted our original proposal to design "break the mold" schools in February 1992. There were nearly 700 original entries. Two years ago, as we were on the river bank about to embark on a Colorado Outward Bound river rafting course with the Harvard/Outward Bound Project and educational leaders from around the country, a park ranger came down to the canyon with a phone message for us: we had won.

In the twenty-four months since, our expedition has widened its circle and moved at an incredible forward pace with significant accomplishments along the way. We have kept our word.

In September 1993, new Expeditionary Learning schools opened in Denver and New York City. In Dubuque, Iowa; Portland, Maine; Boston; Baltimore; Decatur, Georgia; and San Antonio, public schools (K-12) are transforming themselves entirely or gradually into Expeditionary Learning centers working with local design partners, including Outward Bound schools and urban centers.

Our design principles and program components remain our givens, our "non-negotiables." In each site, teachers, administrators, students, parents and design partners are unleashing what Frederick Law Olmsted referred to as the "genius of local place." Expeditionary Learning design principles and program components continuously inform every aspect of school culture, space, time and curriculum.

One of the best things about being on an expedition is the permission slip one grants oneself and one's colleagues to keep learning, inventing and improvising. We have no single-answer books in Expeditionary Learning; instead we have design principles and program components we take very seriously.

Central to our undertaking is an expansive and deep commitment to fieldwork. Not only do we advocate replacing the traditional practice of field trips with student fieldwork which is directly related to an ongoing learning expedition, but we envision our collaboration with teachers, administrators, parents and students as valuable fieldwork for public education for the next century. We are learning a great deal from our successes as well as our failures, and we are committed to sharing what we are learning with our colleagues. This is the chief intent of this book.

One of our accomplishments has been the creation of a monthly newsletter, *The Web*, edited by Emily Cousins and Melissa Rodgers. *The Web*, as its name suggests, is one way for us to strengthen our connections to each other. The primary intended audience is teachers and administrators, because in our design ongoing professional renewal is central.

Fieldwork: An Expeditionary Learning Outward Bound Reader includes selections from *The Web*, our original proposal, and other reprints. It is intended as a resource for those who are Expeditionary Learning guides now and in the future. We hope you will find it useful and that you will share with us your suggestions on how we might improve it.

We offer *Fieldwork* in the spirit of shared dialogue, inquiry and reflection. We invite you to join us as we go forward, and as we pause along the way.

—*Meg Campbell*
Executive Director
Codirector Harvard/Outward Bound
Harvard Graduate School of Education
July 1994

Acknowledgments

We thank the New American Schools Development Corporation and the DeWitt Wallace Readers' Digest Fund for their generous support which makes our work possible.

Our President Allen Grossman and our Council of Senior Advisors continue to share with us invaluable support, ideas, and advice. We thank David Beim, John Collins, Eleanor Duckworth, Thomas James, Mieko Kamii, Harold Howe II, Diana Lam, Larry Lewis, Mimi Levin Lieber, Jerome Pieh, Geraldine Robinson, Suzanne Schwerin, Dennie Wolf, and Virginia Worden.

We also thank our many design partners who contributed time, creativity, and passion to shaping and implementing Expeditionary Learning in these first few years:

Academy for Educational Development; Richard Ackerman; Baltimore Public Schools; Boston Public Schools; City Year, Boston; Colorado Outward Bound School; Cooper Union College, New York; Denver, Cherry Creek, Littleton and Douglas County Public Schools; Decatur Public Schools; Dubuque Community Schools; Educators for Social Responsibility; Facing History and Ourselves; Harvard/Outward Bound Project, Harvard Graduate School of Education; Hurricane Island Outward Bound School; Institute for the Infrastructure at Cooper Union, New York; Linda Nathan; New York City Outward Bound Center; New York City Public Schools; New York Mission Society; North Carolina Outward Bound School, Atlanta Center; Portland Public Schools; Project Adventure; Public Education Coalition, Denver; San Antonio's Harlandale ISD, North East ISD and Southwest ISD; Robert Snyder; TERC; Thompson Island Outward Bound Education Center; Tri-College Consortium, Dubuque; Trinity University, Smart Schools Network, San Antonio; University of Colorado, Boulder; University of Southern Maine, Portland; Voyageur Outward Bound School.

Introduction
Expeditionary Learning: A Design

Expeditionary Learning^{SM} is a comprehensive school design that transforms every aspect of a school. It draws on the pedagogy and tradition of Outward Bound® and the writings of Eleanor Duckworth, Kurt Hahn and Paul Ylvisaker. Expeditionary Learning teachers, students, administrators, parents and community members create a school culture that embodies all of the ten design principles as well as key program components. Students' primary daily experiences are as crew members embarked on rigorous, purposeful, multi-disciplinary and project-based learning expeditions which include strong intellectual, service and physical dimensions.

Expeditionary Learning centers have significant school-based decision-making authority and operate within districts where the leadership actively supports implementation of this design. Over time, this design builds community understanding, interest and commitment to public education by offering parents and community members meaningful and rewarding involvement in supporting students' intellectual and character development and growth.

❖ Mission Statement

Our endeavor is to transform schools into centers of Expeditionary Learning.

Over a five-year period, we will work with schools to design and implement expeditionary curricula, models of student assessment, new forms of school organization, programs for staff development and systems for evaluation, replication and dissemination.

❖ Preamble

Learning is an expedition into the unknown. Expeditions draw together personal experience and intellectual growth to promote self-discovery and construct knowledge. We believe that adults should guide students along this journey with care, compassion and respect for their diverse learning styles, backgrounds and needs. Addressing individual differences profoundly increases the potential for learning and creativity of each student.

Given fundamental levels of health, safety and love, all people can and want to learn. We believe Expeditionary Learning harnesses the natural passion to learn and is a powerful method for developing the curiosity, skills, knowledge and courage needed to imagine a better world and work toward realizing it.

❖ Expeditionary Learning Design Principles

1. The Primacy of Self-Discovery

Learning happens best with emotion, challenge and the requisite support. People discover their abilities, values, "grand passions" and responsibilities in situations that offer adventure and the unexpected. They must have tasks that require perseverance, fitness, craftsmanship, imagination, self-discipline and significant achievement. A primary job of the educator is to help students overcome their fear and discover they have more in them than they think.

2. The Having of Wonderful Ideas

Teach so as to build on children's curiosity about the world by creating learning situations that provide matter to think about, time to experiment and time to make sense of what is observed. Foster a community where students' and adults' ideas are respected.

---

[1] The above principles have been informed by Kurt Hahn's "Seven Laws of Salem," by Paul Ylvisaker's "The Missing Dimension" and by Eleanor Duckworth's *The Having of Wonderful Ideas" and Other Essays on Teaching and Learning* (New York: Teachers College Press, 1987).

3. The Responsibility for Learning

Learning is both a personal, individually specific process of discovery and a social activity. Each of us learns within and for ourselves and as a part of a group. Every aspect of a school must encourage children, young people and adults to become increasingly responsible for directing their own personal and collective learning.

4. Intimacy and Caring

Learning is fostered best in small groups where there is trust, sustained caring and mutual respect among all members of the learning community. Keep schools and learning groups small. Be sure there is a caring adult looking after the progress of each child. Arrange for the older students to mentor the younger ones.

5. Success and Failure

All students must be assured a fair measure of success in learning in order to nurture the confidence and capacity to take risks and rise to increasingly difficult challenges. But it is also important to experience failure, to overcome negative inclinations, to prevail against adversity and to learn to turn disabilities into opportunities.

6. Collaboration and Competition

Teach so as to join individual and group development so that the value of friendship, trust and group endeavor is made manifest. Encourage students to compete, not against each other, but with their own personal best and with rigorous standards of excellence.

7. Diversity and Inclusivity

Diversity and inclusivity in all groups dramatically increases richness of ideas, creative power, problem-solving ability and acceptance of others. Encourage students to investigate, value and draw upon their own different histories, talents and resources together with those of other communities and cultures. Keep the schools and learning groups heterogeneous.

8. The Natural World

A direct and respectful relationship with the natural world refreshes the human spirit and reveals the important lessons of recurring cycles and cause and effect. Students learn to become stewards of the earth and of the generations to come.

9. Solitude and Reflection

Solitude, reflection and silence replenish our energies and open our minds. Be sure students have time alone to explore their own thoughts, make their own connections and create their own ideas. Then give them opportunities to exchange their reflections with each other and with adults.

10. Service and Compassion

We are crew, not passengers, and are strengthened by acts of consequential service to others. One of a school's primary functions is to prepare its students with the attitudes and skills to learn from and be of service to others.

❖ Program Components

1. Schedule, Structure, Teacher-Student Relationships

Expeditionary Learning requires a complete reconsideration of the relationships among staff and students, as well as the schools' arrangements of time and space. Schools must eliminate the fifty-minute period and replace it with a schedule organized to accommodate learning expeditions that may engage students full-time for periods of days, weeks or months. Tracking is eliminated. Expedition guides teach the same group of students for periods of several years.

2. Curriculum

Expeditionary Learning engages the learner in situations that provide not only context but consequence. Interdisciplinary learning expeditions replace subject-separated classes. The curriculum makes intellectual learning and character development of equal importance and encourages self-discovery.

3. Assessment

Expeditionary Learning uses real-world performance as the primary way to assess student progress and achievement. Assessment reflects world-class student performance standards, as well as world-class standards for curriculum, instruction and opportunities to learn.

4. Staff Development

Expeditionary Learning depends upon and invests in the ongoing development and renewal of staff. An apprenticeship model, flexibility in hiring or reassignment and a substantial investment in year round staff growth is required.

5. Linkages to Community and Health Service Organizations

To provide necessary support to students and their families, Expeditionary Learning centers will develop working relations with the appropriate service agencies.

6. Budget

Expeditionary Learning achieves its goals through reorganization of existing resources and should not require significant additional funding after an initial period of transition.

Expeditionary Learning may be implemented in existing schools which commit themselves to school-wide transformation as well as in newly created schools organized around the philosophy embodied in the ten design principles and key program components. Educators must choose Expeditionary Learning; it cannot be mandated. Once school-based councils and faculties have decided to create new or to transform existing schools into Expeditionary Learning centers, in concert with the active support of the district's leadership, the design process begins. Local partners, including higher education institutions, often play significant leadership roles as well.

Expeditionary Learning has an impact on human relationships, standards, curriculum, pedagogy, assessment and school organization. The principles and program components are non-negotiable; they are the roots that nourish this design. The commitment to redesign time and space and to deepen and restructure every relationship is the trunk of the tree. The design components are the branches that offer height and breadth. One element cannot be separated from another. Each part of this design is integral to the whole. Because it calls for so many changes, it requires more than an alteration in curriculum or scheduling or any isolated aspect of school reform. Our design calls on adults and students to embark on an expedition themselves, in the process renewing themselves as individuals, as a school and as a community.

The power of our design is the creativity, confidence, teamwork and imagination unleashed through the collaborative, supportive and challenging process of embarking on different kinds of expeditions as well as designing and guiding learning expeditions consistent with rigorous standards. Human and natural resources are enlisted in this effort; virtually any parent or community member may become a significant participant, and any natural or community setting may become a field site in the course of a learning expedition.

The design calls for a dramatic paradigm shift, particularly for the implementing teacher, who must make the commitment to teach students for at least two consecutive years. School schedules are changed so there are longer blocks of flexible time and common teacher planning time. The teacher's self-definition and role is expanded to that of a collaborative curriculum designer whose own ongoing professional development is fueled by the continuing intellectual growth required to create learning expeditions for, and ultimately with, students.

Every educator who works in the school, whether specialist, Chapter I teacher, special needs teacher, librarian or counselor, is also engaged in designing and supporting learning expeditions. Designing learning expeditions becomes a shared experience for the entire faculty and offers a common vocabulary, understanding and approach which in turn rests firmly upon the foundation of the design principles and program components. The process and act of writing *Learning Expedition Guides* with colleagues is a difficult, engaging and deeply rewarding intellectual and social experience. Issues of standards, assessment, technology and pedagogy are addressed, and more critically, owned by the teachers themselves through this process. These works-in-progress are available for sharing across Expeditionary Learning sites, and the directory by topics is frequently updated.

Since educators play a central role in implementing the design and creating learning expeditions, staff development is the keystone of Expeditionary Learning. Traditionally, staff development has focused on isolated techniques or programs without addressing the fundamental issues of personal and professional transformation or learning how to learn.

This inner transformation accelerates and supports the outwardly visible changes in every aspect of school design. Individual change in turn facilitates and accelerates group change and vice versa.

Structured professional development experiences for educators and community leaders and partners vary in length from one day to more than one week. They foster and support inner transformation, thoughtful reflection and imaginative collaboration. "If it makes sense, it can be done" becomes the operating mode, so that what were previously seen as barriers and obstacles now appear as challenges to be navigated around or through. Traditional turf issues are recast as problems for the group to solve. The thread throughout the work is higher standards for students' intellectual achievement and character development. The backdrop is compassion, perseverance, integrity, joy, adventure and challenge.

Professional Development Experiences

Our design calls for a sequence of professional development experiences for teachers and administrators that includes a combination of newly designed and specially tailored professional development and renewal courses. Every professional development institute or course that we offer seeks to model the design principles by inviting educators to be learners. As educators build their own, experience-based understanding of the Expeditionary Learning design principles, they can use them to create schools that embody them. We also use a "Full Value Contract," the tool developed by Project Adventure, whereby Expeditionary Learning teachers and administrators construct their own ongoing contract to foster communication and integrity in implementation of the design principles and program components.

A one-day community exploration experience is recommended as a first step for all faculty in Expeditionary Learning schools. This one-day experience allows participants the opportunity to work in small groups to identify, interview and compile potential field sites and resources for future learning expeditions as well as reflect on the implications of the design principles in their own work.

The mini-sabbatical conducted by Expeditionary Learning Outward Bound is a five-day, nonresidential, intensive curriculum-writing institute that simulates an Expeditionary Learning classroom where the teacher becomes the learner. Twenty to twenty-five teachers work together in small groups to design multi-disciplinary thematic projects which are consistent with district outcomes and Expeditionary Learning standards and design principles. Teachers identify community resources and experts to assist them in carrying out the learning expedition. Teachers are afforded the opportunity to present their work-in-progress to colleagues to support a culture of revision and excellence.

The ten-day summer institute also facilitated by Expeditionary Learning Outward Bound is site-specific but includes redesigning existing schedules so they support Expeditionary Learning, sequencing learning expeditions consistent with rigorous standards, and further developing learning expeditions.

Additionally, educators participate in one or more of the following courses which are offered by design partners and which are tailored to support implementation of Expeditionary Learning design principles and program components: Outward Bound immersion courses in the wilderness and the city, designed and offered by Colorado Outward Bound School, Hurricane Island Outward Bound School, New York City Outward Bound Center, North Carolina Outward Bound School, Thompson Island Outward Bound Education Center and Voyageur Outward Bound School; Adventure in the Classroom

Samidh Guha, a teacher at Winston Middle School in Baltimore, takes earth samples at the Geology Summit. Photograph by Elizabeth X. Maynard/Expeditionary Learning.

and Adventure-Based Counseling five-day residential courses conducted by Project Adventure; and residential summer institutes with a strong curricular focus offered by Facing History and Ourselves and Educators for Social Responsibility. Teachers participate in five-day residential intellectual expeditions or "summits." Principals also participate in specially tailored expeditions offered in conjunction with Outward Bound schools.

The Web, a monthly professional development newsletter, serves as a communication tool for Expeditionary Learning sites, Outward Bound schools, and other partners and interested parties. An electronic mail network is another avenue for cross-site communication.

Lisa Rankin, a ninth-grade student at the School for the Physical City, an Expeditionary Learning school in New York City's District 2, takes notes in her journal during fieldwork. Photograph by Leah Rugen/Expeditionary Learning.

Part One

A Design, Not a Program

Building an Expeditionary Learning School Culture

by Emily Cousins

Expeditionary Learning is not a program for enhancing existing structures. It is a design that transforms every aspect of a school. It reconfigures time, space, and relationships. Expeditionary Learning impacts standards, curriculum, assessment, and school organization. Because it calls for so many changes, it requires more than an alteration in curriculum or scheduling or any one piece of school reform. Expeditionary Learning teachers, students, administrators, parents, and community members create a school culture that embodies all of the ten design principles as well as the key program components.

Since teachers play a central role in implementing the design, staff development is the keystone of Expeditionary Learning. Traditionally, staff development has focused on isolated techniques or programs without addressing the fundamental issue of personal and professional transformation. This inner transformation accelerates and supports the outwardly visible changes in every aspect of school design. The Expeditionary Learning summer development institutes triggered that transformation for many teachers.

Like the mini-sabbaticals in the spring in which teachers designed learning expeditions, the summer institutes modeled the design principles by inviting the teachers to be learners. As the teachers experienced the principles firsthand, they discovered they could use these principles to become the creators of their schools. These principles are the tools they can use to build a school community that has scaffolding for challenge, shared space for collaboration, and room for growth.

❖ The Challenge

This summer, every Expeditionary Learning teacher ventured into the unfamiliar, whether it was the New York teachers searching for water in the Catskill Mountains or the Denver team creating the schedule for a new school. These challenges called for a great deal of courage, for they demanded that people think and work together in ways they never had before. People who had lived in New York City all their lives learned to understand the flow of mountain streams. Administrators whose schedules had always been dictated by Denver-area stipulations worked in the absence of rules and regulations. People were willing to take these risks because of a sense of personal commitment and group support.

Expeditionary Learning is not a program. It is a design that transforms every aspect of a school.

They believe the challenges helped them understand the meaning of the design principles. When teachers discussed their experiences this summer, they expressed a sense of achievement. They believe that with each challenge they surmounted, they contributed to the Expeditionary Learning culture in their school.

❖ Outward Bound Wilderness Expeditions

The Outward Bound expeditions offered the teachers firsthand experience of the design principles. Many of these experiences will have far-reaching effects on how teachers will interact with their colleagues and students. The New York City teachers went on an Outward Bound expedition into the Catskill Mountains. "It was very rugged and physically challenging," describes Leah Rugen, formerly of New York City Outward Bound. "The group responded to the challenge and I think they are only just beginning to tap the benefits of that group experience. You could see it in the way they

Mary Lynn Lewark, from the Rocky Mountain School of Expeditionary Learning in Denver, on the school's ropes course. Photograph by Scott Hartl/Expeditionary Learning.

related to each other throughout the summer and in their amazement at what others were able to accomplish."

Kathy Sheth, the mother of a Central High School (Dubuque) student, also felt the benefits of teamwork and collaboration. Sheth was one of 50 Dubuque teachers, administrators, parents, and community members to attend a Voyageur Outward Bound canoeing expedition in the Boundary Waters of Minnesota. On the trip, she sprained her ankle and aggravated an old knee injury. Instead of letting that slow her down, she soaked her ankle in streams, elevated her ankle with rocks, and distributed some of the weight in her pack to the rest of the group. "We made do with what we had," she explains. "We all worked as a team." Sheth makes a connection between the successes and failures on the trip and the first year of implementing Expeditionary Learning. "It sounds like it is going to be fantastic. I realize it is not going to be perfect in the first year. They are going to have to work up to it. Just like we did on the expedition. We were all ready to go, but we had to make stops along the trail."

Sheila Schultz of Central Alternative High School (Dubuque) says the Boundary Waters expedition demonstrated the importance of self-discovery. "We expected our guides to have all the answers," Schultz explains. "Even as adults we waited around to be told what to do. It struck me how important it is for teachers to ask the kinds of questions our guides asked us. When we asked them a question, they would ask us, 'Well, what do you think? Do you have another idea about this?' When the guides let us figure out the answers, we got to experience the thrill of learning. It made me rethink my role as a teacher. It helped me put the focus back on the students."

❖ Summer Institutes

Every Expeditionary Learning site participated in summer institutes designed to address scheduling and the designing and sequencing of learning expeditions. Many teachers also attended professional development institutes hosted by design partners Facing History and Ourselves, Educators for Social Responsibility, and Project Adventure. While the institutes explored many topics, Scott Hartl, an Expeditionary Learning school design specialist, believes that writing learning expeditions was the cornerstone of the summer development.

In learning expeditions, students and teachers combine intellectual inquiry, physical activity, and community service to explore a particular topic or theme for a period of at least three weeks. The process of drafting an expedition has the design principles embedded within it. When the teachers write their expeditions, they experience the same learning process that they will provide for their students. Once they know how their students will be learning, they know what kinds of schedule, planning, sequencing, and development are needed to support it.

◆ ◆ ◆

A closer school culture is needed to make Expeditionary Learning work.

◆ ◆ ◆

"Working on the expeditions injects Expeditionary Learning into the heart of the school," Hartl explains.

After designing expeditions that include periods of solitude and reflection, the teachers now make sure there is time for it in the schedule. "During the first institute," Central High School (Dubuque) principal David Olson says, "solitude and reflection were scheduled in after lunch every day. But in the second institute, it was up to the teachers to schedule them in within their working groups, and they made sure they did it." Now that teachers have expeditions that require a flexible schedule, they are willing to work hard to use it well. "Flexibility requires great things on the part of the professionals who are going to operate a flexible schedule to make sure that it yields the results that we want," remarks Barbara Volpe of the Denver Public Education Coalition. "It has been very challenging, but it also has incredible opportunity attached to it."

> If the principles fail to become a way of life, then we have negated all that we have put into Expeditionary Learning. What makes this school different should always comes back to these principles.
>
> — *Lesley Stephens*
> *Bryant Elementary School*

Discovering new possibilities and the having of wonderful ideas are central tenets of Expeditionary Learning. As the teachers work to provide these experiences for their students, they realize they too can benefit from them. Helen Shelton, assistant principal of Winston Middle School in Baltimore, says, "I tell the teachers that we are the forerunners in developing expeditions for the middle school setting, and that we shouldn't be afraid just because there is nothing ahead of us. Don't be afraid to be creative and think of new things. If it doesn't work, we'll turn it around and do something different."

❖ Building a School Culture

In order for expeditions to be successful, there has to be a supportive learning culture alive within the schools. Throughout the summer institutes, teachers turned to the principles of intimacy and caring, the responsibility for learning, collaboration and competition, and diversity and inclusivity to help map out an Expeditionary Learning community. Ron Berger, a teacher at Shutesbury Elementary School in Shutesbury, Massachusetts, and a facilitator at the Dubuque Summer Institute, observes, "The teachers all acknowledged that a closer school culture was needed to make Expeditionary Learning work. They understood that Expeditionary Learning is not just about designing themes. It is also a new way of working together as a staff. It is making sure that the staff is not isolated in the way it was. It is team teaching and collegiality. It is supporting fellow teachers to take risks on academic and emotional levels."

Berger was impressed with the Dubuque teachers' level of commitment to Expeditionary Learning. "I have been a part of a lot of restructuring initiatives and generally some people are on board and some of them are not. But in Dubuque, everybody was on board. Everyone on staff was really enthusiastic and interested in trying all of this."

Teachers at the institute could feel a change in the atmosphere, says Dubuque Bryant Elementary School teacher Fran Kennedy. "The biggest change that occurred in the summer institute was that we had a caring learning community. We got to know people in other schools and to appreciate their expertise and hard work. If you are having trouble, you know you can call them. That is what I want for my students: a place where they can learn and where they are cared for."

Many of the staff and teachers present at the institutes wanted to underscore the connection between the supportive atmosphere and the design principles. Bryant Elementary School principal Lesley Stephens said, "I want people to come into the school and ask, 'What is it that makes our school unique?' I want to be able to say it's because we take time for each other, we have intimacy and caring, solitude and reflection, service. I want our school to be a hallmark of those principles. I don't want to have service when it fits into the day. I want it to be a way of life. If the principles fail to become a way of life, then we have negated all that we have put into Expeditionary Learning. I think we should be able to say that what makes this school different always comes back to these principles."

❖ Team Building

Team building is the life-blood of a supportive school culture. People are willing to take risks and strive for high standards when there is trust and respect among colleagues. Unfortunately, working as a team has not always been encouraged in schools, and collaborating in new ways can seem difficult. Many teachers found that the structure of the institutes helped them work together in way they never had before. Jean Cobb, a teacher at Winston Middle School who comes to teaching from the military, explains, "I am not used to getting consensus on things. I am used to saying, 'Okay, this is what you need to do, this is how you do it, and we'll make corrections at the end.' I am changing my way of thinking, and it is hard." While it may be difficult for some teachers to learn how to work collaboratively, Cobb thinks it is essential. "If we are going to teach students how to build consensus, we have to know how to do it ourselves."

The trust that results from working in a team can help teachers rethink how they work together. As Maria Campanario Araica, director of instruction at the Rafael Hernandez Bilingual School (Boston), points out, people in a team have to be flexible. At the Hernandez summer institute, she worked in a team in which the new members of the group wanted to make changes in a learning expedition that the other members had already started. "It really strengthened us in terms of working together, because it made us feel like we had to get consensus. It was all right if we pulled the expedition apart and put it back together again in a bunch of different ways until we felt we were all happy with it."

School counselors in Dubuque are also exploring new teaming arrangements so they can support the Expeditionary Learning culture. For instance, a teacher who is doing an expedition on families, instead of simply asking a counselor for a packet of information, will invite the counselor to get directly involved with the expedition. Counselors will work with the students who need individual or small group interaction, but they will also work with the adults to teach them the valuable skills of conflict resolution and initiative debriefing.

Lincoln Elementary School principal Kathy Kolarich sees the counselor's office as a model for the whole school. "When you walk into a counselor's office, as a child or an adult, you know you are going to have a listener. There is a trusting environment. I want an Expeditionary Learning school to have that kind of feeling. I want it to feel like a counselor's office where you have the trust and support of everyone."

Cal Chaplin, the principal of the Portland Regional Vocational and Technical Center, wants to make sure that teachers pass on the lessons they are learning about working as a team. "The culinary arts teacher came back from an Expeditionary Learning event and said, 'I assign students in teams, we do a little preliminary work, and then I wonder why it falls apart. I want to be more deliberate about making sure team-building happens every day and that we spend time with it.'"

The teachers discovered that they could use the design principles to become the creators of their schools.

Expeditionary Learning is a design because it influences everything from the way the culinary arts teacher works with his or her students to the way solitude and reflection are scheduled into the day. The principles are not simply suggestions. They are the roots that nourish this design. The commitment to redesign time and space and to restructure every relationship is the trunk of the tree. The design components are the branches that we climb upon. One element cannot be separated from another. Each part of this design is integral to the whole.

What We Are Learning about Learning Expeditions

by Leah Rugen and Scott Hartl

"I felt like a real scientist looking into a microscope and when I found the specimen I felt awesome. When you are done with the expedition, you go home and tell your mom and dad what you learned and they practically don't even know what you are talking about. It's like you wrote a new chapter in the encyclopedia. Six weeks ago I would never have known about pond life." (Journal entry by Dallas Kalmes, a fifth-grade student, Dubuque, Iowa.)

In Expeditionary Learning schools, students like the one above spend most of their days in school embarked on purposeful, rigorous "learning expeditions" which include strong intellectual, service, and physical dimensions. Learning expeditions are sustained, in-depth studies of a single theme or topic that generally take four to nine weeks and are the core of the curriculum. Intellectually rigorous projects and purposeful fieldwork are the center of each expedition, and are part of a vision and strategy for assessment that is fully integrated with curriculum and instruction.

Expeditionary Learning Outward Bound was one of nine projects funded for five years by the New American Schools Development Corporation in 1992 to create "break-the-mold schools." A design team of educators from Outward Bound, schools, universities, and educational organizations from around the country shaped a plan for school change and created ten design principles and components (see the Introduction, "Expeditionary Learning: A Design") which encapsulate Expeditionary Learning's purpose and philosophy. As we begin our second year of implementation, Expeditionary Learning is taking root in eleven elementary, middle, and secondary schools in five primary sites around the country: Boston; Denver; Dubuque; New York City; and Portland.

We have found that an intensive focus on teaching and learning through the development of learning expeditions has been a lever for whole school change. As we collaborate with teachers in planning and thinking through a new structure for curriculum, we are simultaneously immersed in questions of professional development, the organization and support of school change, and the communication of ideas within local sites and across a national network.

The conscious use of fieldwork is perhaps the most visible and radically different dimension of learning expeditions.

At the Rocky Mountain School of Expeditionary Learning in Denver and the School for the Physical City in New York, teachers are involved in creating whole new schools as well as learning expeditions. No aspect of school design—schedule, governance, physical space, transportation, or attendance systems—can be taken for granted. And in transforming schools, teachers have quickly realized that the implementation of learning expeditions has implications for every aspect of their schools, particularly for the use of time and space.

Expeditionary Learning did not materialize on a mountain top. It has deep roots in a tradition of active learning which includes the history and ideas of Outward Bound. It is also part of a growing national initiative to make active learning more intellectually rigorous and accountable. The learning expedition, as a new concept of curriculum design, owes much to research and practice in theme and project-based learning, early childhood education, cooperative learning, writing process and whole language theory, and interdisciplinary curriculum development. Through its explicit joining of intellectual and character development, and its tapping into the metaphor and structure of an expedition, the learning expedition has the potential to extend students' learning in powerful new ways.

The equal value and importance of intellect and character ring throughout Expeditionary Learning's ten design principles, calling for attention to dimensions of learning that have rarely received explicit acknowledgment in schools. Service, time for reflection and solitude, and the personal attention of small groups are integral parts of the learning process, not just supplements. As a metaphor, an expedition draws students and teachers out into the world.

❖ The Shape of Learning Expeditions: Getting Students to Think Deeply and Work Cooperatively

Within a range of different school settings—elementary, middle, and secondary; urban and smaller city—Expeditionary Learning teachers are testing the boundaries of what it means to plan and implement learning expeditions. Some expeditions focus on two academic disciplines, while others tie together multiple disciplines such as math, science, humanities, and arts. Some are four to six weeks in length, others last three months. All share the common goal of getting students to think deeply, work cooperatively, and serve the wider community by creating a meaningful context and purpose for learning. All are prompting teachers to raise common questions and face common obstacles.

The organizing center of the learning expedition is the theme or topic. A good theme is intriguing and open-ended. It defines the territory of the expedition but also generates questions. It naturally cuts across disciplines, though some themes lend themselves more to one discipline than another (*Our City, Ourselves*; *Pond Life*; *Water*; *Urban Renewal*). Guiding questions shape a theme and give it further definition. They are the basic tools of intellectual exploration and give a learning expedition a structure of inquiry. At the School for the Physical City middle school, the question "How can we tell when a community is thriving?" gave focus to the theme *Our City, Ourselves*. Across all sites, as the initial learning expeditions unfold, teachers are weighing which themes and questions work and which seem too broad or narrow. They are considering the role of the student in developing guiding questions and in shaping the expedition plan. At Dubuque's Central Alternative High School, teachers include students in planning meetings, offering them academic credit for effective participation.

Teachers quickly realized that the implementation of learning expeditions had implications for every aspect of their schools, particularly for the use of time and space.

Sifting through the spectrum of possibilities for learning goals and developing a focused set of priorities is one of the toughest challenges of planning a learning expedition. When a team of teachers at King Middle School in Portland, Maine, recently convened to plan a learning expedition, they wanted to ensure that they could still satisfy the major objectives of their school for each discipline. One of the team members, a social studies teacher, discovered she had the flexibility to address aspects of world culture, but not American history, which was the school-wide focus of the following year's curriculum. Similarly the science teacher needed to focus on biology. The language arts teacher knew her students should focus on writing a major research paper and persuasive essays.

After a lively discussion of possible themes that would allow the teachers to address each of these needs, they settled on *Endangered Species*. Through this theme, students, in their social studies work, would examine the complex interactions between humans and the environment of endangered species in selected non-American cultures using a case study approach. Their science work would focus on the ecological issues; and math would include the collection and presentation of data on endangered species.

A learning expedition is shapeless until ideas for projects are developed. Working on projects comprises much of the intellectual journey and destination of a learning expedition. Projects within a learning expedition unify and ignite student learning by calling for concrete products or actions which address authentic problems and situations. Ron Berger, a sixth-grade teacher from Shutesbury,

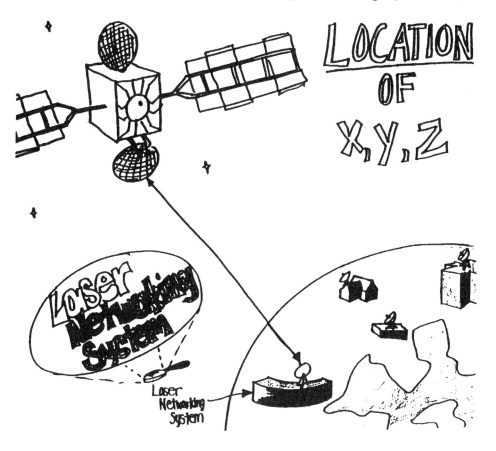

For a learning expedition combining physics, pre-calculus and computer science, Sarah Palmer, Sara McIlveen and Zack Keefe asked, "How are satellite dishes aimed in order to receive information from satellites?" These students from Deering High School, an Expeditionary Learning Spirit school in Portland, Maine, made this drawing to help demonstrate the answers they found.

Massachusetts, and a consultant to Expeditionary Learning, refers to projects as "the main arena in which students apply, extend, and showcase their skills and understanding."

After the group of King teachers chose their theme, they brainstormed ideas for projects that would integrate the social studies and science content with writing. The projects on which they agreed included a debate, a campaign to inform the school and community about endangered species issues, and an in-depth research paper on an endangered species. Although they had included research papers in their curricula many times before, the teachers realized that the common focus and interdisciplinary connections would give the paper added power as a learning tool.

One of the tensions in developing projects is finding the balance between group and individual assignments. The experience of many teachers points to the value of designing projects which include a significant amount of individual work. Such work ensures student engagement and gives teachers the opportunity to obtain information on the strengths and challenges of each student, providing a body of work from each student for assessment purposes. Individual projects do not mean that students work in isolation. Rather, students can help each other through sharing skills and resources and critiquing each other's work without sacrificing their individual products.

It is also possible to plan group projects that have specific components which are clearly the responsibility of each individual student. For example, in the field guide to a local pond completed by fifth-grade students at the Table Mound School in Dubuque, each student was responsible for his or her own page in a common field guide. As students become accustomed to project work and develop strong work habits and high standards for their work, group projects inevitably grow stronger.

A driving question in the planning of learning expeditions has been how best to prepare students for sophisticated projects. Such preparation occurs over time through an array of tasks and experiences which develop and stretch students' background knowledge and skills. It requires the cultivation of habits of work, thinking, and judgment that come through the daily rituals of reading, writing, problem-solving, and discussion. Most important, preparation for sophisticated work relies on the development of a strong school culture and community with a common vision and experience.

The conscious use of fieldwork and service is perhaps the most visible and radically different

Two students at the Rafael Hernandez Bilingual School in Boston use a microscope. Photograph by Brian Smith/NASDC.

When fieldwork is joined with meaningful service, the consequences and purpose of learning are made even clearer to students. Middle school students at the Hernandez School in Boston surveyed community members to determine the best uses for several vacant lots near the school. When they presented their plans and scale models to parents and community members, a local environmental organization decided to use one of the proposals in actually developing one of the lots. Not only did the students feel that their ideas had been heard and respected, but they had a chance to make a needed contribution.

However, like every other aspect of learning expeditions, purposeful fieldwork and service are extremely challenging to plan and carry out. They require flexible scheduling and rethinking the grouping of students and the roles of all school staff. Field experiences need not be elaborate or long-distance endeavors. Much can be learned from a walk in the neighborhood surrounding a school, by interviewing the driver of a milk truck, or developing an ongoing relationship with a local nursing home. Visitors from the community—experts, parents, and neighbors—bring the outside world into the classroom.

❖ Beginning with Teachers: Collaboration, Planning, and Time

The complex, collaborative process of implementing learning expeditions must be supported by a new definition of professional development. Rather than something packaged and delivered by experts, professional development at Expeditionary Learning schools is an ongoing, site-based enterprise which taps into a large network of resources and experience and recognizes the central role of teachers. During the school year and summer, in week-long planning institutes or "mini-sabbaticals," teachers collaborate to select themes, define and prioritize learning goals, create guiding questions, develop project ideas and fieldwork sites, and establish interdisciplinary connections.

Perhaps the most important facet of collaborative professional development is ongoing daily and weekly time for planning and assessment, and administrative support in establishing the schedule and school culture to reinforce it. Sufficient time and psychological space to allow for messy, recursive debates and discussion are not found easily

dimension of learning expeditions. It quickly creates a new set of school norms, as clipboards for field notes and journal entries join blackboards and 3-ring binders as essential school equipment. Teachers are discovering the multiple purposes of fieldwork—for immersion into a theme or topic, deeper investigation and research, team-building and adventure—as they find their way through barriers of tradition, planning, logistics and safety, and time. They are throwing away the old, passive model of field trips in which students reluctantly followed a guide through a museum or business. Instead, teachers are guiding students outside to interview passers-by, sketch buildings, measure shadows, and make detailed observations. Students are venturing out to answer questions and follow leads that cannot be looked up or found easily in text books, enriching their project work with evidence gleaned from experience.

amid the clamor and hectic pace of schools. Even when a school schedule has been designed or redesigned to allow for longer blocks of time and common planning, the daily complications of students' needs and demands competes with teachers' needs to reflect and plan. One inevitable dilemma is that teams of teachers must grapple with the tough issues of planning, classroom management, and assessment at the end of a challenging day of teaching.

What does it mean to collaborate? How does one learn how a colleague thinks? How can we develop shared goals and assumptions, and equally divide responsibilities? Key ingredients make the planning process go smoothly and effectively. First, there must be extended periods of time (a week or more) away from the distractions and hectic pace of school life. Second, the planning groups should be kept small (no more than four or five). Third, the teachers should have the autonomy to select a theme and develop the parameters for their learning expedition. Finally, although the creative, professional autonomy of the groups of teachers is key to the process, the role of guiding facilitation is indispensable. Facilitators of the planning institutes help to provide an organizing structure, an outside perspective, and an array of supporting resources. The end result is a powerful, effective, collective enterprise.

The complex, collaborative process of implementing learning expeditions must be supported by a new definition of professional development.

The founder of Outward Bound, Kurt Hahn, had a vision of education that captures the spirit of our endeavor: "I regard it as the foremost task of education to insure the survival of these qualities: an enterprising curiosity, an indefatigable spirit, tenacity in pursuit, readiness for sensible self-denial, and above all, compassion." The hard work and creativity of teachers and administrators working in collaboration are changing every level of school organization and culture. The evidence is found in the way faculty meetings are conducted, in the growth of new structures like community meetings, in the involvement of parents and community members, and most of all in people's willingness to experiment and take purposeful risks.

A version of this article appeared in the November 1994 issue of *Educational Leadership*.

Expeditionary Learning in the Classroom: One Teacher's View

An Interview with Ron Berger

by Emily Cousins

Ron Berger is a sixth-grade teacher and a member of the Expeditionary Learning Outward Bound Teacher Advisory Board. In the following interview, he discusses his interpretation of Expeditionary Learning and his process of designing thematic units. Berger teaches at the Shutesbury Elementary School in Shutesbury, Massachusetts. For over fifteen years, this elementary school has taught all of its students through project-based learning.

There are 215 students in the school, with class size ranging from fifteen to thirty and special needs students fully mainstreamed. Many classrooms have only one full-time teacher, and spending per student is well below the state average. Despite these constraints, Shutesbury's project-based program continues to inspire students of all skill levels to meet rigorous intellectual standards and to create exceptionally polished work.

At Shutesbury Elementary, teachers choose projects based on what their students have done in the past and what they will need to know for the future. At weekly staff meetings, teachers review the projects to insure the students are receiving a well-rounded education. Students work on many drafts until they have a finished product that is so good they want to share it, perform it, publish it, or give it to the community. In this process, each step prepares the students for the next level of their learning.

How do you start designing a thematic unit?

I choose one thematic study, and within that theme, a number of projects. Every teacher in the school uses that approach, but everyone uses it differently. A theme for one teacher may be three weeks; for me it is usually three months or longer. Also, lower grades tend to do shorter units, and the upper grades do longer ones. But the extent to which they integrate all of their work into that theme depends on the teacher's style.

We don't have pre-made themes; teachers invent their own. The process of building thematic units is so important that I really don't like to package them. I do have a few write-ups, but I would never go to a workshop and say, "This is my geology theme, this is how you should do it." I do take students' work and show slides and give an example of a theme and then brainstorm with people about themes they would want to use. But a theme that is being studied has to be managed to suit the class, the local culture, and the teacher's own interests and strengths. Otherwise, it won't be deep and rich.

The notion behind every theme is to have the students become experts in that area.

What level of immersion do you prefer?

I tend to go on to the extreme side of the very long, entire immersion style of themes.

So all elements of the school day are contained within the theme?

Yes, except math. And it is a notable exception. We've played for years with, "Can we integrate all our math?" There is no way to do it without being forced. There is a lot of math in our studies, but there is also a lot of math that kids need to learn that is not connected at all to geology, or oceans, or India, or whatever you are studying. So every teacher has a separate math time in their day.

How do you choose the themes?

The first step is choosing a thematic topic that has some level of intrinsic interest for this teacher. Teachers bargain to get themes they are interested in. The other issues in the bargaining are what themes have the kids had in the past, and what themes do they need to balance out their education. If kids have had a lot of biological science, I will do a physical science. Some teachers have themes they return to on a cyclical basis. I do.

Could you define what you mean by a theme? Is it a topic, a discipline, a subject?

A theme could be Japan. It could be geology. It could be a concept: independence, revolution. I did one on law and justice.

A theme has to suit the class that is being worked with, the culture the class is embedded in locally, and the teacher's own interests.

How do you build a theme?

The first thing I do is go to every teacher I know in every school and ask if anyone knows anyone who has done this theme already. And when I find out who did, I interview them (even if they did the unit for kindergarten) and I find out what resources they used, what books, what projects they did, what local people they used.

I need to learn a lot about the subject, and I start with children's books. Because not only are they handier to use and helpful, but it is easier. And then often I go on to higher-level books. But I often go to the young adults' section and get out every book on Japan. You want to build up a library of the ones you want to use for class later on. You want to look for what fiction and nonfiction books would be important to use with the whole group, either as read aloud or as multiple copy. You can get lots of resources to work with individual children, but finding a book you can use as a general resource is an important step.

For geology I use *Tom Sawyer* because we spend a big portion of geology on cave exploration. It seems like an obscure fit, but it is a great piece of literature, and a lot of it takes place in the cave, and it just meshes so well. So one thing is finding a book that will work as a whole class, and the other is finding a whole resource for informational books on that subject. Where can you get them? Does your school or local library have them? etc.

Every teacher here always brings in outside experts, but usually well into the theme when the kids can appreciate the experts' expertise. And the expert is usually very impressed with the level of expertise of the children, so it is a very nice blend. The culmination of a unit is bringing in that paleontologist or whomever, and having mutual respect and excitement. And it is almost a given that experts who come in get so excited that they want to return, because kids here really do become experts in a way that most adults are not.

How do projects fit into the themes?

Finding a few good projects that will fit with the whole is the most important part. A unit will sink or swim based on the appropriateness and complexity of the projects that you have picked to integrate into the theme. You can know a lot and read a lot about it, but if you don't have really creative, exciting projects for kids to do, it won't work as an expedition. So I often brainstorm with other teachers. I try to make a list of every local expert in the area and figure out which ones will be good resources. Some may be good for me but not with kids.

Then we all plan field trips; as many field trips as we can fit in. We do not have a lot of money for field trips, so we often plan fund raising as well. If you are really lucky you can plan fund raising that fits into your unit. So, a unit takes me a couple of months to put together. I spend most of the summer putting together a new unit, that's why I don't do a new unit every year. And while I am doing a unit, I continue to work on it. The unit I am doing currently is one I've done before, this is my fifth time doing it in fifteen years. And it's a sure fire success. I already have the experts, I have the field trip sites, I have the materials, I have the projects figured out.

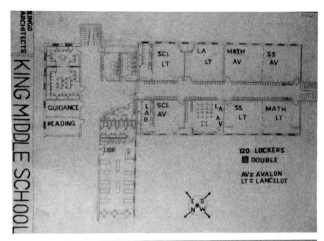

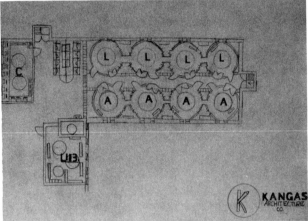

Pictures of the draft process: architectural drawings from King Middle School in Portland, Maine. Photograph by Scott Hartl/ Expeditionary Learning.

Can you talk about what makes a good project?

My idea of a good project is very different from many other people's. When I am sharing my ideas with other teachers, a lot of it is explaining my definition of project. I always set it up as a comparison to the science project model that was around when I was in elementary school. A science project meant that the teacher would say, "In a month you have to bring in a science project." And that was it. That was the level of support. And in that model, the work was outside of school; it had no connection to the curriculum. Kids with a lot of support at home did very well; kids with no support either did well if they were talented or they struggled. They didn't have the organizational skills or resources or abilities to do it. And when the project actually happened, you couldn't compare because every one was unique. Kids couldn't learn from each other very much because every one used a different structure and different style of knowledge. The work was never critiqued and prizes were given and that was it.

The project model here is that projects are done in school primarily. Kids bring projects home to work on, but school is the center for the project. That is so the projects can be the structure through which skills are taught. If the project is done at home and is not connected to school work, then you have to have school work that deals with skills in isolation. So one of the criteria for a project is that it has to be a good medium for teaching the skills you want to teach; researching, writing, editing, reading, or learning to find the main idea of a piece, or a scientific concept. So you need to build a project that uses the skills you want the kids to learn.

The current project kids are working on is about caves, and they are writing a novel about a group of people lost in a cave. They studied caves, as a part of science and geology. And they went cave exploring, so they know what it is really like to be in a cave situation. And we did cave drawings, which were a lot of work. There were weeks of learning how to do drafting work, and doing elevation projections of a cave. So some kids are stronger in the writing section, some kids are stronger in the art section. And some of them are not really strong in either, but were incredibly brave in the caves. It was an area for them to shine, by being strong and heroic when we were actually doing the exploring. Some of the novels are stronger in the fictional part, some are stronger in understanding the geological basis of caves.

> You can know a lot about a topic and read a lot about it, but if you do not have creative, exciting projects for kids to do, it will not work as an expedition.

A good project for me is one that should last a while with kids, with time and care put into many drafts. And we always find a way to share the project with the larger group at the end of it. Maybe an exhibition or a show or reading aloud to parents or other kids in the school, or something on video. Kids always know what they are doing is going to be shared. So there is a reason to do a good job. It may be used for real work in some way. It may be used by the town or a committee. A project might be going out and interviewing all the senior citizens to create a book about what seniors in town are doing. In another project, we mapped the entire downtown, interviewed all the store owners, and made guide books of the downtown for kids. That took all kinds of different skills and strengths. Some were stronger writers, illustrators, mappers, historians; some were better interviewers.

How Much Do the Students Get Involved in Planning the Projects?

I am more uptight than other teachers using this kind of approach, and most of the projects are pretty well spelled out before we even begin. But students always bargain with me about every project. There is a kind of informal family-like atmosphere to the room anyway, so we always have suggestions. I always try to put a little choice within their realm of negotiation; kids can dream up their own things. Let me give you an example. For the geology study, we will probably do about eight field trips, some of which will be expensive. We will be going to New York City to museums and jewelry stores. We need to do some fundraising, so we are going to set up a rock and mineral and jewelry store. Kids will be working over the fall tumbling rocks, collecting crystals on our field trips, and making jewelry. Then we will have a store to sell these things to the people in town.

Now in one way this is my idea. I know what I want, I know how to get the store set up, I know what we will be collecting, I know how to do the tumbling [a process through which rough rocks become smooth and lacquered]. I know how to do the jewelry-making. On the other hand, the kids will be running the store. They'll be setting it up physically, they'll be determining what prices they will use, they will be handling all the money, they'll be depositing the money in the bank, they'll determine all the policies that the store uses. I want the store to be in their hands in a Foxfire kind of way. Eliot Wigginton put kids in charge of Foxfire, and let them make decisions. But it was really his idea. Kids can come up with suggestions, but if I am going to do a unit for a long time, I need to plan it out ahead of time.

The school is the center for the project. That is so the projects can be the structure through which skills are taught.

Last year I did a world geography study the whole year, and the big culminating project was putting together an exhibition, and in the exhibition were many projects that had been worked on during the year. And they each invented a country, but it had to be believable, so believable that no one would know it was fake. They had to be experts in that area of the world, in geography, and history, and politics and distribution of resources.

We ended up setting up a booth for their country. And I told them all this at the beginning of school. The first week of school we discussed that by the end of the year they would be such experts that they would be able to put this together. I had never done this before; it was an entirely new unit for me. But over the course of the year we constantly discussed what should be in their booths. And many of the components I would have thought of, but I just let the kids dream up all the components. We ended up having mandatory components; they had to have a report on their country, they had to have a flag, they had to have some artifacts. Then there were these optional ones; kids did food from their country, they did stamps, clothing, music.

So a lot of it was in their hands. They had to figure out how to set up the fair. Those were their decisions. So as much as possible, I let kids take responsibility. But only within the frame that I feel comfortable with. I am often willing to take suggestions from kids about where to direct things.

What kind of assessment do you use?

I think of assessment first in terms of self-assessment. The most important thing is for kids to be assessors of what's working for them. So we do a lot of work on self-assessment, self-editing, and self-critique.

Is that done on a one-on-one basis, or is it in the overall atmosphere of the room?

It's both. We do conferencing with the teacher, peer conferencing and reading work aloud to each other, and kids edit their own work, and do many drafts of their own work. And lately, in the last few years, we have a lot of self-reflection forms that we give to kids to look at their own project and say what they liked about it, what they didn't. And we do a lot of structured critiques where we pin up work, like an architectural student does, and kids give comments on it. The only difference is that we don't make comments that hurt feelings, like an architectural school. But we do have good critique sessions. And we do a lot of partner and peer critique. Kids are always critiquing each other on their work.

We conference throughout the day. There is informal conferencing continually, and then there is formal conferencing where I ask the kids to bring me their work and we look over it together. When one teacher is working with the same fifteen to thirty kids all day, there is no reason why a teacher would not have a tremendous sense of how every kid is doing, I mean you just see the kids and see their work so much. To me, assessment is not just having a sense of the reading level and writing level of each kid; assessment is an engine for pushing the growth of the children. Good interactive relationship between the teacher and student, and the parent and the student, and the students and each other are vital to be able to recognize what they are working on, what their next step is and how they improve.

Tools of Assessment

◆ Teacher Conferences
◆ Peer Conferences
◆ Group Critiques
◆ Reading Work Aloud
◆ Self-editing and Numerous Drafts
◆ Written Reflection Sheets
◆ Final Presentations and Performances

We do a lot of multi-drafting of work. And my philosophy of projects is that you have a project that has many drafts and a beautiful final copy, rather than lots of final copies. And the components of the project may culminate in a final project and then be saved for inclusion in a larger piece or presentation later. My personal theory is that if it is a half-baked job and the students don't feel like they have succeeded or they aren't really proud of it, then it is not done. They have to draft again.

How do you convey the expectations of the different projects?

The presumption is that each student is going to do their best work. Any way they can get help to do their best work is fine. Cheating is not possible. I have a light table which I built with my students last year so kids can trace. Usually tracing is considered cheating. To me tracing is what they do in graphic design studios all the time. Kids use the copy machine a lot here. Kids have an illustration they want to use, but don't know how to draw it. We find it somewhere, we blow it up on the copy machine using the enlarger, and they copy from there. Anything you can do to make your work accurate and presentable and careful; use your resources.

Some teachers feel like my project model is very restrictive, and they allow kids to choose all different kinds of projects or go through different steps to get there. There is a lot of strength to that and it allows for more creativity. Functionally, it doesn't work for me, because if all the students are going through the same steps, then we can do a critique session and every student is at the same place and I can teach the skills. If I am teaching scale design and using drafting equipment every student can learn from each other. When students are all doing separate things, there is no atmosphere of critique. If you are all writing a novel, or doing a certain experiment with rocks or animals, kids can constantly share the techniques they learn along the way.

Could you tell me about the theme you are working on now?

The second day of school we went cave exploring, so it was a kind of Outward Bound beginning. Parents came. It was all day, very scary, very challenging. Immediately after that they started learning scientifically about caves, and they were pretty involved after having been in the caves. The trip was

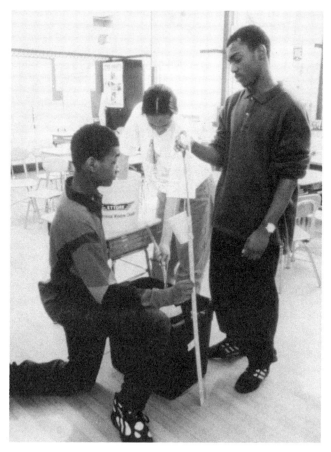

Middle School students from the Rafael Hernandez Bilingual School in Boston working on the Waterwheels learning expedition. Photograph by Brian Smith/NASDC.

great for community building. As soon as they got back, they started writing their cave novel about kids lost in a cave because they could remember what it

◆ ◆ ◆

Assessment is not just having a sense of the reading level and writing level of each student; assessment is an engine for pushing the growth of the children.

◆ ◆ ◆

felt like to be in those caves, and immediately started rough-drafting the cave drawings. By the time they got to the final draft, they knew a lot about cave formation, and how to make the drawings accurate. For weeks they worked on writing their novels, and drawings. And we have also been reading *Tom Sawyer.*

We've expanded the land form geology into a whole study. We've gone mountain climbing as a group and looked at the glacier formation of the valley that we are in, and kids have done a lot of research and essay work. We are about to move into mineralogy and rocks themselves.

A connected project is tumbling stones; we've been running rock tumblers and students are in charge of maintaining the tumblers. The kids know that I have invested about $250 of my own money in tumbling materials and jewelry materials, and that I have to make it back in the jewelry store. They are a bit worried about the investment, but I'm not. I've done the store before, and we made over $1,000. So this is part of their mineralogical work. And there are art activities connected to it; rock painting and rock soap stone sculpture. We'll be writing children's books about geology, and running this rock and mineral store, and going on a field trip to a local rock museum. We have two local geologists coming in to speak.

What does the structure of your day look like?

There's usually a basic schedule for the day. We start with a morning meeting that lasts for about forty-five minutes. We talk about the plan for the day. We read the newspaper; I bring in *The Boston Globe* every morning, and we discuss international, national, and local events. Kids do personal sharing about what's going on in their lives. We all sit on the floor; there's kind of a family feel to it. Also, we talk about a lot of bureaucratic things; such as lunch count attendance, and field trips, and who needs their slips. It's sort of a family feeling for about forty-five minutes. There's a lot to cover in that time.

From there, we usually go to a reading component of the day which might be in reading groups or independent reading, to a writing and drafting component, then to recess. After recess, there is a math block, and then the afternoons are science and social studies; lectures, research, project work. That schedule is similar every day, but the more kids get invested in a project, the more flexible the schedule becomes. When kids are working on the blueprint of a house, for example, sometimes we start the day working on them and at 2:00 we are still working on them. I love it when they are really

Students bargain with me about every project.

—*Ron Berger*

gripped by their projects. I often let them go work for the day. And they will often bargain: "Can we work through math today, and do math tomorrow or for homework?" I like being flexible, if as a manager of the classroom, I can see that it is going well.

As kids show their level of responsibility, they often bargain for more flexibility. If it is a reading period and they come to me and say, "Can I do my reading tonight and work on my draft?," if they have proven themselves responsible in that regard, I can reward that responsibility by relaxing the curriculum.

A Successful Project

- Uses the skills that need to be taught.
- Draws upon the different talents and strengths of each student.
- Uses local resources, such as field trip sites or local experts.
- Contains some mandatory and some optional components.
- Allows for flexibility in scheduling, so students can pursue what they are really interested in.
- Has built-in structures of self-assessments, such as multi-drafts, critique sessions, etc.
- Requires that students work in some similar areas so knowledge is easily shared.
- Includes a forum for presenting final work so students strive to do the best job possible.
- Has an end product that has important uses in the community, such as teaching other students or sharing with the town.

What are some of the strategies you use to make the projects run smoothly?

One strategy is having a project that has mandatory and optional components to it. So that when kids finish their work, it is not an issue of what they do next. The project is broad enough that there is always something more that they could do to deepen it. Other strategies are critique sessions and peer critiques, multiple drafts, and requiring a certain amount of drafts. Making expectations clear. Sometimes making expectations entirely rigid, for some things, so you can be flexible on the other things. For example, the cave had very specific expectations. You had to do the first draft on this size paper in pencil, the second draft on this size paper in pencil, and the third draft had to be done in pencil, razor point, then in color pencil. And if kids did any one of those drafts wrong, it wasn't accepted. And that intensity of structure allowed kids to relax about other aspects, because the entire cave was up to them as long as they followed that form. They felt very secure about the flexibility within it. They liked the rigidity; kids like structure in ways, and I don't want it to be unstructured. I want the steps to be absolutely clear.

There is some flexibility in the deadlines, because the projects usually have mandatory components and then optional components, since I can't expect every kid to finish the projects at the same time when some novels have forty chapters and some have ten chapters. So quite often, when kids were creating their own countries, for example, there were all these mandatory components; they had to have this, they had to have that. But then there were all these optional components, and when they finished their mandatory components, they could move on to the optional. So there was a flexible period of finishing. Some kids are slow workers, or they have handicaps, they are learning disabled, or they have physical handicaps and they need a lot more support to have a successful project. Those kids get fewer optional components done. Some kids are really on top of things and work constantly at home and get the mandatory things done at home, so I have to have lots of optional components that they can do to elaborate the projects. And it's done with every level of need; everyone writes a cave novel; some of them will seem as if they were written by college students and some by third graders. When you have a fully mainstreamed special education program, you have every level of child. The project is not a success in my eyes unless it is a success for every student, so that each student feels individual pride and whole class pride.

Geology Outcomes

- Demonstrate an understanding of earth formations, plate tectonics, basic astronomy, and the geological forces that create mountains, valleys, and rivers.

- Master drafting techniques and scale design in order to create geologically accurate maps of caves, rivers, and mountain ranges.

- Develop an understanding of experimental technique and scientific analysis through rock and mineral identification.

- Demonstrate an understanding of *Tom Sawyer*, through essay writing, discussion, and performance.

- Practice the expressive skills needed to transform their cave experience into a novel of their own.

- Learn to structure the complexity of language and knowledge for certain audiences by writing a geology book for children.

- Develop aesthetic appreciation and craftsmanship through jewelry-making, rock painting, stone sculpture, and color illustrations.

- Master the mathematical skills needed to handle unit-pricing and bookkeeping in the class jewelry store.

- Begin to understand the procedures of the adult business world by establishing their own geological consulting firm complete with business letters, calls to local geologists, and mock payment transactions.

- Demonstrate responsibility and cooperation through shared risk taking in the caving experience and other field explorations.

Outward Bound Enters the Classroom

by Thomas Duffy

From the outside, the Rafael Hernandez School looks like any number of urban schools: dingy brick, barred windows, locked door and no playground. But the gloomy facade masks a school that is alive with the voices and ideas of a radical education experiment.

Step by tentative step, teachers and students at the bilingual school on the Roxbury–Jamaica Plain border are reinventing the very notion of education based on the ideals of Outward Bound.

The Hernandez is one of three Boston public schools experimenting with the approach to education inspired by Cambridge-based Expeditionary Learning Outward Bound. The group is sponsoring similar projects at Mattapan's Lewenberg School and the Blackstone Elementary School on Shawmut Avenue and is in the process of starting a fourth program at South Boston High School.

The projects are part of a national school reform effort begun two years ago when President Bush called on businesspeople to develop model schools. The result was the New American Schools Development Corporation, which is sponsoring Expeditionary Learning and eight other projects across the country with private money.

To get a sense of just how radical the approach is, look no further than the classroom of Hector Soto and Brian LaFerriere, who teach a group of sixth, seventh and eighth graders. When a student assembling a structure with Lego-like blocks asks if the walls have to be matching heights, LaFerriere refuses to dictate.

"However you make your building is up to you," he tells the student, repeating, "It's up to you." The girl quietly returns to her work.

Or look inside the classroom of Blanca Burgos and James Hunt, where students are building models with straws and paper clips. In a twist that owes more to college physics than arts and crafts, the students later will be required to estimate how much weight their structures can support and test their predictions with a box of nails.

"We thought we would give them an hour," Burgos says with a glance at the busy students. "But it's already been 90 minutes."

Both cases illustrate two of the guiding principles of Expeditionary Learning: Students are physically involved in their work, not just receiving information passively, and they are partners in the process of learning, with a strong voice in how that learning takes place.

Like learning itself, reinventing a school is a messy process that requires teachers to learn with the students. There is much trial and error.

"We're not quite sure how to evaluate some of the work that's being done, and we're not quite sure how all the lessons are going to work," says Hunt. "There's not a standardized text for this with lesson plans."

Guided by ten design principles, the approach replaces traditional subject-by-subject learning with what are called "expeditions" that draw on a variety of subjects and involve students in the community.

At the Hernandez, students in the sixth, seventh and eighth grades are designing a plan to develop three vacant lots in the neighborhood as part of an expedition called "structures."

Armed only with string, they mapped out and measured the lots on a crisp October morning. They asked residents what they would like to have there. They have met with planners and architects and researched the property at City Hall.

They also are reading *The Young Landlords*, a novel about a group of children who buy a building for $1 and develop it. When their project is finished, they will make a presentation to the neighbors.

Meanwhile, first- through fifth-grade students at the Blackstone's are involved in an expedition on whales; a spring expedition will focus on black women. At the Lewenberg, the fall expedition focused on dinosaurs, while the spring expedition will focus on the Salem witch trials.

December 26, 1993; pp. A37-A38, *The Boston Globe*. Reprinted with permission of the author.

With a budget of $1.2 million this year, Expeditionary Learning has begun similar projects in seven other cities: Dubuque, Iowa; Portland, Maine; Decatur, Georgia; Baltimore; San Antonio; New York; and Denver.

The ten principles that guide the experiment were culled from the ideas of educators and the philosophy of Outward Bound, an outdoor education organization. The principles are self-discovery, having wonderful ideas, the responsibility for learning, intimacy and caring, success and failure, collaboration and competition, diversity and inclusivity, the natural world, solitude and reflection, service and compassion.

Khesha Hamilton, a sixth grader at the Hernandez, may not be able to list the principles, but she is enjoying her role in the experiment.

"It's hard work, but I kind of like it," she says while working on her straw structure. *"The Young Landlords*, that's what I liked best."

Although it is too early to tell whether the ideas of Outward Bound can be brought into the classroom, educators are intrigued by the possibilities.

"There are some really powerful ideas associated with it," said Jerome T. Murphy, dean of Harvard University's Graduate School of Education. "I'm hopeful that with some kids it can have a big impact."

While the teachers foster social skills and awareness of the world outside the classroom, they do not ignore traditional academics. There are still tests and plenty of homework. Backers say commitment to quality work sets Expeditionary Learning apart from other attempts at progressive education.

◆ ◆ ◆

There are some really powerful ideas associated with it.

— *Jerome Murphy*
Dean, Harvard Graduate School of Education

◆ ◆ ◆

"We want to have the caring, compassion and courage, but we really want to focus on the quality of the students' work as well," says Meg Campbell, director of Expeditionary Learning Outward Bound.

The Expeditionary Learning program is designed to be implemented with little additional cost to the schools, according to Campbell. The group has provided extensive consulting services as well as several thousand dollars for initial training costs.

Because the program constantly is being refined, there are plenty of kinks still to be worked out. The hands-on approach has limited the opportunities for teaching Spanish, according to some teachers. Others said the emphasis on group projects makes it hard to track the work of every student individually.

Still, Jenny Silverman, whose daughter, Rachel Racusen, is in the sixth grade, is pleased with the program.

"I would pay for this education," Silverman said. "I think the group-building experience has been very positive. There's more of a sense that they are a team and that they have team leaders rather than a class with a teacher."

Ideally, in five years the Expeditionary Learning model will be spread throughout the schools and across the school year. But expansion of the program depends upon the interest and commitment of the schools as well as funding.

Implementing the new approach has required hard work and commitment from the teachers. The teachers develop the curriculum and constantly revise and fine-tune. Last-minute meetings to work out difficulties and share new insights are the rule rather than the exception.

"It's not just the kids that are on the expedition, it's the teachers, too," says Maria Campanario Araica, director of instruction at the Hernandez. "It's risky and it's frightening. So when you see the success, it's exhilarating."

Expeditionary Learning: A Design for New American Schools

Submitted by Outward Bound to New American Schools Development Corporation, February 1992. Revised 1993.

1. Introduction

Expedition: the action of helping forward or accomplishing; the condition of being expedited or set in motion; a journey, voyage or excursion made for some definite purpose.

—*Oxford Dictionary*

The right question at the right time can move children to peaks in their thinking that result in significant steps forward and real intellectual excitement. Although it is almost impossible for an adult to know exactly the right time to ask a specific question of a specific child—especially for a teacher who is concerned with 30 or more children—children can raise the right question for themselves if the setting is right. Once the right question is raised, they are moved to tax themselves to the fullest to find an answer.

— *Eleanor Duckworth*
The Having of Wonderful Ideas

❖ Understanding the Bubonic Plague: An Example of an Expedition

While reading aloud to her class *A Distant Mirror: The Calamitous Fourteenth Century*, by Barbara Tuchman, the teacher hears the questions unfolding. What caused the bubonic plague? How did it spread? How many people died? The students, with guidance, plan an expedition that will help them answer their own questions.

Students decide first to create a fictional, historically accurate village peopled with characters they know and understand. They identify and acquire specific skills that include using a microscope to study germs, computer modeling and projections, drafting and research. Students interview a public health epidemiologist who suggests connections to the AIDS epidemic. A medieval historian shares her slide collection of art and architecture.

Drawing on their research in primary and secondary documents and resources, students first create characters by writing biographies, generating house plans and scale models, drawing portraits, writing up daily schedules, projecting life cycles, expressing the fears and dreams, designing clothes, identifying the rituals and beliefs, outlining the power structure, making currency and household objects, playing the games, cooking the food and demonstrating the mathematical and scientific understanding of their fictional characters. What did they know? What did they do? What didn't they know? What did they care most about? One student's work on a baker from the Middle Ages leads to the discovery that no one would have known how to multiply numbers, instead using the common and tedious practice of doubling. "They lived too long ago to know about germs," laments another student, having a sudden appreciation for that scientific discovery. After students have created this village, they are ready to hypothesize, discuss and debate the plague's impact on one community.

They grapple with thorny issues of superstition, public health and the role of church and state making connections to the AIDS epidemic today. These students are distressed as they complete their simulation forecasts on the computer and realize that almost every one of their characters—now beloved—meets death prematurely and gruesomely. They decide to conclude their expedition with a moving memorial to the victims of the bubonic and AIDS epidemics. Grief is not banished from this classroom. Instead, these lives from the Middle Ages touch their own.

The depth of experience, reflection, and discussion of these topics traditionally would have been deferred to upper-level high school or college classes. Middle school students ordinarily would not have enough background knowledge or have been sufficiently engaged emotionally by the subject to sustain lengthy and impassioned inquiry and dialogue.

This is Expeditionary Learning, that broad range of intelligences and relationships necessary to generate, undertake and complete the arduous challenge of an intellectual or physical expedition. We offer an example of this learning because it is the key concept in our design for New American Schools. We believe it responds to the failure in public education today to engage students in their own quest for learning and their personal best, while also motivating and accelerating the acquisition of the skills and knowledge required for expeditions.

Expeditionary Learning is based upon the principles and pedagogy of Outward Bound, with the added insights of TERC, Project Adventure, Educators for Social Responsibility, Facing History and Ourselves, Harvard Graduate School of Education faculty and staff, a Wheelock College professor, the early childhood director from the Boston Children's Museum and practitioners from an urban superintendent to teachers.

Outward Bound, founded in 1941 by Kurt Hahn in England and brought to this country by Joshua Miner and Charles Froelicher in 1962, offers a different antidote to the problems that challenge public education, particularly for those students most alienated from schools. Outward Bound has been built on a longstanding relationship with formal education originated by Hahn, who founded Gordonstoun, a secondary school in Scotland, after his exile from Nazi Germany, where he had founded his first school in Salem. Outward Bound has a history of innovation as a private sector initiative attempting to influence public institutions. The nascent Outward Bound schools, fiscally infinitesimal compared to even the smallest jurisdictions in the public sector, have been able to spread ideas and implant programs in public schools as well as private schools, universities, public agencies and businesses, thus making a limited but distinctive contribution to the practice known theoretically as the pedagogy of experience.

There are six independently chartered Outward Bound schools in the United States, with a national headquarters in Greenwich, Connecticut. These schools are Colorado Outward Bound in Denver; Pacific Crest based in Portland, Oregon, with urban centers in Los Angeles and San Francisco and a program in San Diego; Voyageur in Minneapolis; North Carolina Outward Bound in Morgantown,

with an urban center in Atlanta; New York City Outward Bound and Hurricane Island in Rockland, Maine, which also operates Thompson Island in Boston and an urban center in Baltimore. This extensive network of schools and centers, all of which have working relationships with public schools, affords our design effort a readymade dissemination network.

This is Expeditionary Learning, that broad range of intelligences and relationships necessary to generate, undertake and complete the arduous challenge of an intellectual or physical expedition.

The promise of the experiential principles of education has been well documented throughout the last 20 years. Project Adventure, an interdisciplinary school program founded on Outward Bound principles in 1971, was awarded National Diffusion Network status in 1974, showing statistically significant improvement on the School Climate Survey, on self-reported participation in discussion, critical attitude and depth of understanding, and on the Tennessee Self-Concept Scale. Hundreds of schools have adopted the Project Adventure model since 1974 and have shown clear gains. Recently, two urban elementary schools in Columbus, Ohio, that have used Project Adventure's interdisciplinary curriculum approach in the academic classrooms as well as in physical education classes have shown dramatic gains. Average Basic Skills tests have increased 20 percentile points or two grade levels in reading and 30 percentile points in math since the program's inception three years ago, despite a turnover rate of approximately 30 percent. Our design will take inspiration from examples such as this and the many others from existing Outward Bound programs and those programs based on the principles of Outward Bound, and leverage their potential for

Fourth-grade students from the Rafael Hernandez Bilingual School in Boston gather specimens for their learning expedition on pond life. Photograph by Brian Smith/NASDC.

breakthrough learning by transforming the entire school structure and learning process. The principles of Expeditionary Learning are not new, but our design will start a revolution in learning by making them the core of the whole education process.

Our design breaks the mold in three dramatic and fundamental ways: first, its hierarchy of values puts human beings' learning and character development together at the pinnacle. Second, it requires the complete reorganization of time, space and relationships among persons, across disciplines, between persons and learning technology and between the school and community. Third, its high level of expectation for student achievement and character development is manifested in our requirement for student demonstrations of intellectual, physical and character competencies at three major transition points: the end of the grades two/three/four cycle; the end of the grades seven/eight/nine cycle and at the conclusion of secondary education. Each of the national education goals is addressed in our design.

Our design is based upon a shared set of principles. These are our "givens." As articulated by the late Harvard dean Paul Ylvisaker: values must be clear and the value of values clearly demonstrable; there is no learning without emotion and challenge; it must be done with intimacy and caring; the collective and the individual can be brought together; there must be a fair assurance of success. Harvard professor Eleanor Duckworth has called attention to the spirit of infectious intellectual excitement and inquiry; and Kurt Hahn's work and writings insist on our final guiding principles: the importance of solitude and reflection; and the need to develop community and social vision.

After outlining the design principles in Section 2, we explain in greater detail our key concept of Expeditionary Learning by its features, how it would be organized and its benefits. One of our ideas is to keep teachers and students together for three-year cycles and to organize students in groups of 8–10, each called watches, using the nautical term for a crew on duty. Section 3 also addresses what we want our students to accomplish, including the final senior service expedition. The expertise of TERC, Project Adventure, Educators for Social Responsibility and Facing History and Ourselves will be especially crucial as we develop a curriculum of expedition prototypes.

Expeditions cannot begin or succeed without guides. In Section 4, we offer our apprenticeship proposal for teachers and our emphasis on ongoing professional and personal renewal of administrators and teachers. Since we view teaching and learning as the heart of every school system, we outline a proposed organizational framework utilizing a web where all staff consider themselves "teachers first" rather than a rigid hierarchy for school systems.

◆ ◆ ◆

We are on an expedition ourselves in designing New American Schools.

◆ ◆ ◆

Our design calls for a marked change in how schools view parents and community. Section 5 highlights this expanded view and notes its benefits for society and democracy. World-class standards and the national education goals are addressed in Section 6 within the context of our overarching goal, in Lawrence Cremin's words, "to make human beings who live life to the fullest, who will continually add to the quality and meaning of their experience, and who will participate actively with their fellow human beings in the building of a good society."

Section 7 addresses the change process either by way of chartering a new school or by way of transforming an existing school. We address the question of how to persuade others to use our design. Change, particularly of the magnitude we are envisioning, entails conflict. We will draw on the expertise of Educators for Social Responsibility as we work with local schools to implement Expeditionary Learning on-site.

Section 8 outlines our proposed organization for the design team. We note, especially in this context, that we are on an expedition ourselves in designing New American Schools.

We do not have all the answers, but we believe we are asking the right questions. As we uncover answers, we will document and share them. Section 9 addresses the issue of how we will know if our design works. We draw particularly on the Academy for Educational Development's expertise in evaluation, and submit the entire design process to extensive documentation, review, evaluation and dissemination.

2. Design Principles

Outward Bound's cardinal principle is that education should reflect and respect the passions of the young by giving them authentic and tangible opportunities to experience the joy of learning. Only when they are impelled into experience on terms they can accept and understand will students take to heart the academic learning of the school program.

— *Thomas James*
Brown University

The first step in breaking the mold of current school design is to articulate a set of principles that will guide our new design process. These are unlike the traditional principles and underlying assumptions that have governed and shaped public schools for the last century. Courage, intellect and compassion are our guideposts. We assume not only that every child can learn but that all children can reach their fullest potential as persons. Our design principles are lofty, like the peaks we seek to climb, one step at a time.

❖ The Value of Values

A dominant feature of our proposed New American School is an ethos where character development and universal intellectual achievement are viewed as the central mission of a school community. All education is moral education and all moral education is grounded by necessity in human experience, intelligence and reflection. Unless thinking and values connect vitally with the continuum of experience in human lives, the ideas quickly become disembodied, unthinking, inhuman. People lose sight of who they are and what their roots are. They act with habitual disregard, both for their own well-being and for the needs and dignity of others. The school has a supreme duty to counteract these tendencies. Every step forward in intellectual growth should be accompanied by a strengthening of moral perspective and a more fully activated life of learning in pursuit of humane ends. Every word and symbol, each gesture that makes meaning, the entire tree of knowledge must send its taproot down into this reality: we go to school to learn how to create the good society, a world in which we can all live freely and responsibly to our greatest potential.

The good society is built by locating, respecting and strengthening the learning dynamic within a family and community. It may require humility on the part of teachers and administrators to recognize the multicultural and gender expressions of courage in the nuance, language and terms of a particular community.

◆ ◆ ◆

> We assume not only that every child can learn but that all children can reach their fullest potential as persons.

◆ ◆ ◆

❖ Learning Requires Emotion and Challenge

The supporting structures of authentic experience that once formed the rite of passage to adulthood are gone. The young people who lack positive experiences with adults in a community context have a strong predisposition to every pathology from substance abuse to suicide, from remorseless violence to unthinking consumption of mass media and consumer goods.

Our answer to these tendencies is the conviction that intellectual and social learning must be built upon a firm foundation of active experience in young people or, for that matter, in all people. Experience is not the end of education, but it is a means without which other goals are not attainable.

Exploring itself involves a willingness to draw and build upon one's knowledge and understanding and an openness to risk. Young children are quintessential explorers with their curiosity and freshness about what many adults have come to view as mundane. Young children generate questions and do not think in terms of compartmentalized learning. We intend to nurture and foster a voyage of that spirit from childhood through adolescence and on to adulthood by using Expeditionary Learning.

The rich and varied experiences of working with real scientists and artists, climbing real rocks, reading books that make one laugh and cry, writing, discussing, charting maps, reasoning mathematically, spending time alone, designing and carrying out lengthy experiments with peers, conducting business in school, bringing history to life, going out of school to offer service to one's community and coming back to create an artistic reflection of, or intellectual response to, that experience will cumulatively shape one's character, knowledge and aspirations. These moments can be exhilarating if they are accompanied by consciousness of the significance of human accomplishment. When one not only discovers but also takes pride in and can share these feats with others who care, learning becomes purposeful and lifelong. This is true whether one is 4, 14 or 54.

For students the deep lessons of responsible selfhood are necessary preconditions to growth of the mind. To teach such lessons, education must impart to the young greater capacities not only for positive action, but for overcoming the constraints within themselves, and for working constructively with others to surmount the obstacles that may lie before them in their lives. Outward Bound teaches that to strengthen the will to prevail against adversity, we must learn persistence in turning our disabilities into opportunities, our weakness into strength, our incomprehension into a devotion to truth. For the underachiever or the intellectually gifted, this insight from the founder of Outward Bound represents a Magna Carta of school success.

Two students from the Rafael Hernandez Bilingual School in Boston work together during the Pond Life learning expedition. Photograph by Brian Smith/NASDC.

❖ Learning Occurs with Intimacy and Caring

Deeper relationships foster deeper and clearer thinking. Friendship best nourishes self-renewal both for adults and children. For this reason, our design proposes keeping teachers and students together for at least three years to create continuity and foster friendships for both. The antidote to insularity and alienation is not competition but friendship, the discovery of bonds and mutual commitment among human beings. The educational philosopher Maxine Greene points out that friendship, as Aristotle saw it, was "a way of getting pleasure from another's achievements, celebrating what another authentically chooses." This spirit of celebration will permeate our schools, creating even larger circles of friendship, reaching out to families and communities with new initiatives to build the understanding necessary to sustain a democratic society. The reasons for cooperation are not only found in pedagogy, though they are fully evident there in improved student performance. The best reasons have to do with the kinds of human beings we are capable of becoming through education—sensibly defending the dignity of persons, stewards of civility as we sift through our many differences, always ready to act together to strengthen the moral and political basis of the community that sustains us.

❖ The Collective and the Individual Can Be Brought Together

Kurt Hahn, who founded secondary schools in Germany and Scotland as well as Outward Bound, told students, "You are crew, not passengers." When students are genuinely needed in a group, they respond with higher levels of commitment and performance. This fact has been validated in thousands of Outward Bound courses conducted throughout the world and in related fashion in the research on cooperative learning. Outward Bound has pioneered a pedagogy that addresses the severe motivational and self-esteem issues which prevent some students from learning how to learn as well as enhancing the growth of those who almost intuitively learn well. Outward Bound does this by putting all students on equal footing, with competition subordinated to cooperation, and with genuine opportunities for students at all levels of learning skill to test themselves and their deepest-held values.

◆ ◆ ◆

> Adults, as well as students, should have the opportunity to learn from both triumph and defeat.

◆ ◆ ◆

❖ A Fair Assurance of Success

Educators find Outward Bound intriguing because it offers a curriculum in which towering standards of human performance are paradoxically joined to an assumption that everyone can succeed. Those contentious categories of educational reform—excellence and equality—are fused into a program single-mindedly devoted to improving human character and performance among all kinds of learners.

This is accomplished through the sequential cycle of Expeditionary Learning, where ambitious yet realistic goals are set by participants. The teacher's role shifts from ensuring that students are adequately prepared to complete their challenge or problem with success to guaranteeing the safety of an expedition. Much as the Outward Bound instructor has safety paramount in his or her mind, teachers in our school will think and assist students in designing challenging intellectual, physical and service expeditions where students' intellectual and emotional safety as well as their self-esteem is respected.

Adults, as well as students, should have the opportunity to learn from both triumph and defeat. It is through overcoming defeat that we learn some lessons best, instead of merely pampering self-esteem with easy victories over modest challenges. To experience only an unbroken chain of comfortably limited successes that never challenge or strengthen the human spirit is not nearly as valuable as learning to push beyond our perceived limitations for a worthy cause to solve a problem or to help another human being in need. As they try to strengthen the will of the young to prevail against adversity and intellectual challenge, expedition advisors must teach students to go beyond their weaknesses and strive for learning and truth.

◆ ◆ ◆

> I know of no better metaphor for life than rock climbing. You see all the behaviors in a very short time: the reluctance to challenge themselves, the problem-solving skills or lack thereof, the willingness or unwillingness to give up. And we see lots and lots of behavior changes as we progress through the year.

— *Ian Lipson*
Thompson Island Outward Bound Education Center

◆ ◆ ◆

❖ The Having of Wonderful Ideas

We view children neither as receptacles to be filled nor damaged goods to be patched. Instead, we are deeply respectful of the ideas children, adolescents and adults generate and the strengths and weaknesses they bring to every experience. Ideas are the sparks to start campfires which can light the darkness and warm us all. We view all children and teachers as scientists, inventors, writers, mathematicians, leaders, artists, linguists and deeply compassionate human beings who are in the process of discovering and becoming. We want them to become more thoughtful, more knowledgeable, more confident and more courageous as they develop their minds, bodies and character to their fullest potential.

"Intelligence cannot develop without matter to think about. Making new connections depends on knowing enough about something in the first place to provide a basis for thinking of other things to do—of other questions to ask—that demand more complex connections in order to make sense," Eleanor Duckworth notes in *The Having of Wonderful Ideas*. Referring to curriculum, Duckworth observes, "The difference can best be characterized by saying that the unexpected is valued."

We want to design schools that are homes to ideas, including the unexpected ideas of children and adults.

❖ Solitude and Reflection

Reflecting on one's experiences is a major road to building a person's own values. If students are to tap into their own creativity, personal renewal and thoughtfulness, schools must structure time where meaningful reflection is valued. At Salem, the school Kurt Hahn founded in Germany, each day students took 30-minute walks alone to replenish their minds, bodies and spirits.

Every aspect of education must have times when people can be quiet, alone and reflective, not only to refresh their nervous systems, but to ask questions about themselves, to examine their own inner lives and to discover for themselves their own springs of growth and self-renewal. Our schools—and hence our professional development as well—will help people to discover the talents they naturally possess, and show them how they might learn to work together, now and in the future, to use their talents most effectively. Those straining ever forward at the head of the pack have no greater privilege than to discover how to help shoulder the burden of stragglers, strangers to success.

"I don't retreat from the world to escape," Robert Frost said, "but to return stronger." Solitude is cocoon time. It requires silence, commitment and an imaginative use of existing space. It does not cost any money; it can happen every day. While younger children's developmental needs prescribe significantly shorter spans of solitude, persons of all ages reap its benefits. Scientists and artists alike attest to the "click"—the unanticipated connections—they make when constructively immersed in solitude. This experience is virtually unknown today in public schools, and without the strength-giving experience of breaking out of its cocoon, a butterfly cannot survive.

◆ ◆ ◆

Every aspect of education must have times when people can be quiet, alone and reflective.

◆ ◆ ◆

❖ Social Vision

The young can learn best when they are allowed to place their formidable energies in service of the common good. One of the greatest needs in education today, the one on which intellectual achievement and lifelong learning importantly depend, is to involve young people in real service experiences that will teach them the bonds of social life and connect them constructively to their future education and employment. When presented with an authentic choice, the young choose not to be spectators and will gladly embrace the rigors of an arduous quest. They want to learn. They crave self-discovery and are willing to work hard together to achieve it when they feel they are truly called upon to generate questions. Meeting challenges in which they have invested themselves, they will act vigorously to work out the problems they encounter as they strive to accomplish goals they believe are worthy.

Nicole Caldwell, a sixth-grader at the Rocky Mountain School of Expeditionary Learning in Denver sits in a chair donated by parents as she works on her journal during the first week of classes. Photograph by Jay Koelzer/Rocky Mountain News.

The foundation for school improvement is to be found in the lives of people who work in and around schools—students, teachers, administrators, community leaders, parents. For students, no growth in the capacity for school learning will occur until they are disposed to seek it. For teachers, no change of any worth will come to the process of education until they discover within themselves the social vision that makes improvement necessary. For administrators, the lines of constructive change must be located within themselves as a personal quest, or change will not happen. For parents and community leaders, all these things must happen in believable ways, not as top-down mandates to be implemented without regard to local customs. Whatever rules we might ever seek to impose on them, schools are fundamentally democratic at the "shop floor" level. Schools will improve only as people discover in themselves, and then work out together, new understandings and more effective forms of active cooperation.

It is imperative that our schools train the imagination and organize structurally so that staff can deliberate their intentions, visualize goals and act decisively upon their vision of things to come, instead of merely succumbing to the immediate pressures and circumstances of the moment. Social imagination, as distinguished from the passive, isolating and destructive forms of fantasy now so prevalent and commercially available to the young, is essential to the survival of a democratic society. Adults must experience social imagination firsthand within themselves if they are to have any hope of imparting its development to students.

To activate learning, school reform should not impose a new set of constraints but help people learn how to learn in supportive settings where their individual and collective genius can flourish. Our stance is crystal clear on this point. To meet the challenge of school improvement, people must be able to visualize themselves as active learners in a common quest that will carry them together over the barriers that loom high in their lives. They must experience themselves unforgettably as members of a community worth defending against the negative influences they see everywhere around them and within them. This is the essence of school improvement, but as anyone can see, it is missing from many current efforts to improve the schools and influence the young lives that need it most. By viewing families and communities, as well as individual children, as possessing a reservoir of talents, strengths, passions and dreams, our design engages entire communities in a process of development and in the realization of its aspirations through a changed relationship to its schools.

3. Our Key Concept: Expeditionary Learning

Expeditionary Learning is that broad range of intelligences and relationships necessary to generate, undertake and complete the arduous challenge of an intellectual, physical or service expedition. Our design fuses the principles of Outward Bound pedagogy with the intellectual rigor and inquiry delineated by Duckworth in *The Having of Wonderful Ideas*. Students make idea expeditions, drawing on multiple intelligences. These intelligences include at least the seven identified by Howard Gardner in *Frames of Mind*. They are linguistic (the capacity to be verbally fluent), mathematical-logical, musical, spatial and body kinetics; the final two intelligences are personal: the capacity for introspection and reflection and the capacity to empathize and to read other people. Through Expeditionary Learning, our goal is to educate young people to realize all of their intelligences, not just the linguistic and mathematical modalities that have been the traditional domains addressed in public schools.

❖ Features of Expeditionary Learning

We will develop a sequence of interdisciplinary intellectual expeditions for students in pre-kindergarten through grade 12. These will interrelate the major academic disciplines and the performing and applied arts and will include service and physical dimensions. Experiential learning, intellectual inquiry, reflection, service and performance will be characteristics of all expeditions, regardless of length or site. A cumulative, up-to-13-year framework of

Our schools will serve as base camps for students and teachers, and often parents as well, who will experience school as the springboard for a sequence of sustained and challenging interdisciplinary expeditions to peaks of learning and growth.

expeditions will correlate with our rigorous academic and service diploma requirements and will, in most cases, exceed state curricula mandates.

- Intensive, real-life challenges
- Interdisciplinary focus
- Intellectually rigorous
- Animated by strong service ethic
- Highly adaptive so learning will transfer to new situations
- Rapidly building upon growth
- Cooperative as well as individually challenging
- Time for silence and reflection
- Placing high value on fitness and craftsmanship
- Student-centered and -directed
- Constructive risk-taking
- Flexibility in site, timetable and grouping
- Multi-year cycle with students and teacher
- Preparation for the unknown

Expeditions require preparation and teamwork and are intensive and immersing. They demand persistence and include elements of suspense and the unknown. Participants must depend on each other to fulfill a mission, and actions have immediate consequences. No single school, prescribed curriculum, social service agency or family system can prepare a student for every challenge in the workplace and society of the twenty-first century. In Expeditionary Learning schools, we can equip students with the necessary self-confidence, integrity, skills, knowledge, imagination, compassion, creativity and discipline to summon their best character and intelligence in the face of challenges, problems, danger and the unknown.

Learning and service are the mission of our schools. At its best, learning is an emotional as well as cognitive experience, tapping the individual talents and the passions of students. Our schools will serve as base camps for students and teachers, and often parents as well, who will experience school as the springboard for a sequence of sustained and challenging interdisciplinary expeditions to peaks of learning and growth. Expeditions will activate students in learning how to learn and *how to serve* in the major domains of democratic citizenship, natural and social sciences, mathematics, technology, humanities, languages, geography, arts, craftsmanship, physical education, introspection and empathy.

Although group work will be the primary experience for our students, they will also participate in individual expeditions. Every expedition will also include reflection and solitude. Unlike in many conventional schools, students will have ample opportunity not only to "move around" but to set and meet demanding intellectual, physical and emotional goals for themselves so that total fitness becomes not only a part of their routine, but a source of renewal in their daily life. Our centers of Expeditionary Learning teach students how to learn, but that is not enough. Because knowledge is gained in service to the individual and community, we couple that important goal with learning how to serve. We will design schools for citizens of the future era, which calls for an unprecedented degree of global cooperation and compassion.

Students will not only learn by doing, they will demonstrate what they have learned by reflecting, synthesizing and expressing the highlights of their learning experience for others. Learning and then teaching or sharing what one has learned is a truer demonstration of mastery than traditional pen and paper tests. For this reason, expeditions will conclude with a performance or presentation as an indication of students' accountability for their learning and as a tangible way for students to share what they have learned with peers, teachers, parents and the larger community. If, for example, an expeditionary group returns unprepared to answer the questions posed by its peers and expedition advisors, the students will venture out again until they can demonstrate that they have completed the intellectual, service and physical fitness goals of the particular expedition. These goals may include completing expedition logs and reading lists, solving a sequence of problems, undertaking research or experiments, and creatively answering a challenging question which crosses academic and artistic disciplines.

> Recognizing that many students do not have access to swimming instruction, we would teach our students how to swim, in the process acquiring a lifesaving skill. We also want our students to be academic swimmers where, through practice and coaching, they know all the strokes of the various academic disciplines by heart and have developed a strong feel for their own bodies in water. They do not all swim alike. Not everyone aspires to be a racer. But no water will frighten them because each one—whether reading, writing, problem-solving or being better related to two-thirds of the earth's surface—has demonstrated he or she can manage. Swimming is owned as a lifetime skill and source of pleasure rather than a submerged terror that any day one might fall in and drown.

Experiential learning, joined with accelerated academic work as well as preparation in the skills needed for expeditions, can improve school performance. Expeditionary learning is rich with the possibility of interdisciplinary connections coupled with in-depth study over time. Since Expeditionary Learning is performance-based and cumulative, ongoing and varied assessment measures will be an integral part of our design. We will design portfolios that document oral, visual and written problems and measures of the student's best thinking and emotional work over time. These may include oral or video interviews, books authored by students, research reports, computer programs designed by students and art or music created by students. Expedition logs, annual goal-setting pledges, expedition advisor evaluations and outside evaluations will be included. We may interrupt our routines to interject unexpected expeditions of service or problem solving or personal growth. The only diploma we will award will utilize as frameworks a final senior service expedition with an intellectual aspect, and our world-class standards.

Fourth-grade students from the Rafael Hernandez Bilingual School in Boston gather specimens for their learning expedition on pond life. Photograph by Brian Smith/NASDC.

◆ ◆ ◆

Learning and then teaching or sharing what one has learned is a truer demonstration of mastery than traditional pen and paper tests.

◆ ◆ ◆

We will identify and design materials and resources to support the various expeditions from early childhood through secondary years. These materials will include but not be limited to books, tapes, interactive computer programs, scientific equipment, artistic supplies and a wide range of recycled industrial materials. We will design a framework of school/community interaction to support and extend Expeditionary Learning at sites other than school facilities. This framework will foster coordinating the delivery of social services to parents on-site to strengthen the school as a multi-service institution within the community. Not only will our students go into the community to learn, but the community will also come into school, offering students and parents tangible and important support for learning and family cohesion. As a consequence, aspects of our school may need to remain open and active around the clock and throughout each week of the year.

❖ How Will Expeditionary Learning Be Organized?

Expeditionary Learning will be characterized by intimacy, continuity, spontaneity, sustained effort over time and commitment. To achieve this, the fundamental unit of our schools will be expedition watches of approximately eight to twelve students, so named after the nautical terminology for a crew on duty. Emulating the best of today's work force, small groups of students will share responsibility for presenting research reports, solving problems, serving school and community and working, playing and performing together. Students will learn that having a great idea is the first step to implementation and that communicating that idea effectively to others is a key skill. The give and take that comes with sharing opinions and ideas fosters deeper thinking, more precise expression and the testing of one's beliefs. Students do not only learn discussion skills; they learn a fundamental lesson in democracy.

Two to three watches will comprise a crew of approximately twenty-five students and one expedition guide who will remain together for at least three years. For teachers to draw the best from their students, they must know them well, and this is not best done in 40-minute periods. While expeditions will adapt to the needs of specific situations, we propose the following: in the primary grades, a teacher would work with one group of eighteen to twenty-five students spanning pre-kindergarten through second grade. Later, a second teacher would work with the same group of students, spanning grades three through five. In the middle grades and high school, students, still working in watches within crews, would be affiliated with a core group of teachers for three or more years. Groupings of students could be multi-age, with older students sharing with and leading younger children.

In the elementary grades, a crew may convene daily for a meeting and meals, whereas older students may meet weekly. School size will purposefully be small, no more than 350 students. Larger facilities would become separate schools sharing one physical site. Our school communities will develop special identities, rituals and traditions and will have ample opportunities for gatherings to view expeditionary performances and presentations which are deserving of a larger audience.

> Emulating the best of today's work force, small groups of students will share responsibility for presenting research reports, solving problems, serving school and community and working, playing and performing together.

Flexibility is a hallmark of our centers of Expeditionary Learning. Expeditions will take place in a variety of sites including cultural museums, businesses, hospitals, airports and community-based agencies. Staffing may be reconfigured, for example, so that an expedition guide is based at a cultural museum full-time. Expeditions will be age and developmentally appropriate, although they may include students of differing ages. The length of each expedition will vary depending on the scope of its problem or mission. The traditional daily schedule will be abandoned in order to foster in-depth study and experiences.

Since learning is mobile and elastic, residencies by area artists, professionals, scholars, scientists and others will be integrated into our schools. Our schools will become more vibrant and interesting communities by sponsoring service projects and small businesses on site, such as a recycling center, puppet theatre, bookstore, homeless shelter, food cooperative or day care facility.

When students are not on an expedition, they will be engaged in purposefully preparing for their next planned expedition by learning a particular set of skills. A key feature of our design is the immediate application of knowledge and skills introduced at the base camp. Going out and returning from learning expeditions will demonstrate that, for students to learn, there must be a balance between learning how to learn and acquiring skills, and the sharp slap of experience that challenges what one has learned.

❖ Link to Productive Employment

Our design also reinforces the bridge between studies and the world of productive employment. These connections will be made explicit through expeditions which challenge students, again beginning in the primary grades, to explore and set ambitious career and postsecondary education goals for themselves. Work-site internships have been demonstrated to be an effective transition to later employment for community college and university students. For example, La Guardia Community College students, who spend three quarters of their two-year education on-site in a workplace, have a 77 percent rate of employment in one of those sites. We believe internships of varying lengths structured into the school experience of our students will also make concrete the connection between studies and work. We even suspect that our accelerated patterns of learning may move a number of students into further education or work well before current schools are able to do so.

❖ Special Populations

Expeditionary Learning is a pedagogy that benefits any group of students, including special needs, remedial and bilingual students. We view students holistically. We have high expectations for all students' character development and achievement. But we also recognize that a small percentage of students require highly individualized learning contracts, in close consultation with parents, that recognize certain severe physical or intellectual challenges that preclude reaching certain academic goals. For example, a student with Down's syndrome would be integrated into expeditions but might meet vocationally oriented goals rather than all the requirements of the International Baccalaureate. We will have high expectations for our special needs students and monitor their progress closely. We will not give up on them. The fact that character development counts and is recognized in our schools for *all* students will mean that special needs students will be evaluated and documented in this domain as well.

◆ ◆ ◆

> Learning how to read differently for different purposes is a prime task for fluent readers; reading scientific material, for example, calls on different skills than reading poetry. Regardless of one's age or reading ability, the act of reading is a purposeful tool, and for that reason the books and materials we select will be challenging and of high quality.

◆ ◆ ◆

Clearly, academic learning and cognitive development must be at the core of the experience for students. Ultimately, what students will be taught in the schools we propose is not how to thrive in the mountains or at sea, but how to flourish in school. That such a result can be achieved is strongly confirmed by research which recognizes experience-based pedagogies as a promising intervention for students needing academic remediation. We relish the opportunity to explore the relevance of these experiences to the needs of these students.

◆ ◆ ◆

> Surprise, puzzlement, struggle, excitement, anticipation, and dawning certainty—those are the matter of intelligent thought. As virtues, they stand by themselves—even if they do not, on some specific occasion, lead to the right answer. In the long run, they are what count.

— *Eleanor Duckworth*
The Having of Wonderful Ideas

◆ ◆ ◆

❖ Reading within Expeditionary Learning

As a contextual skill, reading is particularly adaptive to Expeditionary Learning. Learning to love reading and how to read for meaning is the first task for children. Engaging children in literacy experiences all day long accelerates this process: reading aloud by and with the teacher, selecting favorite books to read alone, reading with a partner, receiving specific instruction in strategies, writing, rewriting, oral reading, storytelling, dramatic play and puppetry are some of the techniques which will be utilized for novice readers. In revamping the schedule, we will celebrate reading and stories and will create opportunities for one-on-one instruction to ensure that all students become avid, fluent readers. Learning how to read differently for different purposes is a prime task for fluent readers; reading scientific material, for example, calls on different skills than reading poetry. Regardless of one's age or reading ability, the act of reading is a purposeful tool within Expeditionary Learning, and for that reason the books and materials we select will be challenging and of high quality.

A student from the Rafael Hernandez Bilingual School in Boston reads a book that he is working on for the Young Authors Project. Photograph by Brian Smith/NASDC.

❖ What We Want Our Students to Accomplish

Students will complete several major interdisciplinary expeditions each year, with the number and duration varying. Students' portfolios will cumulatively reflect their work from their first expeditions. Portfolio assessment will be multidimensional, including written, oral, visual and technological dimensions. For example, at the beginning of every year a student will set goals in a videotape interview responding to the questions "What do you want to learn this year?" and "What do you most love to do?" Every year the new interview will be added to the same tape, creating a panoramic and immediate view of a child's aspirations and growth over as many as fourteen years. These tapes will be enormously useful for new teachers as they prepare to meet their new cycle of students and tailor expeditions to individual students' needs. By having all students participate, this goal setting becomes an Expeditionary Learning ritual and important school tradition. We also believe these tapes will be treasured by students and their families as more meaningful snapshots of learning over time.

Our students will become confident speakers, fluent readers and writers by the fourth grade, be able to demonstrate mathematical and scientific problem-solving and reasoning, demonstrate familiarity with geography and social studies, express their ideas artistically and technologically, demonstrate their ability to participate and contribute in service projects and meet individual physical fitness goals appropriate to their developmental age by the end of middle school. Planning and responsibility are such fundamental skills in our design that students will have had many opportunities from their earliest schooling to explore and map out educational and career plans beyond high school, but these skills will receive accelerating focus later in secondary school.

At grade eight, our students will demonstrate these same domains in much greater depth and breadth. Students will solve interdisciplinary problems and defend their solutions before a panel of expedition advisors. Portfolios will include such things as expeditionary logs and other writings, art, music, things they have made, service projects, documentation of completion of reading lists, scientific experiments and research, and mathematical reasoning, including the content in the first year of Algebra I.

To receive our diploma, our graduates will successfully complete an individually designed and approved senior service expedition as well as other demanding requirements.

❖ Testing

We view the role of most traditional standardized testing as problematic because it has been misused to track, sort and segregate students on the basis of facility in high-speed recall of segmented facts. These tests are administered in highly artificial settings of limited time without access to resources. They cannot reflect the full range of students' thoughtfulness, resourcefulness or multiple intelligences. We do acknowledge standardized tests' usefulness, on a limited basis, for comparing *schools*, as opposed to individual students.

We want students to be able to answer the toughest and most thoughtful questions we pose for them as well as the ones they pose for themselves. We advocate that students have open-ended time and access to resources such as libraries to answer questions and demonstrate competencies. This is a truer test of their range of abilities and intelligences, and it is more consistent with real situations in later employment, family and community life.

We want to move beyond the gatekeeping function of SATs for individual students. We will call upon higher-order thinking skills by requiring demonstrations of competencies at major transitions, usually, although not exclusively, at the end of grades four, eight and twelve. The concluding demonstrations may be based upon sophomore-level university examinations. If students do not pass their written and practical tests, they practice and study until ready to try again. The complex problems and challenges people confront in the workplace cannot be solved with multiple choice answers spit out in five seconds.

Students in our schools may be required to participate in state-mandated standardized tests which measure school performance; but even in this case, we would propose that the testing be administered on a statistically valid sample basis rather than require every single eligible student to take every mandated test. Students' time is precious in our design, and we see no value in preparing for traditional standardized examinations. Test achievement may have little value except to fuel competitive, nationalistic rivalries of dubious merit.

4. Why Teachers Are Key To Expeditionary Learning

Teachers are the lifeblood of any good school. Their professional development and renewal are crucial to the growth of student learning. The capacity of teachers to be lifelong learners is the mainspring of the high standards and *esprit de corps* without which school improvement is impossible.

When one looks closely at effective schools, people in such places are a team. They know how to act together with high levels of commitment and mutual respect to achieve something they believe in. They are dedicated to their own growth as individuals but they have also devised ways of putting their energy behind others to constitute and nurture the learning community as a whole. Most important, they care collectively about their students. They create a web of collegial understanding that sustains growth and learning beyond the walls of particular lessons, school subjects and classrooms.

A crucial point must be made here. Teachers themselves must be impelled into experience for changes to happen in their teaching. An inner transformation must precede the outwardly visible improvements in the professional lives of teachers. Fullan (1990) argues that only when staff development is seen as "part of an overall strategy for professional and institutional reform" can a staff development strategy succeed. Our Expeditionary Learning model is predicated on changing "the culture of the school as a workplace," consistent with Fullan's findings. He outlines four characteristics upon which such a culture is based: collegiality, shared purpose, belief in continuous improvement, and appropriate structures (roles, policies and organizational arrangements). As noted by Sashkin and Egermeier (1991), "The link between the classroom and the school is the teacher as learner. To Fullan this means that teachers take an inquiring approach, collaborate among themselves and with administrators, constantly refine and develop new technical skills and engage in self-learning through reflective practice. These four elements of the teacher as learner are, according to Fullan, rarely addressed all together in the same setting."

> *We shouldn't have teacher training. Training is for dogs. We want teachers to be co-discoverers with us and with students.*
>
> — *Harold Howe II*
> *Former U.S. Commissioner of Education*

We have joined these elements in our design concept by changing the role of the teacher to expedition guide, reinforcing the teacher's responsibility for ongoing growth as a learner as well as the students in their charge.

❖ We Are Teachers First When We Are Learners First

Regardless of central office responsibility, all professional staff will have some direct teaching responsibility in one of "their" schools. While these teaching responsibilities may be flexible, they should be representative of the full range of students. In the medical profession, the most esteemed professors and administrators continue to carry a patient case load. Indeed, it is the constant challenge of new patients that is seen as fodder for development of new treatment modalities. Similarly, trial lawyers do not reach a level of excellence and then completely cut themselves off from courtroom practice. We are teachers first, and nowhere should this be more evident than in the central office. Teaching, like law and medicine, is a practitioner's profession. We have lost sight of that fact in layers of bureaucracy.

Teachers and administrators will become expedition guides, lead guides and principal guides. Those seeking to enter the profession may serve an apprenticeship year in a school. We will draw on Outward Bound's tradition where instructors share a core of idealism and high expectations for student achievement and personal growth. Expedition guides must be knowledgeable, flexible and engaged both by the process and content of their teaching. They will be steeped in understanding the developmental needs of children across the age span and will exhibit mastery of content areas by designing expeditions which feature their discipline and by preparing students for expeditions in their areas.

Principal guides will have primary responsibility for leadership and administration, including teaching themselves. For example, principal guides might work with a watch on a short expedition or might team with an expedition guide in undertaking a lengthier venture.

Mr. Hill will no longer see himself as a fifth-grade teacher; he will be an expedition guide for the same group of students for three years. He will be held accountable for their effective learning. To draw the best from one's students, one must know them very well.

The nomenclature we have chosen of guides underscores another feature of our design: staff will assume mentoring responsibilities in a fashion appropriate to each site. A student's guide may be his or her primary expedition guide, or it may be another staff member. Every student needs to know there is at least one adult whom he or she can confide in and who has responsibility for checking in with the student academically, socially and physically.

❖ Teacher Education and Renewal

In *Tomorrow's Schools*, a report by the Holmes Group, one teacher notes: "I have yet to find a place to work that values any sort of intellectual activity

At the Geology Summit, teachers measure stream depth to understand erosion caused by flooding. Photograph by Elizabeth X. Maynard/Expeditionary Learning.

on the part of teachers. Thinking is a pretty risky business. Who's going to say that inquiry is a major part of teacher's work? If you're devoting a large part of your time to thinking, you're not a teacher."

If we are not devoting a large amount of our time to thinking—observing, questioning, connecting and reflecting—we have no right to call ourselves educators or students. Our minds are not yet elastic enough.

◆ ◆ ◆

Our central goal is personal renewal along with professional growth, so that educators recover the zest of learning in their own lives and dedicate themselves to educational goals they find worthy and challenging.

◆ ◆ ◆

When students begin law school, their professors tell them the purpose of law school is to learn how to think like a lawyer. You cannot possibly learn all of the law. Once you learn to think like a lawyer, you will apply this thinking to every legal problem and issue you face. Scientists speak of the scientific method and remind young scientists that they cannot possibly learn every scientific fact. What is more important is that they learn the scientific method, or how to think like a scientist.

Features of teacher renewal

- Apprenticeship model
- On-site
- Performance-based assessment
- Builds trust
- Stimulating communication among professionals
- Fosters greater self-confidence in taking risks and adapting to change
- Develops personal and group capacities essential to professional growth
- Career path—teaching at core
- Three-year renewable contracts
- Professional and personal renewal

We propose that we borrow from these practitioners when preparing the next generation of teachers as well as students. Expeditionary Learning is also a way of thinking. The process includes a cycle of conscious experiences: observing, questioning, connecting and reflecting. Learning threads each experience to the next. If we are not learning as we teach, we are not teaching. We are play acting. We are pretenders.

Each part of this sequence of observing, questioning, connecting and reflecting is integral to teaching and, in fact, defines teaching by extending its boundaries. The question is, How do we assist adults as well as children in internalizing this way of thinking, whether they are veterans or novices?

Opportunities for ongoing professional development and renewal will be one of our highest priorities. Teachers in our schools will test themselves in new ways and, as with other Outward Bound experiences, find unexpected rewards as they shift their view of themselves and others. Teachers will experience and learn the fundamental community-building skills that are applicable to the classroom and school. Teacher preparation and renewal will include development of close observational skills of one child over time, a practice advocated by Duckworth and widely used in the classrooms in Reggio Emilia, Italy.

Every exchange is an opportunity for teaching. Time, whether over lunch or in a service project, is ripe with opportunities for the meaningful connections that draw students into the abstract forest of intellectual growth. For schools to be a home to ideas, students must believe that ideas are welcome and that the expression of their ideas will be met respectfully. It is this panning for gold, in terms of finding a student's hidden passion, character and ideas, that is exactly what our educators will envision as their primary charge.

If we are not learning as we teach, we are not teaching. We are play acting. We are pretenders.

We recognize that people themselves must bring about the change to Expeditionary Learning. To do this, they must see the challenge of improved performance and the excitement of expeditions brought into clear focus within their own lives in ways they can understand and act upon. This is most true for teachers and administrators who in our design will become guides. These roles create a fluid career path for educators that keeps teaching—both adults and students—at its core. Research has confirmed the value of learning through challenge, cooperation and service as a way of developing the academic self-concept of underachievers and potential dropouts. What is true for the student at risk of dropping out is equally true for professionals at risk of burning out. The inner logic that defines our design springs from an interest in "defeating defeatism," as Hahn put it, and developing one's inner resources. The unique feature of our teacher development program is that it combines this logic, by necessity dramatically personalized, with the collective, highly organized human resources that make up our schooling institutions in the United States. It is our contention that a fusion—bringing together dynamic experiential learning with highly organized human resources—is crucial to the improvement of school performance for faculty members, school leaders and students.

We view teacher education as evolutionary and the advent of new teachers into the profession as an opportunity to advance the state of knowledge of the profession, much the way the training of new physicians is viewed as a catalyst for experienced practitioners to upgrade their own thinking and knowledge. Our schools will host teacher education programs, acting as on-site developers to new teachers and experienced teachers who cycle through the school for apprenticeships and short or extended professional sabbaticals. In our design, lead guides are experienced and highly accomplished practitioners who will continue to lead student expeditions but will be selected also to mentor apprentice expedition guides.

To become an expedition guide, apprentices must have a bachelor's degree in liberal arts; demonstrate an understanding of child development organizational and interpersonal development; successfully apprentice for at least two six-week interdisciplinary expeditions under the direction of a lead guide; and design and lead their own expedition with students. This expedition will be evaluated by their lead guide, principal guide, participating students and potentially a college faculty member. As a concluding challenge, apprentices will be expected to design and execute a culminating personal expedition advancing in some small way our understanding of teaching and learning. The apprenticeship model offers rich rewards for the lead guide as well, who has the opportunity to reflect upon and articulate his or her practice and decision-making.

◆ ◆ ◆

> The three-year cycle also recognizes that there are many talented individuals who would like to teach but also would like to pursue professional opportunities in other fields.

Given our multi-year cycle with students, all expedition guides must make a conscious decision every three years whether or not to continue teaching students. Introducing three-year usually renewable contracts is an important feature of our ongoing professional development and renewal model for the following reasons: a self-assessment mechanism is built in that is synchronized to teachers' relationships and work with students. Expedition guides must want to teach. The three-year cycle also recognizes that there are many talented individuals who would like to teach but also would like to pursue professional opportunities in other fields. Many recent college graduates have been shut out of public education because they do not wish to devote their entire lives to teaching. Similarly, persons mid-career or returning to the work force have much to offer the field. Artists may rotate between producing art and teaching. We believe the high level of energy, commitment and expertise many of these bright and accomplished individuals can bring into expedition centers, even if for only one three-year cycle with students, should not be lost.

Our apprenticeship model will be linked to existing and emerging college and university training programs. The North Carolina Outward Bound School, for example, has a continuing and expanding role with the North Carolina State Teaching Fellows which selects undergraduates in North Carolina colleges and universities for special funding, curricula and support service designed to channel them into teaching jobs in the state and toward careers as educational leaders. Much as in the 1960s, when Outward Bound was one of the main planks of the Peace Corps training experience, the pedagogy of experience is being used to bond and energize this group, as well as to cultivate intensive and well-grounded knowledge of experiential learning for the professional future of members. A concomitant strategy is to draw more minority teachers into the profession in North Carolina so the Outward Bound process offers a strategy for interracial team-building and multicultural awareness.

Our centers of Expeditionary Learning will focus on building trust, stimulating more discerning kinds of communication among professionals, fostering greater self-confidence in taking risks and adapting to change, and developing other personal and group capacities essential to professional growth. We will also focus on specific attributes of growth, offering challenges tailored to the need for teamwork and problem solving that entails human relations and technical challenges. We will offer leadership development for expedition guides, lead guides, principal guides and site-based management teams involved in rapidly changing institutions. Other themes include multicultural understanding, community service, risk prevention for "at risk" populations (as well as for professionals themselves) and environmental awareness. Our central goal is personal renewal along with professional growth, so that educators recover the zest of learning in their own lives and dedicate themselves to educational goals they find worthy and challenging. If we are successful in this effort, we anticipate even the possibility of sharing our approaches within the community with, for example, the police department or the work force in a factory or the researchers in a research and development center.

❖ Organizational Structures

Power, when shared and linked to competence or good ideas, illuminates. For schools to become high-performance organizations well grounded in the experience and knowledge of those who work there, the power must be shared, not only empowering faculty to act, but also creating the kind of supportive organization in which educators will be alerted and enabled to seek life-giving experiences for themselves. This sharing is part of the process of continuous renewal. Continuing administrative support is crucial to success, along with the initiative of teachers and students.

The key to school improvement is not to be found in systems, technical knowledge or the authority of experts. All these things can be helpful, but they can also be misleading if the foundation of the learning community is left to disintegrate. Students, teachers, administrators, parents and community leaders are human beings. To "break the mold," these people need something rarely mentioned in discussions of educational reform. They need to be impelled into the experience of working together to develop a shared vision of how teaching and learning can make their communities better places to live. They need a kind of community expedition much like an advocacy planning or character experience.

Structural features

- Web structure instead of rigid hierarchy
- Responsibility pushed down the organizational ladder
- Every adult has responsibility to "stop the line"
- Assumption that every child can and will learn and succeed
- Principal expedition advisor responsible for every child in his or her school
- Expedition advisor responsible for one group of students over three years
- Expedition advisors and principal advisor work in teams
- Central office function shifts to coordination and equalizer of resources
- Redefine career path with teaching most revered
- School-initiated curriculum and instruction

Schools function within systems. For our New American Schools to flourish as centers of Expeditionary Learning, new organizational structures within schools and school systems must be designed and implemented. Three complementary concepts would inform the organizational apparatus we will design to support Expeditionary Learning. First, we adapt the principles of Taiichi Ohno's "lean production" outlined by MIT authors Womack, Jones and Roos, who, after a five-year study of "Japan's revolutionary way of making and marketing cars," argue that "this will have a profound effect on human society—it will truly change the world." Second, we

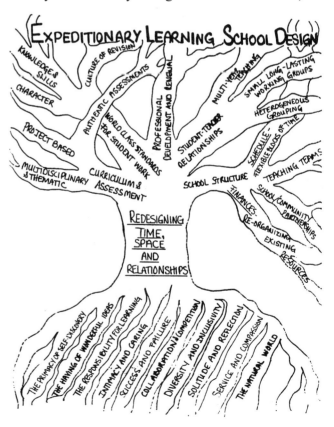

Drawing by Hannah Hopkins of the Expeditionary Learning Tree.

utilize the concept of an organizational web, instead of a hierarchy, as suggested by Sally Helgesen as a way to implement principles of decentralization. Third, we put teaching and learning at the heart of our enterprise, calling on all adults to see themselves as teachers first, supporting Expeditionary Learning in whatever capacity they can, and on all students to regard producing the basic work of the enterprise as their charge, as learners.

> Teaching, like law and medicine, is a practitioner's profession. We have lost sight of that fact in layers of bureaucracy.

Since American public education owes its organizational roots to the ideas of mass production based on an assembly line factory model, we find it useful to look to the cutting edge of business organization and service delivery as we design New American Schools.

In his lean production model, Taiichi Ohno's workers, who are virtually guaranteed life-time employment—much like tenured teachers—are organized to work in teams. Ohno instructed the teams to stop the whole line immediately if a problem emerged that they could not resolve. Ohno had no patience with factories where errors were treated as random events, to be repaired and forgotten. He taught the workers to trace every error systematically back to its cause and to devise a fix so that it would never happen again.

> "How can we help?" will replace "Here's another form for you to fill out."

"We are accustomed to thinking of our careers in terms of a climb toward ever higher levels of technical proficiency in an ever narrower area of specialization, accompanied by responsibility for ever larger number of subordinates. The career path in lean production leads to continuous broadening of one's professional skills, and they are applied in a team setting rather than in a rigid hierarchy," according to the MIT authors.

Children are more important, more complicated and more fragile than automobiles. Nevertheless, public education has treated children as if they were cars filing past on an assembly line. A high number of rejects and failures—whether in high drop-out or retention rates—was expected. The "output" of schools was seen as graduates, not as learning. Looking to lean production, we see a shared sense of responsibility for outcome and customer service. Every principal expedition guide would have ultimate responsibility for every single student; responsibility for the learning of special needs, bilingual, Chapter I, talented and gifted or any other labeled group of children would not be abdicated to a central office. We would strip out the bureaucratic layers traditionally interposed to oversee the mass production system in order to move resources into the classroom.

Instead, the role of the central office shifts to coordination and balancing of resources to ensure equity among schools. The central office or department of education must balance compliance issues with forging a meaningful partnership offering help to schools in meeting educational goals. "How can we help?" will replace "Here's another form for you to fill out."

According to Helgesen, the web model places leaders "in the middle reaching out" rather than "at the top reaching down." The contrasting models also reveal different notions of what constitutes effective communication. Hierarchy, emphasizing appropriate channels and the chain of command, discourages diffuse or random communication: information is filtered, gathered and sorted as it makes its way to the top. By contrast, the web facilitates direct communication, free flowing and loosely structured, by providing points of contact and direct tangents along which to connect. A prime example is in information gathering. In a top-down management model, information flows upward through channels; authority is established by having access to this progressively filtered information. The chain of command is broken, however, if the authority bypasses established channels in order to ask direct questions down the ladder. By contrast, being at the center, connected to every point in the whole, makes it possible for one to gather information directly from all sources. The most important aspect of this direct contact is that there is no filter, no supervisory layer through whom "lower-downs" are expected to go. Members of a web learn to balance action and communication so as to avoid paralyzing the centrally placed leader in overwhelming, trivial detail.

Compilation of a data base of community agencies and resources is a concrete responsibility best fulfilled in the central office, for example. Traditional central office roles, such as director of social studies or other curriculum-related titles, would be eliminated as we push responsibility down the organizational ladder to the school site. The central office should play a leadership role in facilitating communication and cooperation among individual schools and appropriately would convene curriculum task forces of expedition advisors, publish professional journals by teachers, and otherwise promote the rapid dissemination of successful practices and materials. Staff developers/liaisons would rotate and work as facilitators, change agents and "teachers of teachers" at individual schools which were most in need of additional resources to implement Expeditionary Learning. Central office responsibilities would also include keeping schools abreast of research; leveraging additional resources and services to schools; providing technical assistance; making sure funds were spent efficiently; and seeking additional funds to support these efforts.

5. Role of Family and Community

Our design views parents as powerful allies in educating their children. We value parents' experience, ideas, dreams, opinions, support, participation and perhaps most of all their stories, especially their own expeditions. We do not want parents simply to hold bake sales after school; we want parents *with us* preparing for and undertaking expeditions as valuable guides and revered keepers of stories. We do not admit a child to our school; we admit an entire family. The child's entire background is valued as a springboard for learning. Parents, through the local change teams, will help in the planning and implementation of an Expeditionary Learning school.

Since our centers of Expeditionary Learning tear down the barrier between school and the community, we hope to be able to offer parents an array of social services on-site. Time for parenting is the scarcest of commodities. It is treated with great care in our schools. We would rather help make time for a single parent by bringing the family care provider or social service worker to the school site than keep agencies and family help at bay and create transportation and logistical hardships for parents. The time that is thus saved may mean that a parent may listen to her student's group read aloud from works-in-progress or have the opportunity to share an expedition. We are committed to reaching out to existing services and finding concrete ways to strengthen and support families within schools, particularly families under poverty's grinding duress.

Drawing on Outward Bound's experience of bringing diverse groups of people together to solve problems in a demanding but supportive environment, each school will develop and commit to its own vision statement. Parents will be key players in shaping this site-specific covenant. The meaningful participation of parents and community members in school communities strengthens not only one school, but practiced widely enough strengthens our democratic society.

❖ My Child's Passion

We believe every parent wants "the best" for his or her child, including access to the widest possible opportunities. Every parent has a special expertise regarding his or her child. Our teachers and administrators must work with parents to draw upon that expertise.

For students, there will be no growth in their capacity for school learning until they are disposed to seek it. Whether schooling is compulsory or not, students will not learn unless they are willing to do so. Only children can change themselves, and the change, not always perceptible at first, unalterably takes place one child at a time. Like the duckling painstakingly pecking its way free of its shell, the child must struggle on her own and, in the process, strengthen her folded wings enough to one day fly.

◆ ◆ ◆

Every child has a deeply felt passion. The task of adults is to nurture and foster its realization.

◆ ◆ ◆

"What is your child's passion?" is one of the most important questions staff will ask parents in conference or telephone conversations each year. The answer for a seven-year-old might be "fishing" or "art." This is invaluable information for a classroom teacher. By recording the change and development in interests and passions over time, through a simple cumulative record, *My Child's Passion*, kept with school records, the parents' expertise begins to be validated in the official world of school. Parent observations and insights are counted and weighed beside the evaluations of teachers. Together all of these adults will be able to paint a fuller, more accurate picture of student progress and development.

❖ Homework Assistance Center

Expeditionary Learning will generate different kinds of homework assignments. Rather than

As one of their final projects for the initial learning expedition Our City, Ourselves, ninth-grade students created a map entitled "SPC and Me." Each map is both a personal statement about the student's view of New York and an accurate depiction of the student's route from home to school and of the geography of the city. Esmil's map is one outstanding example of this project. The descriptions on Esmil's map read:

- "The Empire State building and the word Macy's stand for 34th Street, where I buy most of my stuff."
- "Manhattan is where I live, and the blue line shows how I come and go to school every day just to get an education."
- "The Twin Towers stand for Battery Park and Battery Park City, where my friends and I hang around."
- "This airplane stands for a wish that I would work at the JFK airport one day."
- "This boat stands for South Street Seaport, where all my friends and I go to meet people and do a lot of crazy things."
- "This flower stands for Peace and Love."
- "The words Pearl Jam stand for my favorite group called Pearl Jam, which I love a lot."
- "If you look at it from a distance, the whole picture looks like an E. That E stands for my name, Esmil."

Map drawn by Esmil Feliz, student at the School for the Physical City in New York. The original dimensions are 18" × 24".

sheaves of worksheets, students will continue their project development outside school with the assistance of other students, parents and community members, with the option of visiting a homework assistance center located either on-site or in the community. Not often do parents and children have an opportunity to engage in intellectual pursuits together. By coming to the homework assistance center, families will share Expeditionary Learning. We will also explore low-cost applications of technology, including cable television as a means of offering call-in, interactive homework assistance for students and their families.

❖ Family Expeditionary Nights

Many of the journeys our students take will be into their communities, where they will gain understanding of the cultural, civic, business and non-profit sectors. These journeys will not end when the school day is over. Our goal is to enlist parents as active expedition guides as well.

Participating schools will host free family evening expeditions to science, cultural and children's museums as well as to institutions of higher education, industry and business. The entire family will have the opportunity to explore the community together. Evening hours, as well as time on the weekends and during the summer, recognize the needs of working parents to participate in school-related events outside the work day. Many parents are unfamiliar with the rich resources available in their community and, for any number of reasons, may be reluctant, unlikely or unable to venture into these institutions on their own. However, parents are much more likely to participate in a tour of the local newspaper plant, television station, aquarium or university if it is a school-sponsored event with their children. These evening expeditions will be tailored to draw on the resources of the particular site. This is a concrete example of schools and community institutions joining together to give families shared experiences of learning.

❖ Business Partners

Business partners will also be valued in our design for Expeditionary Learning schools. We will use shadowing, internships and apprenticeships as a way of weaving work experience into the fabric of expeditions so that students feel connected to the reality of their future and the skills necessary to succeed. For example, an advertising firm may work with students designing a radio advertising campaign that addresses the causes of violence and substance abuse in a community.

6. World-Class Standards and Assessment and National Education Goals

❖ 1993 Supplement

As a more comprehensive and overarching goal that reaches beyond the International Baccalaureate or the specific national education goals, we want to give practical meaning to the statement by Lawrence A. Cremin:

> "... the aim of education is not merely to make parents, or citizens, or workers, or indeed to surpass the Russians or the Japanese, but ultimately to make human beings who will live life to the fullest, who will continually add to the quality and meaning of their experience, and who will participate actively with their fellow human beings in the building of a good society."

Expeditionary Learning Outward Bound defines world-class standards as what we want students to know, be able to do, seek, and value, so that when they enter the postsecondary international receiving communities of the twenty-first century, they are competitive with any high school graduate in the world. We include among those receiving communities four-year colleges and universities, educational institutions offering one- and two-year academic and apprenticeship programs, and the workplace.

To validate our understanding of the kinds of competencies required by these receiving communities, we contacted leading colleges, international corporations and international service organizations, and found that rather than specifying knowledge and skills in the five core academic disciplines (English, mathematics, science, history and geography), they concentrated on competencies which included but went beyond them.

◆ ◆ ◆

In today's world, effective communication includes fluency in a second or even third language.

◆ ◆ ◆

We therefore chose to frame standards in general areas: communication; quantitative reasoning; scientific thinking; cultural, geographical and historical understanding; fitness; arts and aesthetics; technology; organization; and character. Our research indicates that framing standards from this broader vantage point better reflects the demands of the world beyond K-12 schooling than does setting content, performance and delivery standards for the core disciplines. In addition, it creates a much better fit with our design principles and our approach to curriculum and instruction. We briefly describe each of the content areas below, noting that the understanding and use of technology cuts across all of them.

Communication involves making meaning for oneself as well as conveying meaning to others. Communication is used for a variety of purposes (informing, expressing feelings artistically, formalizing quantitative relationships, etc.) and takes place in a variety of modes (oral, written, visual, etc.). In today's world, effective communication includes fluency in a second or even third language.

Quantitative reasoning utilizes problem-solving strategies, and includes creating relationships among quantifiable phenomena and communicating mathematical ideas using multiple representations. It involves making connections between mathematical ideas and those encountered in the sciences, social sciences, humanities and arts, and using them to study real world problems.

Scientific thinking undergirds scientific inquiry, experimentation as a mode of studying "answerable" questions, respect for evidence, thinking analytically and critically about data and suspending judgment until alternative possibilities have been explored. It involves consideration of how science both transforms and is transformed by the world we live in.

Cultural, geographic and historical understanding highlights the necessity of viewing people, objects, physical environments, events, and beliefs from multiple perspectives, whether in historical or contemporary times. It underscores the constructed and contextual nature of knowledge, and encourages the interrogation of all cultural myths, beliefs and creations.

Fitness refers to physical and socioemotional health and well-being, and knowing about, respecting and protecting one's body, spirit and social relationships. Included here are physical dimensions such as exercise, nutrition and protection against disease and pregnancy, and socioemotional aspects such as maintaining healthy habits of mind, social relationships and relationships with nature.

Arts and aesthetics calls attention to recognizing and transforming human experiences into artistic forms of expression, and gaining from these expressions greater insights into the meaning of human existence. Included here are music, the visual arts, dance, theater, poetry and other artistic modes of communication.

Technology influences the gathering and transmission as well as the creation of new information. Technological resources such as sophisticated software, video disks and interactive television help

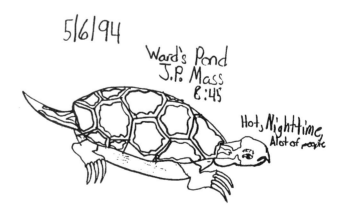

Drawing by Walter Coleman from his natural history journal for the Pond Life learning expedition at the Rafael Hernandez Bilingual School in Boston.

students and teachers make the discoveries and connections that are a necessary part of forming new ideas.

Organization emphasizes the importance of teaching students strategies for organizing time and space. It also fosters an approach to challenging tasks that calls for breaking them down into manageable elements and completing entire projects with success and pride.

Character refers to the attitudes, values and dispositions which influence the judgments, decisions and choices that individuals make. It recognizes the deep connection between intellectual development and character development and calls for students to develop their capacities for empathy, perseverance and courage.

We are developing content standards in each of the above six areas, and as we are progressing, and as they are published, we are also referring to nationally developed discipline-specific or domain-specific standards such as the Curriculum and Evaluation Standards for School Mathematics (National Council of Teachers of Mathematics, 1989).

In the interim each school will continue to use existing district and/or state outcomes. At this time, and particularly in schools that practice tracking, the vast majority of students in all but the highest tracks do not achieve district outcomes. We believe that our schools, committed to teaching all students and to eliminating tracking, will provide the kinds of educational experiences that will enable many more students to achieve those outcomes. This in itself would arguably constitute achieving world-class standards.

❖ Assessment of Student Performance

Expeditionary Learning's model for assessing student performance in each of these content areas is derived from the Literacy Bands endorsed by the Ministry of Education, Victoria, Australia, which outline a continuum of nine successive levels of competency in the development of reading and writing abilities in children. The Literacy Bands are developmental rather than age- or grade-specific and illustrate the concept of continua of growth that we are applying to all of the areas.

Standards-setting prompts teachers, parents and administrators to articulate their expectations and to think constructively about the consequences when a student's achievement, or the achievement of a class as a whole, falls short of the standard.

This model assists teachers in setting clear goals, whether for individuals or for a class as a whole, underscoring the fact that standards-setting is both descriptive and prescriptive. It prompts teachers, parents and administrators to articulate their expectations and to think constructively about the consequences when a student's achievement, or the achievement of a class as a whole, falls short of the standard. Furthermore, making reference to this model allows a teacher to write a profile that emphasizes valuable information about the actual skills and understandings possessed either by the class in general or by an individual child in relation to expectations, instead of simply assigning a percentile score.

❖ Performance Standards

Expeditionary Learning has drawn on existing exemplary high school models, extending themes that are used by them, such as "the autobiography," to apply across the K-12 spectrum. In Expeditionary Learning schools, a progression of experiences will be established as checkpoints at grades three or four, eight, and twelve, connected by the continuation of themes in the passage experiences, and addressing each of the six content areas specified above. Thus certain thematic challenges in on-demand tasks, along with portfolio samples of students' work, will form the basis of student performance data.

We recognize that these new authentic assessment practices require comprehensive teacher development. We will continue to develop standards and assessments this spring in collaboration with principals and teachers from our sites, and in consultation with Professor Dennie Wolf of the Harvard Graduate School of Education and Performance Assessment Collaboratives for Education (PACE). The real work of collecting samples of student performances and developing rubrics will begin in earnest in one year.

Teach what you love to teach, share what you love to share, test your readiness to do the unknown.

❖ Senior Service Expedition

The individual senior service expedition is a demonstration of a student's particular passion in service to others. It is evidence of readiness to go on to the next step. "Teach what you love to teach, share what you love to share, test your readiness to do the unknown" is the advice given to students as they generate their plans. As a rite of passage, it serves as one bridge over which adolescents cross—one by one—from student to teacher. The prerequisites structure a base of skills and experiences, including completion of an outdoor wilderness course with a solo, passing the intermediate level Emergency Medical Technician and Red Cross Junior Lifesaving courses and successfully participating in group service expeditions. From this base, it is our hope and expectation that the students themselves will climb to great heights.

Prerequisites for the individual senior service expedition:

1. Successfully completing an Outward Bound or equivalent wilderness course which includes a solo.
2. Documenting active participation in group service expeditions.
3. Meeting the requirements for certification as an intermediate level Emergency Medical Technician.
4. Passing the Red Cross Junior Life saving exam.
5. If a United States citizen 18 years or older, registering to vote.

Sample of a Senior Service Expedition: Never Too Late

Juan loves computers and he has proposed that he offer a ten-week computer class in an elderly housing complex. His proposal includes a reading list on teaching methodology, gerontology and computer instruction. His advisor suggests he add *Nobody Asked Me*, Kenneth Koch's book about teaching writing in a nursing home. Juan approaches the housing administrator and together they identify two computers he can use for his weekly class. He solicits a donation of a third computer from an area business by meeting with the owner. Juan will serve as expedition guide to a group of elders he has recruited to take his course.

Initially residents do not respond to the registration notices he has posted. Juan tries going door to door to introduce himself and invite—and cajole—residents to come on Thursday. "But I don't know how to type!," "I'm too old for computers" and "What's the use of learning that at my age?" are some comments elders offer as reasons for not attending. Juan must generate countervailing reasons that they should take a risk and come. Five senior citizens show up and Juan welcomes them with refreshments he has made. He uses team-building and trust exercises he has learned from his many previous expeditions.

"Why did you come? What would you like to learn?" he asks his new students. From their answers—which range from "I was curious and I thought maybe I could write my son a letter" to "What you said about needing my help so you could graduate made me decide I might as well come"—Juan shapes a curriculum. They generate a list of uses for the computer in their own lives. They begin with making notecards, notices, invitations; writing letters; and designing menus for the cafeteria. One woman designs a business card for herself because she "always wanted one." Juan is concerned that he is not connecting with them at a deeper level, so he decides to ask students if they would like to work on a booklet filled with their best advice to people his age. By the next session, Juan has recruited three new students to join the project. Juan's expedition log documents, reflects and analyzes his reading and experience as well as his ongoing discussions with his advisor. By the last class, the group has decided to continue meeting without Juan, though they invite him to return often. They join him at school for his presentation of his senior service expedition and read excerpts from their booklet, *Never Too Late*.

❖ ❖ ❖

> We believe every child has the capacity to graduate from our schools, and our goal is 100 percent completion.

❖ ❖ ❖

❖ National Education Goals

Our design for schools is consistent with the national education goals. Our goal is not just to get students ready to learn in the early childhood years, but eager to learn. "By the year 2000, all children in America will start school ready to learn," will be specifically addressed through the creation of Expeditionary Learning centers for pre-kindergarten and kindergarten age students inspired and modeled upon the pedagogy in use in the internationally recognized public pre-schools of Reggio Emilia, Italy. These schools, which "rest on the idea that all children are different" (*Newsweek*, December 2, 1991), view the nutritional, language, scientific and artistic development and physical well-being of young children in an integrated and developmentally appropriate manner, and lend themselves well to our Expeditionary Learning design.

We believe every child has the capacity to graduate from our schools and our goal is 100 percent completion, more than the 90 percent in the second national goal. We will engage all students in the experience of learning through demonstrated dropout

Students at the Rafael Hernandez Bilingual School in Boston hold up their work from the Young Authors Project. Photograph by Brian Smith/NASDC.

prevention measures, including keeping students with a core of teachers for several years.

The third goal states that "By the year 2000, American students will leave grades four, eight and twelve having demonstrated competency in challenging subject matter, including English, math, science, history and geography; and every school in America will ensure that all students learn to use their minds well, so they may be prepared for responsible citizenship, further learning, and productive employment in our modern economy." We will meet and in many cases exceed the third goal, through rigorous academic and service requirements. Fluency in the arts and fluency in a foreign language, important routes to knowledge and expression, are integral expectations for our students. Since we view mental well-being and physical fitness as important personal and civic responsibilities, our students will set and meet their own individual physical fitness goals, in many instances again exceeding the President's goals.

**Sample expedition:
Mapping and navigation expedition**

Principal theme: *Scale and Structure*. The study of scale and structure of Earth, landforms, the solar system and beyond allows students to develop an appreciation of their relationship to their geographic surroundings. It also extends their frontiers beyond their immediate surroundings.

Principal objective: Develop an ability to describe movement from one location to another in a community, on Earth, in the solar system, in the galaxy and in the universe.

Activity objectives: Upon completion of a series of activities in the expedition, a student will be able to:

- Trace the development of our knowledge of mapping and navigation.
- Compare and contrast ancient and modern methods for determining geographic and magnetic direction.
- Construct models of ancient astronomical instruments and observatories.
- Compare and contrast ancient and modern maps of Earth.
- Measure Earth's circumference.
- Determine exact location on Earth's surface.
- Construct and interpret topographic maps of specific geographic areas.
- Use instruments to measure location, distance and time.
- Compute values for direction, distance, time and speed.
- Construct a true-scale model of the solar system.
- Predict the positions of the planets in the night sky.
- Plan an interplanetary expedition.
- Compare the size of the solar system with the Milky Way galaxy and the entire universe.
- Apply the concept of scale to the design of a structure.
- Design an orienteering course for the community.
- Assist community agencies in the planning and preservation of parks, gardens, building sites and so on.

Our design integrates scientific and mathematical reasoning and capability across disciplines in accordance with the recent standards adopted by the National Council of Teachers of Mathematics. Expeditions feature a strong hands-on science and technological dimension, especially with calculators, computers and interactive video, consistent with the fourth national goal: "By the year 2000, U.S. students will be first in the world in science and math achievement." Every year every student will study mathematics and science not to demonstrate memorization of unconnected data but to demonstrate scientific and mathematic reasoning and capability in the solution of a problem or challenge.

Central to our pedagogy is the corollary belief that the best discipline is self-discipline.

Parents and community members are vital learners in our expedition centers, reflecting our commitment to address the fifth national goal: "By the year

2000, every adult American will be literate and will possess the knowledge and skills necessary to compete in a global economy and exercise the rights and responsibilities of citizenship." We are prepared to conduct literacy expeditions for our students' families and for other adults as well.

"Freedom only comes through self-discipline," Isaac Stern noted. Central to our pedagogy is the corollary belief that the best discipline is self-discipline. The use of drugs, violence, alcohol and cigarettes is inconsistent with our values and pedagogy. Students will specifically explore negotiation skills, mediation, violence prevention, substance abuse, fetal alcohol syndrome, smoking, parenting skills and goal setting beginning in the early grades. This is consistent with the final national goal: "By the year 2000, every school in America will be free of drugs and violence and will offer a disciplined environment conducive to learning."

7. How a School Becomes a Center of Expeditionary Learning

❖ How We Will Persuade Others

Persuasion is an organizing task, one which is most effectively coupled with opportunities and incentives. We are asking people to change. As a design team we will model what we are asking schools and schools systems to do. We will offer opportunities and incentives and place a high premium on communication.

Utilizing the team's existing network of affiliations with school systems, we will select at least three to five systems within which to implement Expeditionary Learning. School systems that have been working with Outward Bound and that have expressed interest in piloting our design include Portland, Maine; Boston; New York City; Decatur, Georgia; and Douglas County, Colorado. We will work with school systems and state departments of education in our pilot sites to facilitate the changes necessary for state and district structures to support active implementation in their jurisdiction.

In the first year, we will collect, create and lead sample expeditions at all levels (pre-K to 2, 3-5, 6-8 and 9-12) in pilot sites. We will host a working conference on Expeditionary Learning for the three to five pilot schools/systems. We will fund joint planning time for the design team and the local schools as well as providing on-site schoolwide team building for parents, teachers and administrators. We will co-host with the pilot school systems family expeditionary nights and invitational local conferences on the implementation of Expeditionary Learning for community organizations and cultural institutions. We will offer on-site technical assistance and comprehensive communication, including electronic mail among sites, a hotline for teachers, parents and community and technical assistance in securing funds for planning. There is also the potential for cable television and radio programming developed for parents, depending on the community. In any case, we will reach out to all parents in the schools that have been selected to enlist their ideas and participation in the design process. Through the course of joint planning, persons will serve on work groups to develop local adaptation in these four areas:

1. Curriculum and assessment
2. Policies and governing structure
3. Community and parents
4. Teacher renewal

Following on-site meetings, we will select three to five pilot systems and we will sign a Memorandum of Agreement with each school system chosen. One of our first activities together will be participation by individuals from those school systems and design team members in a special Outward Bound course designed to accelerate teamwork. The idea of Expeditionary Learning must be experienced firsthand if it is to be truly owned by those seeking to implement it.

Why chartered schools as well as existing schools?

The opportunity to start at least one school from scratch holds great appeal. The change process can be significantly accelerated if a school is specifically chartered as a new center for Expeditionary Learning. We are asking people to go to places they have never been. The dissemination and replication process will speed up if we have at least one school that can share its lessons. With little to stand in its way, that center would have been able to go further, deeper and faster than its colleagues in existing schools. We will try to charter our own school and then, perhaps, several model schools while also working with individuals who are interested in pursuing a chartering option.

Nevertheless, our design holds promise for existing schools that commit themselves to a transformation process. Change is often painful and yields conflict before harmony. We will work on-site to assist in conflict resolution, as well as implementation of the myriad details involved in a change of this dimension. How shall we arrange the schedule? How shall we look at staffing patterns? What should be the length of the school year or day? These questions have local answers. We will help schools and communities find the answers that best adapt our design principles to their sites and conditions.

Clearly, neither chartering nor transformation occurs in isolation. We will work closely with school systems to nurture and sustain the dramatic school-based change our design requires. There are many concrete steps that school systems can take to encourage the creation of schools based upon our design. Central office administrators and staff must willingly expand their roles, and in some cases, change or waive regulations, if these changes are to take root. The most fundamental change is an expansion of administrators' view of themselves, regardless of their position or bureaucratic responsibility, as teachers with a stake first and foremost in Expeditionary Learning and students' lives.

8. Our Structure

We will organize ourselves consistent with the organizational structure we advocate for school systems and schools. Every design team member will have a responsibility to stop the line, bringing our process to a momentary halt while we trace back to the origin of a problem so that we resolve it completely and do not repeat it. All team members will teach, drawing on the broadest talents of our group. Our organizational structure will be a web rather than a hierarchy. The design team of core members will have primary responsibility for creating these frameworks for Expeditionary Learning. The design team will work with at least three local change teams from different school systems that have applied and been selected to implement our design. The local change teams will plan implementation of the design with comprehensive technical assistance from design team members.

We will seek and value the advice of a Council of Senior Advisors as well as a Teacher Advisory Board, two groups we will convene for the purpose of sharing their best thinking and providing us with feedback throughout the design process. One advantage of the web structure is the cross-pollination of ideas.

Our schematic of our proposed organization puts students in the center. The design team and local change teams will work most closely together, centering efforts on students' learning, character development and achievement. The Council of Senior Advisors and the Teacher Advisory Board, which respectively will meet quarterly, create a communication and broader accountability loop around the design team and local change teams.

9. Evaluation and Self-Assessment

Evaluation and self-assessment are integral to the process of any expedition. Did we meet our goals? What would we have done differently? What did we learn when faced with the unexpected? What would we advise others who are undertaking expeditions similar to ours?

- ◆ Qualitative "telling the story"
- ◆ Documenting design process
- ◆ Look at transformation
- ◆ Focus groups
- ◆ Continuous feedback

The expedition is not complete until we can answer these questions to our own satisfaction and to the satisfaction of others. Assessment of children, and by extension educational reform efforts for students' achievement, have traditionally entailed standardized results and statistically measure outcomes. "What is the single right answer we are looking for?" often drives an assessment. We propose asking something different: What are the questions we should be asking? What would assist us in documenting and measuring what we have accomplished during the five years of our design effort? What was successful and on what terms? On the one hand, we view evaluation as ongoing so that we can continually assess our progress, stopping the line if necessary, and learn from our mistakes as well as our successes. We also value evaluation as an opportunity for final reflection and cumulative assessment

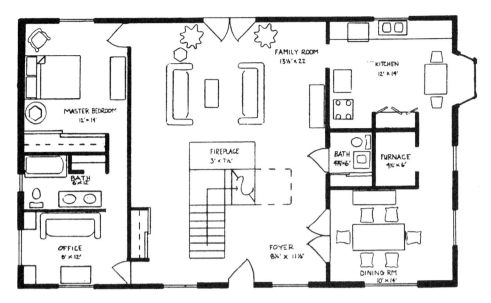

Architecture Summit blueprint by Barbra Lail, a teacher at Clairemont Elementary School in Decatur, Georgia.

at the end of our work. While all team members actively contribute to the evaluation process, we designate one team member with primary evaluation responsibility. The Academy for Educational Development is particularly suited for this charge.

In the first year, we will document the design process and prepare an evaluation plan for the entire project. We will utilize focus groups, collect socioeconomic, ethnographic data on the districts in which schools are being developed and conduct interviews with design team members, local change committees, the Council of Senior Advisors and members of the Teacher Advisory Board.

Bibliography

American Federation of Teachers. *Education Reform Overseas* (video recording). Producer, Jamie Horwitz; director, Charles Stopak. Fairfax, VA: Media Associates, 1988.

Bacon, Stephen. *The Conscious Use of Metaphor in Outward Bound*. Denver: Colorado Outward Bound School, 1983.

Brandt, Ron. "On Research and School Organization: A Conversation with Bob Slavin." *Educational Leadership* 46, No. 2 (October 1988).

Caine, Renate Nummela, & Geoffrey Caine. *Making Connections: Teaching and the Human Brain*. Alexandria, VA: Association for Supervision and Curriculum Development, 1991.

Coleman, James S. "Experiential Learning and Information Assimilation: Toward an Appropriate Mix." *Journal of Experiential Education* 2 (Spring 1979): 6-9.

———. "Differences Between Experiential and Classroom Learning." In *Experiential Learning: Rationale, Characteristics, and Assessment*, edited by Morris Keeton, pp. 49-61. San Francisco: Jossey-Bass, 1976.

Comer, James P. *A Conversation between James Comer and Ronald Edmonds: Fundamentals of Effective School Improvement*. Dubuque, Iowa: Kendall/Hunt, 1989.

———. *School Power: Implications of an Intervention Project*. New York: Free Press; London: Collier Macmillan, 1980.

Cremin, Lawrence Arthur. *Popular Education and its Discontents*. New York: Harper & Row, 1980.

Dewey, John. *Experience and Education*. First published by Kappa Delta Phi in 1938. Reprint. New York: Collier Books, 1963.

Dillard, Annie. *The Writing Life*. New York: Harper & Row, 1989.

Duckworth, Eleanor. *"The Having of Wonderful Ideas" & Other Essays on Teaching and Learning*. New York: Teachers College Press, 1987.

Fullan, Michael, ed. *Understanding Teacher Development*. New York: Cassell, 1990.

Gardner, Howard. *Frames of Mind: The Theory of Multiple Intelligences*. New York: Basic Books, 1983.

Godfrey, Robert. *Outward Bound: Schools of the Possible*. Garden City, NY: Anchor Press/Doubleday, 1980.

Graham, Richard. "Youth and Experiential Learning." In *Youth: The Seventy-Fourth Yearbook of the National Society for the Study of Education*, Part I, edited by Robert J. Havighurst and Philip H. Dreyer, pp. 161-193. Chicago: University of Chicago Press, 1975.

Greene, Maxine. "Maxine Greene on Leadership: An Interview." *Klingenstein Newsletter* 1 (Winter 1990).

New York: The Klingenstein Center on Independent School Education, Teachers College, Columbia University.

Hahn, Kurt. "Origins of the Outward Bound Trust." *Outward Bound*, edited by David James. London: Routledge and Kegan Paul Ltd., 1957.

———. "Outward Bound." In *World Year Book of Education,* pp. 436-462. London: Evans Brothers, 1957.

Hamilton, Stephen F. "Raising Standards and Reducing Dropout Rates." In *School Dropouts: Patterns and Policies*, edited by Gary Natriello, pp. 148-167. New York: Teachers College Press, 1986.

Helgesen, Sally. *The Female Advantage: Women's Ways of Leadership.* New York: Doubleday Currency, 1990.

Hinckle, Pia. In Barbara Kantrowitz and Pat Wingert. "The Best Schools in the World." *Newsweek*, December 2, 1991, pp. 50-64.

Holmes Group, The. *Tomorrow's Schools: Principles for the Design of Professional Development Schools: A Report of the Holmes Group.* East Lansing, MI: Erickson Hall, Holmes Group, 1990.

International Baccalaureate Office. *General Guide to the International Baccalaureate.* Geneva: International Baccalaureate Office, 1980.

James, Thomas. *Education at the Edge: The Colorado Outward Bound School.* Denver: Colorado Outward Bound School, 1980.

———. "An Urban Strategy: Outward Bound in New York City." Fund for the City of New York. Unpublished paper, October 7, 1987.

———. "Outward Bound and Public Education." Education Department, Brown University. Unpublished Paper, March 1989.

Koch, Kenneth. *I Never Told Anybody: Teaching Poetry Writing in a Nursing Home.* New York: Random House, 1977.

Kolb, David A. *Experiential Learning: Experience as the Source of Learning and Development.* Englewood Cliffs, NJ: Prentice-Hall, 1984.

Lentz, Robert R. "Outward Bound—Education Through Experience." In *Models for Integrated Education,* edited by Daniel U. Levine, pp. 77-88. Worthington, OH: Charles A. Jones, 1971.

Marsh, Herbert W., Garry E. Richards, J. Barnes. "Multi-Dimensional Self-Concepts: The Effects of Participation in an Outward Bound Program." *Journal of Personality and Social Psychology* 50 (1986): 195-204.

Means, Linda Klein. "Outward Bound Enters the Public Schools." *The Boston Globe*, Sunday, January 26, 1992, Learning Section, pp. 32-34.

Miner, Joshua L. & Joe Boldt. *Outward Bound USA: Learning Through Experience in Adventure-based Education.* Philadelphia: William Morrow, 1981.

Moore, David Thornton. "Discovering the Pedagogy of Experience." *Harvard Educational Review* 51 (1981): 286-300.

Olson, David R. & Jerome Bruner. "Learning Through Experience and Learning Through Media." In *Media and Symbols: The Forms of Expression, Communication and Education: The Seventy-Third Yearbook of the National Society for the Study of Education,* Part I, edited by David R. Olson, pp. 125-150. Chicago: University of Chicago Press, 1974.

Sashkin, Marshall & John Egermeier. *School Change Models and Processes: A Review of Research and Practice.* Washington, DC: Office of Educational Research and Improvement, Working Draft, November 1991.

Schulze, Joseph R. "An Analysis of the Impact of Outward Bound on Twelve High Schools." Mankato State College, Mankato, Minn., September 1, 1971.

Senge, Peter M. *The Fifth Discipline: The Art and Practice of the Learning Organization.* New York: Doubleday/Currency, 1990.

Tinker, Robert F. *A Curriculum for Science Instruction.* Cambridge, MA: Technical Education Research Centers, 1981.

Tuchman, Barbara W. *A Distant Mirror: The Calamitous Fourteenth Century.* New York: Knopf, 1978.

Wehlage, Gary G. & Robert A. Rutter. "Dropping Out: How Much Do Schools Contribute to the Problem?" *Teachers College Record*, 87, 3 (Spring 1986): 374-92. New York: Teachers College Press.

Womack, James P., Daniel T. Jones, Daniel Roos. *The Machine that Changed the World: How Japan's Secret Weapon in the Global Auto Wars will Revolutionize Western Industry.* New York: Harper Perennial, 1991.

Ylvisaker, Paul. "The Missing Dimension." Outward Bound International Conference, Keynote Address, September 9, 1988.

Part Two

Self-Discovery

The Only Mountain Worth Climbing

An Historical and Philosophical Exploration of Outward Bound and Its Link to Education

by Thomas James

Outward Bound is more than a set of methods and activities. It represents a core of values, a philosophy of education. In this broader sense, as well as in its applications as a specific method of learning, Outward Bound has a deep historical affinity with conventional schooling.

The historical background is useful to consider when trying to understand the power of Outward Bound for improving schooling processes today. The moving spirit of Outward Bound, Kurt Hahn, employed challenge and outdoor adventure not for their own sake, but as a way of teaching perseverance, skill, teamwork, leadership, and compassionate service to the students at Gordonstoun, the school he founded in the 1930s. Having provided equipment and training, Hahn then established watch patrols for emergencies along the Scottish coast using teams of the privileged students from his high school. Hahn also decided to include other children from poor families living near Gordonstoun. He created a sense of moral community around demanding personal commitments to such things as fitness, craftsmanship, and service. He later widened this program into more systematic proposals such as the County Badge Scheme, Outward Bound, and the Duke of Edinburgh Award. Hahn's inclusion of poor children along with the rich established a cardinal principle that became part of Outward Bound in later years: bring together people from different social classes in common pursuits leading to self-discovery and service to others.

With the coming of World War II, Kurt Hahn became aware of the devastating toll that German submarines were taking on the British ships in the North Sea. Building upon his experience as an educator who had used challenging outdoor activities requiring cooperation and craftsmanship along with academic learning, he and others devised a program of intensive training from initiatives he had been running at this school. The program became Outward Bound, which took its name from the nautical term for a ship leaving port on a sea journey.

Outward Bound developed into a separate organization during the war and eventually became a worldwide movement in its own right, resulting in several dozen schools all over the world. But it is significant that the program first took shape, pedagogically, as an educational innovation arising from a secondary school.

Your disability is your opportunity.

To understand the potential of Outward Bound for helping teachers and learners in schools, it is useful to look more closely at Hahn's educational values. This chapter considers Hahn the educator, the roots of his educational vision, and the relevance of his ideas to classrooms and schools today. Since only a brief introductory sketch can be provided here, I will also suggest some references at the end for readers wishing to explore Hahn and his educational vision in greater depth.

Let us begin by looking more closely at Kurt Hahn's life and times. Born in 1886, Hahn was the second of four sons in a Jewish family in Berlin. Schooled with conventional German rigor at the Wilhelms gymnasium, he graduated in 1904, the year in which he experienced a sunstroke that left

---

Copyright © Thomas James, Brown University, 1992. All rights reserved.

Reprinted with permission of the author and Outward Bound®, Inc. Material from this article was also included in the *Journal of Experiential Education* and in a book under the author's copyright.

him with a recurring disability for the rest of his life. Hahn went on to Oxford from 1904 to 1906 to read classics, with the support of his father, Oskar Hahn, industrialist and anglophile. From 1906 to 1910 he studied at various universities—without, however, completing any degree. Returning to England in 1910, he continued to study at Oxford, and convalesced during the summers at Moray in northeastern Scotland, until the beginning of the Great War in 1914 called him home to Germany. Kurt Hahn never achieved a degree beyond his secondary schooling.

During the war, Hahn served as a reader for the German Foreign Office and then the Supreme Command, reviewing English-language newspapers to gauge popular opinion. Politically, he allied himself with those inside the German government who were seeking a negotiated peace in Western Europe instead of protracted war. Perceived as a liberal within the political spectrum of his day, Hahn advocated greater restraint in pushing German war aims. He espoused a code of responsibility that would be equally binding in war and peace; he used his influence behind the scenes to remind those in power about conciliatory factions at work within the governments of enemy nations.

At the end of the war, Prince Max von Baden asked Hahn to become his personal secretary. An articulate and enterprising young man, Hahn helped Prince Max, Germany's last imperial chancellor, to complete his memoirs, probably writing as much as editing. Whatever the form of their collaboration, the two men left a record of tough-minded idealism and political vigilance. When Prince Max returned to spend his last years at the ancestral castle of his family at Schloss Salem, by Lake Constance, he took Kurt Hahn with him and they discussed projects to renew the ethical traditions of German social life, traditions they believed were threatened not only by extremism on the right and left, but by incomprehension, moral failings, and lack of will in the middle. In 1920, with Prince Max as benefactor, Hahn opened Salem School in part of the castle.

Salem School, which still operates today, was influenced by the educational ideas of Plato, Cecil Reddie's Abbotsholme and other English schools started by German educators under the leadership of Herman Lietz. Salem represented an attempt to create a healthy environment in which young people could learn habits of life that would protect them against what Hahn saw as the deteriorating values of modern life. He identified the worst declines as those in fitness, memory and imagination, and compassion.

Directing the school from 1920 until 1933, Hahn placed greater emphasis on noncompetitive physical activities and democratic forms of social cooperation than was the case in conventional German schools. At the urging of Prince Max, he incorporated egalitarian aims into the design of the school; while Salem naturally attracted the children of the wealthy, it also made space for, and actively sought, less privileged students. Emulating the Cistercian monks who had inhabited the castle for many centuries, the students and teachers at Salem School helped the surrounding communities through various forms of service, including a fire brigade.

Among the unusual assumptions underlying all forms of instruction at Salem was Hahn's conviction that students should experience failure as well as success.

The curriculum at Salem prepared young people for higher education, but not without laying the groundwork for a life of moral and civic virtue, the chief aims of the school. Among the unusual assumptions underlying all forms of instruction at Salem was Hahn's conviction that students should experience failure as well as success. They should learn to overcome negative inclinations within themselves and prevail against all adversity.

He believed, moreover, that students should learn to discipline their own needs and desires for the good of the community. They should realize through their own experience the connection between self-discovery and service. He also insisted that true learning required periods of silence and solitude as well as directed activity. Each day the students took a silent walk to commune with nature and revitalize their powers of reflection.

To keep mental and physical growth in balance, Hahn developed the notion of training play for his students, each of whom committed himself to an individually designed, gradually more challenging regimen of physical exercise and personal hygiene. Unlike the physical education program of other schools, the aim of the training plan was simply to establish good living habits, not to produce high levels of performance in competitive games.

An assassin failed to end Hahn's life in 1923. Still in his early thirties, the schoolmaster was controversial, a gadfly, a target because he was a moral leader far beyond the lives of his students and teachers. The director of Salem—the school's name means "peace"—idolized few men in his lifetime, but one incident he often recounted was the confrontation between Max Weber, Germany's most distinguished social scientist, and an angry crowd of leftist demonstrators in 1918. Weber shouted that he had never crawled before kings and emperors in the past, and he was not going to crawl before any mob now.

Similarly, Kurt Hahn refused to back down from the moral aims that animated every aspect of education as far as he was concerned. In a nation frighteningly polarized by the right and the left in political debate, Hahn forced educational issues into the larger discussion of how society should be organized, and what people must do to maintain human decency in a world of conflict. No idyllic schoolmaster's life awaited him.

When it finally came, in the early 1930s, the controversy that pushed Kurt Hahn out of Germany involved the right, not the left. As the Nazis rose to power, the director of Salem School became an outspoken opponent. In 1932 a group of fascist storm troopers kicked a leftist activist to death before the eyes of his mother. Adolph Hitler immediately praised the action of his followers. Kurt Hahn wrote to the alumni of Salem, telling them to choose between Salem and Hitler. A man who knew Hahn at the time called it "the bravest deed in cold blood that I have ever witnessed." When he became chief of state in 1933, Hitler imprisoned Hahn. Fortunately for the embattled educator, he still had friends in Britain who remembered his idealism and his hopes for friendship between the two nations. Prime Minister Ramsay MacDonald and others helped to arrange for Hahn's release and timely emigration to England in 1933.

Within a year of his arrival, Kurt Hahn started another institution, Gordonstoun, which became one of Britain's most distinguished progressive schools and served as a model for similar schools in other countries. In the following decades, Hahn's educational vision served as the moving spirit for new

Sculpture by Laurie Sevigny from the Facing History and Ourselves Summit. Photograph by Scott Hartl/Expeditionary Learning.

institutions and programs of worldwide renown: the Moray Badge and County Badge Schemes and their successor, the Duke of Edinburgh Awards; Outward Bound; the Trevelyan Scholarships; and the United World Colleges.

Reaching back into this pre-history of Outward Bound, we might well look for the origins of the idea in 1913 instead of 1941, when Outward Bound was founded. For in the summer of 1913, instead of vacationing, as he hoped, with a friend in Scotland, and while recuperating from the sunstroke he had suffered a few years before, Kurt Hahn outlined his idea for a school based on principles set forth in Plato's *Republic*. Hahn was twenty-eight years old and had never run a school, or even taught in one. The ideal school he imagined never came into being, but it exerted a profound influence on all his subsequent efforts as an educator and statesman: Salem School, in Germany, in 1920; Gordonstoun School, in Scotland, in 1934; Outward Bound in Wales, in 1941; and Atlantic College, in England, in 1962.

In *English Progressive Schools*, Robert Skidelsky analyzes Hahn's debt to Plato as follows:

> Plato was a political reformer who sought to recall the Athenians to the old civic virtues eroded, as he saw it, by democratic enthusiasm and soft living. His aim was to educate a class of leaders in a "healthy pasture" remote from the corrupting environment, whose task it would be to regenerate society. Hahn must have been haunted by similar visions of decay as, inspired by these ideas, he drew up a plan in 1913 for a school modeled on Platonic principles. The war that broke out a year later and ended in the collapse of Germany was to give them a new urgency: to convert what might have remained a purely academic speculation into an active campaign for social and political regeneration.

Outward Bound places unusual emphasis on physical challenge, not as an end in itself, but as an instrument for training the will to strive for mastery. There is also the insistent use of action, instead of states of mind, to describe the reality of the individual. Education is tied unequivocally to experience, to what one does and not so much to one's attitudes and opinions.

A thread running from Plato through Hahn and through Outward Bound is the responsibility of individuals to make their own personal goals consonant with social necessity. Not only is the part subordinated to the whole, but the part cannot even understand its own identity, its relations and its responsibility, until it has grasped the nature of the whole. Having stood up to Hitler before being exiled from Nazi Germany in 1933, Hahn believed in individual freedom, but he believed that students should be impelled into experiences that would teach them the bonds of social life necessary to protect such freedom. He took from Plato the idea that a human being cannot achieve perfection without becoming part of a perfect society—that is, without creating social harmony to sustain the harmonious life of the individual.

◆ ◆ ◆

The schools Hahn founded sent bookworms to the playing fields and jocks to the reading room.

◆ ◆ ◆

This is the overall structure of the argument in the *Republic*, and it is also the most important lesson of an Outward Bound course, the lesson without which personal development is of questionable value. In a small group away from the degenerate ways of the world, the individual student comes to grips with what must be done to create a just society. In attempting to construct such a challenge, Hahn placed compassion above all other values of Outward Bound because it among all emotions is capable of reconciling individual strength with collective need.

The prospect of wholeness, the possibility, at least, of human life becoming an equilibrium sustained by harmony and balance, is what makes this form of education even thinkable. Skidelsky again offers a lucid analysis of the source of Hahn's thinking:

> The second idea which Hahn assimilated was Plato's notion that the principle of perfection was harmony and balance. The perfection of the body, he held, depends upon a harmony of its elements. Virtue (the health of the soul) is the harmony or balance between the various faculties of the psyche: reason, the appetites and spirit.
>
> Virtue in the state is the harmony between its functional elements: thinkers, soldiers and artisans. The same principle can be extended indefinitely—to relations between states, and so on.

This passage sheds some light on Hahn's interest in giving his students experiences that would complement their strengths and weaknesses. In his speeches he said he wanted to turn introverts inside out and extroverts outside in. He wanted the poor to help the rich break their "enervating sense of privilege" and the rich to help the poor in building a true "aristocracy of talent."

The schools he founded sent bookworms to the playing fields and jocks to the reading room. He did not produce outstanding athletes, but his students exhibited consistently high levels of fitness, accomplishment and social spirit. He said he valued mastery in the sphere of one's weakness over performance in the sphere of one's strength.

The preceding paragraphs do not record Hahn's debt to other thinkers, such as Rousseau, Goethe and William James, to name a few. William James, for example, in his "The Moral Equivalent of Wars," asked if it is not possible in time of peace to build the kind of social spirit and productivity one takes for granted in time of war. Hahn saw Outward

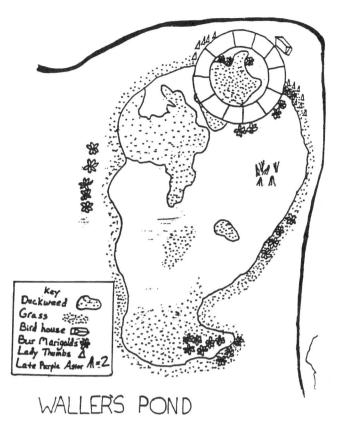

WALLER'S POND

A map from the Field Guide created by fifth graders at Table Mound Elementary School in Dubuque, Iowa, as part of their learning expedition, Pond Life. Students went to local ponds, took samples of pond life, and after identifying their findings, created the Field Guide so other students could learn from their discoveries.

Bound as an answer to that question. Goethe wrote of an education that would need to occur in a place apart, a "Pedagogical Province," so that individuals could be strengthened and given skills to survive, individually and collectively, in the debilitating environment of human society as we know it. Hahn was indebted to Rousseau, both for the idea that awakening an individual's collective concern is the key to healthy personal development and also for Rousseau's assumption that Nature is an educator in its own right, more akin to the true nature of a human being than is the society that humans have built for themselves.

Hahn remarked once that we are in the Western world confronted by a progressive inhumanity of the society in which we live. He said that he saw Outward Bound as a countervailing force against the decline of initiative due, in his words, to the widespread disease of "spectatoritis," the decline of skill and care due to the weakening traditions of craftsmanship, and the decline of concern about one's neighbor due to the unseemly haste with which daily life is conducted. In 1930, three years before his exile from Germany for opposing Hitler, he drew up "The Seven Laws of Salem" to describe his educational methods.

❖ First Law

"Give children the opportunity for self-discovery.

Every boy and girl has *grande passion*, often hidden and unrealized to the end of life. The educator cannot hope and may not try to find it out by psychoanalytical methods. It can and will be revealed by the child coming into close touch with a number of different activities. When a child has come 'into his own,' you will often hear a shout of joy, or be thrilled by some other manifestation of primitive happiness."

❖ Second Law

"Make the children meet with triumph and defeat.

It is possible to wait on a child's inclinations and gifts and to arrange carefully for an unbroken series of successes. You may make him happy in this way—I doubt it—but you certainly disqualify him for the battle of life. Salem believes you ought to discover the child's weakness as well as his strength. Allow him to engage in enterprises in which he is likely to fail, and do not hush up his failure. Teach him to overcome defeat."

❖ Third Law

"Give the children the opportunity of self-effacement in the common cause.

Send the youngsters out to undertake tasks which are of definite importance for the community. Tell them from the start: 'You are a crew, not passengers. Let the responsible boys and girls shoulder duties big enough, when negligently performed, to wreck the State.'"

❖ Fourth Law

"Provide periods of silence.

Follow the great precedent of the Quakers. Unless the present day generation acquires early habits of quiet and reflection, it will be speedily and prematurely used up by the nerve-exhausting and distracting civilization of today."

❖ Fifth Law

"Train the imagination.

You must call it into action, otherwise it becomes atrophied like a muscle not in use. The power to resist the pressing stimulus of the hour and the moment cannot be acquired in later life; it often depends on the ability to visualize what you plan and hope and fear for the future. Self-indulgence is in many cases due to the lack of vision."

❖ Sixth Law

"Make games (i.e. competition) important but not predominant.

Athletes don't suffer by being put in their place. In fact you restore the dignity of the usurper by dethroning him."

❖ Seventh Law

"Free the sons of the wealthy and powerful from the enervating sense of privilege.

Let them share the experiences of an enthralling school life with sons and daughters of those who have to struggle for their existence. No school can build up a tradition of self-discipline and vigorous but joyous endeavor unless at least 30 percent of the children come from homes where life is not only simple but hard."

Writing in 1941, Hahn listed the benefits that such an education offered the individual student: "He will have a trained heart and a trained nervous system which will stand him in good stead in fever, exposure and shock; he will have acquired spring and powers of acceleration; he will have built up stamina and know how to tap his hidden resources. He may enjoy the well-being which goes with a willing body. He will have trained his tenacity and patience, his initiative and forethought, his power of observation and his power of care. He will have developed steadfastness and he will be able to say 'No' to the whims of the moment. He will have stimulated and nourished health interests until they

Outward Bound places unusual emphasis on physical challenge, not as an end in itself, but as an instrument for training the will to strive for mastery.

become lively and deep, and perhaps develop into a passion. The average boy when first confronted with these tests will nearly always find some which look forbidding, almost hopelessly out of his reach; others he will find easy and appealing to his innate strength; but once he has started training he will be gripped by magic—a very simple magic, the magic of the puzzle . . . and he will struggle on against odds until one day he is winning through in spite of some disability. There always is some disability; but in the end he will triumph, turning defeat into victory, thus overcoming his own defeatism."

Kurt Hahn brought intensity to Outward Bound by asking difficult questions: "Can a demanding active service to their fellow man, in need and in danger, become an absorbing leisure activity for an ever increasing number of young people?" And he came up with difficult answers: "We need an aristocracy of service as an example to inspire others to do likewise."

Hahn said he wanted to introduce into the art of life-saving the meticulous care which is generally devoted to the art of war, and he quoted William James to the effect that inspiration tends to evaporate, leaving no trace on future conduct, unless it is translated into action. He suggested to Outward Bound that the secret of education was to teach young people the inner strength that comes from serving others. "There are three ways to win the young. There's persuasion, there is compulsion and there is attraction. You can preach at them: that is the hook without the worm; you can order them to volunteer: that is dishonest; you can call on them, '*you are needed*,' and that appeal hardly ever fails." He reasoned that "the experience of helping a fellow man in danger, or even of training in a realistic manner to be ready to give his help, tends to change the balance of power in a youth's inner life with the result that compassion can become the master motive."

◆ ◆ ◆

> You can preach at them: that is the hook without the worm; you can order them to volunteer: that is dishonest; you can call on them, '*you are needed*,' and that appeal hardly ever fails.
>
> —*Kurt Hahn*

◆ ◆ ◆

Not long after leaving prison in Germany and just after founding Gordonstoun in Scotland, Hahn described the three essential approaches to education that he saw about him. He called them the Ionian, the Spartan and the Platonic. "The first believes that the individual ought be nurtured and humored, regardless of the interests of the community. According to the second, the individual may and should be neglected for the benefit of the state. The third, the Platonic view, believes that any nation is a slovenly guardian of its own interests if it does not do all it can to make the individual citizen discover his own powers. And it further believes that the individual becomes a cripple from his or her own point of view if he is not qualified by education to serve the community."

In school, Hahn asked his students to pledge themselves to the "training plan" establishing personal goals and a code of responsibility. Outward Bound instructors make a similar appeal to their students today, though not in the detailed terms used by Hahn at Salem and Gordonstoun, and it is a crucial aspect of the Outward Bound experience. The individual commitment of the student, the expressed desire to accomplish a worthy goal by means of the course, becomes, in effect, the moral basis of the community, the foundation both of compassion and of achievement.

Another important element that Hahn brought to Outward Bound was adventure—with all the risk it entails. He believed that education should cultivate a passion for life and that this can be accomplished only through experience, a shared sense of moment in the journey toward an exciting goal. Mountaineering and sailing were integral parts of his program at Gordonstoun, and he made space in all his programs for student initiative—an expedition, a project, a sailing voyage. Hahn welcomed powerful emotions, such as awe, fear, exultant triumph. Part of his lifelong aspiration, part of the "whole" he sought through programs like Outward Bound, was that the experience accessible to any human being, at any level of ability, could be charged with joy and wonder in the doing.

Hahn also understood the educational value of working with small groups of students. He probably took this idea from military organization as it came into the youth movements of the late 19th century, especially the Scouting movement of Lord Baden-Powell in England. Hahn saw small groups as a way to develop natural leadership abilities he thought were present in most people, but such an inquiry would eventually miss the point. They were suppressed by the dependency, passivity, and bureaucratic impersonality of modern life. Such groups place heavy social pressures on individual initiative, yet at the same time they require it absolutely. Small groups require tremendous amounts of energy to reach the consensus necessary to meet objectives. Natural leaders emerge when a group must solve real problems instead of playing games with an unnatural reward system. A genuine community begins to appear on a small scale.

A concern encompassing all the rest was Hahn's dedication to community service. As Hahn saw it, the link between individual and school depended for its meaning upon the link between school and society. The notion came into Outward Bound in the form of rescue service, and it has since been applied to diverse needs in communities and the natural environment.

♦ ♦ ♦

Natural leaders emerge when a group must solve real problems instead of playing games with an unnatural reward system.

♦ ♦ ♦

With such distinctive origins, it is only natural that Outward Bound should seek to ally itself more closely with conventional schooling. As the Outward Bound movement expanded after World War II, it was carried into the United States initially by educators such as Joshua L. Miner of Phillips Academy, Andover, and F. Charles Froelicher of Colorado Academy. From the 1960s through the 1970s, Outward Bound sought as an explicit aim to influence American schooling by persuading teachers and administrators to adapt experiential methods from the outdoor program to enhance formal learning.

The aim was not to manage such projects. Outward Bound turned over its ideas to school personnel for development within the schools, both public and private. For example, the Outward Bound schools set up teachers' courses and attempted to transmit ideals and methods in order to make an imprint on the dominant pattern of schooling for adolescents. The responses of participants from conventional schools emphasized the pedagogical vitality of experiential methods as well as the team building and depth of mutual commitment elicited from students on Outward Bound courses. Studies of in-school adaptations produced some alternative models and promising but ambiguous results.

Beginning in the early 1970s, Project Adventure, an offshoot of Outward Bound started by instructors wishing to work more closely with conventional schools, achieved success in applying experiential methods derived from Outward Bound to the schools. Project Adventure, which has been identified as an exemplary model by the National Diffusion Program of the U.S. Department of Education, went on to develop a repertoire of its own, paralleled by other creative offshoot programs, to assist in adventure programming, teacher training, and counseling.

Students from the Rafael Hernandez Bilingual School in Boston observe and document wildlife for a learning expedition on pond life. Photograph by Brian Smith/NASDC.

By the mid-1970s, Outward Bound was part of a larger movement in the United States, referred to broadly as experiential education. The movement had some impact through generating alternative programs for adaptation by public and private schools, including not only outdoor education but such widely implemented strategies as action learning, experience-based career education, and cultural journalism. But while it had philosophical roots in common with these innovations, Outward Bound pursued a strategy of staying apart organizationally, mostly offering ideas and short-term training, then hoping that mainstream institutions would replicate what might prove most effective.

In the remainder of this chapter I would like to offer a personal interpretation of Kurt Hahn's vision of learning, one that attempts to connect the events of his life with his ideas. I believe it is this vision of Hahn's that shows most clearly what Outward Bound has to offer American education.

Kurt Hahn understood weakness better than strength. The goal of learning, in his view, was compensatory: to purify the destructive inclinations of the human personality, to redress the imbalances in modern ways of living, to develop each person's disabilities to their maximum potential, and to place new-found strength in service of those in need. Kurt Hahn was suspicious of presumed excellence; he paid scant attention to the glories of unsurpassed individual performance, whether it be on the playing fields at Eton or the examination ordeal of the German gymnasium. He understood, as few educators have so well, the tender fears of young people, their alienation before the rigors and rituals of adult power. He understood how wrong it was to vanquish them with that power to make them learn. This strategy would only deepen their confusion about the meaning of their lives, making them cynical, lacking in humanity, even if it strengthened them. Hahn's favorite story was the Good Samaritan, wherein the strong, those clearly in a position to help the most, failed to act. It was the outsider, the weak, the despised who taught what it means to be a civilized human being.

Where did Hahn learn this, and if he once felt it himself, how did he convert his own weakness into an enduring vision of education? We must look, I believe, to the most tumultuous time of life to see the emerging center. In late adolescence, on the threshold of higher education and adult life, Hahn felt the impact of three events that changed his life.

The first was an expedition, some days of fresh air and majestic surroundings on a walking tour of the Dolomite Alps. One can well imagine the exhilaration of a boy in his teens on such a rite of passage. Famed for their bold, other worldly shapes, their awe-inspiring hues of light and shadow from sunrise to sunset, the Dolomites imprinted on Hahn an inextinguishable love of natural beauty. As an educator, he would always be devising ways to turn his classrooms out of doors, putting his students into motion and forcing his teachers to come to grips with the healing powers of direct experience.

But something else happened on this expedition. A second event added to these other feelings a specific passion, strong enough to organize his self-discovery into a lifelong vocation. Two English schoolboys who accompanied Hahn gave him a gift, a book called *Emlohstobba* by the German educator Herman Lietz. The title of the book was the name of their school, Abbotsholme, spelled backwards. Lietz wrote rapturously of life inside that school, where he served as master of studies for a sabbatical year under the innovative headmaster, Cecil Reddie. When Lietz returned to Germany, he fathered the country school movement there, inspiring others to begin schools more healthful for young people than the prevailing system of the time.

For Hahn this book was a momentous gift. Along with the living example of the two students from

The Cree Brigade reaches the boundary waters of Minnesota during an Outward Bound wilderness course for Dubuque, Iowa, school teachers. Susan Whitty navigates at the bow while Wendy Miller steers at the stern. Photograph by Mike Krapfl/Dubuque Telegraph Herald.

Abbotsholme, who impressed him with their healthy love of life, and the sheer beauty of their alpine journey together, young Hahn must have felt in himself a new conviction of life's possibilities. Coming at a time when his own formal education was marching lockstep through the authoritarian, rigidly academic curriculum of the gymnasium, the alternative vision of a more humane and democratic school, capable of fostering more perfect human beings, seized his imagination with a force that can be judged only by abandoning strict chronology and looking ahead to the seventy indefatigable years of institution-building that lay ahead of him.

It was not on that trip, however, that Hahn imagined the school he hoped to build. Two years later, the year of his graduation from the gymnasium, a third event completed his initiation. He suffered the life-threatening sunstroke that permanently changed his life. Never again would he have the freedom to trek or sail long pleasurable distances out of doors. Nor was it certain, in the weeks following the accident, whether he would recover enough to participate in normal functions of life. Depression set in, squelching his hopes. One would not be surprised if his boyhood dreams became cruel reminders of all that was not possible now. His life was a washout, a failure before it had really begun.

Here, and not in his later life of so many memorable accomplishments, the educational genius of the man is to be found. The center emerged as a discovery of who he really was inside, the gift of suddenly knowing what he had to do, and would do, when he bumped up against his own limitations. It was the scale of values, the plan of life, the desired future he asserted as his response to adversity when it came.

Adversity came to Hahn in several forms, all of which must have seemed insuperable from his perspective in a darkened room as he recovered from his accident. The physical disability would always be present in his life. It would be necessary for him to wear a broad-brimmed hat to protect his head from the sunlight. Frail in the heat, he would have to flee northward to a cooler climate for the summers. Periodically, he would need to undergo major operations to relieve the fluid pressure within his head. All this he knew, or could well imagine, in those months of convalescence.

In his darkened room, Kurt Hahn regenerated his spirit with a vision of what he could do with his life. He decided that he would someday start a school modeled on principles drawn from Plato's *Republic*, a school that would expand the wholesome influence he identified with Herman Lietz and Cecil Reddie's Abbotsholme. How much of the vision came to him at that time and how much later is not clear, but he grasped the essential outline. The school would harmonize the social and intellectual differences between its students by operating as a community of participation and active service. It would seek out the natural qualities of leadership, skill, and responsibility possessed by all in different ways when they see that they are truly needed. His school of the future would harmonize the wild and discordant personality of the adolescent by demonstrating that true need.

◆ ◆ ◆

Passion must not be treated lightly.

◆ ◆ ◆

Once again, it is difficult to say how much of that vision became evident to Hahn during his recovery and how much came to him as glimpses and inklings which he later converted into plans and traditions. That the center emerged, though, is indisputable, both by his own account and because of the central place he gave to his thoughts during the dark night of the soul in later educational projects.

How could his vision be made believable to the alienated young? Closer to home, how could Kurt Hahn himself, in his debility and depression, bring himself to believe in a better life? Forced by the accident to reflect upon his own childhood, to seek out some deeper matrix of meaning to keep his spirits up, Hahn came face to face with his own youthful passion. That there exists, in everyone, a grand passion, an outlandish thirst for adventure, a desire to live boldly and vividly in the journey through life, sprang forth as the most salient lesson of his lifelong pedagogy.

That was not all, however, and it was not enough. For now the Dolomites and the classics flowed together to become Hahn's vision of the good. Dwelling for a time in his imagined world of Plato as he dreamed of a future school, feeling his spirit awakening to a great sense of purpose in that semi-darkness after the sunstroke, Hahn made the crucial connection. Passion must not be treated lightly. Its deep springs in human nature must not be poisoned. Above all, it must not be misdirected and turned to inhumane ends. The grand passion of the young must be embraced in wholesome ways by adult power. It must be nurtured instead of deformed or punished. Its creative force must be harnessed to the quest for a good society, the aim of Plato's educational designs. To accomplish this purpose would require more than a school in a traditional sense. Some separation from the existing human world, into the intensity of a journey-quest, confronting challenges and transforming opportunities for service, could change the balance of power in young people, Hahn believed. Then they would be more inclined to use their lives, back in the world from which they came, to bring the good society into being.

With the center in view, the chronology of Kurt Hahn's life takes on greater meaning. Expelled from the land of his birth, the schoolmaster continued his career in Britain, which became a second homeland for him. When he opened Gordonstoun in 1934, Hahn carried the Salem tradition to the new setting, and he brought staff and students with him. New features appeared, such as the addition of rescue training to the service program. And some of the old practices changed, or were presented differently, in response to the cultural milieu of the British Isles. All this, of course, is to be expected in transplanting the design of an institution from one place and time to another. Certainly the transition was made easier by the strong affinity of Hahn's thinking with the traditions of Abbotsholme and the English public schools. What stands out, nonetheless, is the fact that Hahn was able in so short a time to create a new institution which, like his first school, would become known around the world for its distinctive educational practices.

If Hahn had not been restless, if he had not felt driven toward wider applications of his principles beyond any school he might ever create, he would perhaps have settled to a longer career as the eccentric headmaster of a school favored by the English aristocracy. But he was not satisfied. He began to organize a constellation of other education forms around Gordonstoun, using the school as a staging ground for programs through which he hoped to instruct the whole society around him in the first lessons of sound living and civic responsibility. The Moray Badge Scheme took form in 1936, followed quickly by the larger and better known County Badge a year later.

◆ ◆ ◆

You will find that the good artisan has a greater horror of unfinished work than the schoolmaster.

◆ ◆ ◆

Along the way, Hahn experimented with short courses to discover the combination of challenging experiences that might help young people discover new ways of organizing their lives and working with other people. In 1941, with Laurence Holt, Hahn started Outward Bound as a short course. Initially, the goal was to strengthen the will of young men so that they could prevail against adversity as Great Britain faced staggering losses at sea during World War II. After the program had demonstrated its effectiveness, it continued to expand during the postwar years, furnishing opportunities for personal and social growth to many people beyond the original clientele of boys and young men.

Chronology alone cannot account for Hahn's widening sphere of educational activity. Only by grasping how he continued to draw both from a sense of weakness and from the strong idealism at the center of his being can we understand his intuitive leaps as he created new programs over the years. Hahn perceived clearly that schools as we know them are not equal to the urgent problem of social life in this century. Even the best schools probably damage as much as develop the volatile inner lives of young people.

One reason for this unintended consequence is that schools represent only a partial solution to a much more pervasive problem. The problem of how to educate the whole person cannot be resolved without learning how to civilize human communities, which in turn cannot be done without preparing the entire world society in the arts of living harmoniously at the highest levels of potential activity and understanding. Hahn's debt to Plato was his conviction that education must embrace all these aspects of human life. A vision of what is most desirable in education must embody not only some notion of how the whole is to be organized, but what it will take for that whole to be good. Without a vision of wholeness, without at least a hope that the

Students from the Rocky Mountain School of Expeditionary Learning in Denver explore their city. Photograph by Cyrus McCrimmon/Rocky Mountain News.

compassionate community might someday be realized on a worldwide scale, people are not inclined to live on humane terms with one another.

Exiled to the British Isles, Kurt Hahn was restless at the center of his being. Carrying with him an unflinching impression of the expanding Third Reich and its effects on European civilization, he could never be satisfied with the auspicious beginning of a school. Soon after his arrival he began to write and speak in public, deploring the general lack of fitness among the British people. He urged his hosts to recognize the need for programs on a large scale that would combine individual training plans with group projects to build stronger civic consciousness.

Out of such concerns he initiated the Moray and County Badge Schemes. The latter quickly expanded and became further elaborated in many counties across the British Isles, spreading even to other countries in the British Commonwealth. The County Badge granted public recognition to young people who completed a planned course of challenges. They first adopted a training plan of physical conditioning and personal health habits. Then they undertook an arduous expedition requiring group decision-making as well as individual effort. They also completed a project demanding new skills and craftsmanship. Finally, they engaged in service activities, experiencing the value of compassion through direct action on behalf of the community or specific people in need.

At the beginning of the war, the County Badge contained most of the essential features of the Outward Bound program as it would develop in the future years. Indeed, the secretary and key promoter of the County Badge Experimental Committee, James Hogan, became the first warden of the first Outward Bound School at Aberdovey, in Wales. Yet there was a difference, and it was more than the residential setting and month-long sustained program of Outward Bound. Although both programs offered models for changing how individuals organized their lives, there was something more universal and enduring about Outward Bound.

Hahn had realized how close are weakness and strength in the most powerful forms of education. In his own day, he perceived clearly, while others did not, the subtle line that distinguishes compassionate service from destructive egotism. On the one hand, he feared the lack of will among those whose lives stood in the path of the advancing Third Reich. Hence his call for programs like the County Badge to build fitness and commit young people to civic ideas. But on the other hand, he recognized the affinity between his methods and those of the Nazis, one used for the good, the other for deadly ends.

There is an irony in this affinity, since Hahn was criticized by some in England for importing the paramilitary methods of the Hitler Youth. The irony is that the Hitler Youth movement did not discover the intensive methods of socialization they used to unleash the energies of the young. Rather, they borrowed from the leading educators of the day and applied the methods to their own goals. Hahn knew this well, for he had seen Hitler Youth before he left Germany. Their leaders had adapted and twisted to demonic purposes the training plan of Salem. Hahn had witnessed, therefore, the effects of reaching the whole person with the fascist plan of life instead of a Samaritan ethic. Hitler and his followers were reinforcing the passion of the young, giving them a spirit of adventure, introducing them to self-development and cooperation in the outdoors, then giving them meaningful opportunities to serve. Hahn recognized that there was no time for complacency. The weakness of the status quo must be acknowledged. All education must be made activist, or else the humane values upon which western democracies were built would succumb to a determined usurper.

Not even in its desperate beginnings before the onslaught of the Third Reich did Outward Bound ever train young people for war, but it arose fully conscious of the challenge presented by the Hitler Youth, that nationwide mobilization of young people to serve the cause of world conquest and genocide. Never did anyone press Outward Bound toward becoming a preparation for violence, and in this respect it would always remain distinct from youth mobilizations under totalitarian regimes. Yet it is difficult to imagine how Outward Bound would ever have come into being if it had not been for Hahn's recognition of the weakness of democratic cultures before well-organized forms of authoritarian education that were appallingly efficient at stirring up the passions of the young for collective violence.

Through Outward Bound, Hahn hoped to foster a deeper intensity of commitment in the rite of passage from youth to adult life. He was intent on creating more dramatic challenges and victories for the young than were available in conventional forms of schooling. Advocating a more arduous quest than was present in the institutions around him, Hahn was working from a disability greater than his own, a collective predicament verging on catastrophe. In England during the German Blitzkrieg, it was by no means apocalyptic to argue that there would need to be a new education, reconstructed on a massive scale, to produce the compassionate army needed to preserve what was left of civilization at home. Hahn believed that an intensive program of training, expedition, reflection and service would make a difference.

◆ ◆ ◆

We need opportunities for active service in peace time.

◆ ◆ ◆

That belief survived beyond the exigencies of war, but Hahn's own direct role quickly receded once the philosophical values were in place to launch Outward Bound. While Hahn continued to influence Outward Bound, it soon took on a life of its own under the vigorous leadership of many people drawn to its idealism and hardy lifestyle over the years. Taking an image from Plato, Hahn likened himself to a midwife of educational projects as he sparked ideas for new endeavors and then left much of the development and maintenance to others. Outward Bound sea and mountain schools proliferated across several continents in the following decades. As it adapted itself to different cultures in later years, Outward Bound lost its wartime urgency, but it maintained a zest for adventure and Hahn's legacy of moral purpose.

Outward Bound has come to mean many things in different places and for the great variety of people who are drawn to it, but at its heart, in every time and place, is Hahn's own center, his conviction that it is possible, even in a relatively short time, to introduce greater balance and compassion into human lives by impelling people into experiences which show them they can rise above adversity and overcome their own defeatism, make more of their lives than they thought they could, and learn to serve others with their strength.

Hahn's postwar contributions include several other projects of which he considered himself more midwife than instigator. It would be most accurate to characterize him as the moving spirit, since his arts of persuasion were decisive in each case. The Trevelyan Scholarships, for example, provided funds for young people to attend Oxford and Cambridge based on experimental as well as academic criteria: applicants were asked to complete a project of their own design, which would be reviewed by a selection panel. Shortly after a recurrence of his sunstroke in the early 1950s, Hahn helped to launch the Duke of Edinburgh Award, a program similar to the County Badge but much more widely developed throughout the British Commonwealth. His crowning achievement after the war was the United World Colleges, which began with the founding of Atlantic College in 1962.

If Outward Bound's origins are to be found in the war, those of the United World Colleges appear in the desire to build institutions that will offer a living example of what it means to be at peace. Taking students from 16 to 19, equivalent to the sixth form in England or the last two years before postsecondary education in the United States, these colleges bring together boys and girls from all over the world, from competing social economic systems, from rivaling cultures and religions. The program fosters world citizenship, an interconnected leadership of people who have experienced a collective life of active dialogue and peacemaking service. The curriculum, like that of Gordonstoun, combines both academic and experiential challenges, but the institutions have developed in new directions under their diverse leadership, leaving some of Hahn's education practices behind while preserving others. Kurt Hahn's original insight that such institutions were possible stands as perhaps the greatest legacy of his influence as they continued to thrive and expand in the 1980s.

◆ ◆ ◆

Through Outward Bound, Hahn hoped to foster a deeper intensity of commitment in the rite of passage from youth to adult life.

◆ ◆ ◆

Returning to Germany for his last days, Kurt Hahn died near Salem, in Hermannsberg, on December 14, 1974. The entry in Britain's *Dictionary of National Biography* calls him "headmaster and citizen of humanity." Hahn's educational influence persists under such organizations as the Round Square Conference, comprised of schools modeled on Salem and Gordonstoun. His genius in devising short-term educational experiences has not stopped infusing energy and inspiration into the Outward Bound Trust, which oversees Outward Bound schools throughout the world. His love of peace flourishes in the United World Colleges, not to mention the many other institutions and individuals who continue to embody his ideals. This man's educational vision remains, becoming like an adventure, arising from weakness to teach about strength, turning self-discovery into acts of compassion, everywhere defending human decency.

Having Wonderful Ideas
An Interview with Eleanor Duckworth

Conducted by Mieko Kamii

Mieko Kamii: *One of Expeditionary Learning's most important design principles is the having of wonderful ideas, an idea that you contributed to the discourse on teaching and learning.*

I am wondering what, in your mind, the having of wonderful ideas means for students, for teachers, for parents, and for schools?

Eleanor Duckworth: My book, *The Having of Wonderful Ideas*, was my response to a six-year-old boy to whom I gave ten soda straws. I intended to ask him to put them in order from littlest to biggest. When he arrived and looked at the straws, he said, "I know what to do with these," and proceeded to put them in order. He worked very hard at it and got it right. When he left, he asked me if he could keep the straws and put them in his shoe box of treasures.

When he first said to me, "I know what to do with these," I had the impression he was saying to me, "I have a wonderful idea about what to do with these." It was very important to play out his own wonderful idea. Ten soda straws are not a treasure to most people. But for him they were a treasure because they manifested this wonderful idea that he had.

I think the having of wonderful ideas can be a guiding principle to what we do with students in schools, right down to the simplest of tasks. We should make sure we respect the way students see ideas. We should respect the way they approach ideas, and give them the feeling that they have wonderful ideas that they are able to follow through with.

That requires, perhaps, that adults listen to and observe children very, very carefully.

It certainly requires that adults listen to children and observe them. This is no easy task for a teacher with many children at once. What it requires is giving students occasions to do things in their own way. Expeditions are a very good example of this. You see that students are different and you get to know those differences.

The more different yes's we have in a classroom, the more everybody learns.

This is an infrequently mentioned reason to steer clear of workbooks. They demand that students do exactly what every other student is doing. They don't help the teacher understand the way a child is thinking, since it is either a yes or a no answer. The more a teacher can set up a classroom so different students can do things differently, the more the teacher can understand the kids.

Does this mean that if parents are in conversation with teachers, then the teachers will understand the students better?

Conversation both ways would be to everybody's advantage. So is conversation between teachers and students. The emphasis of this conversation has to be to let the student tell you what he or she is interested in and how he or she thinks about it. This is related to keeping track of students' work. One of the important things in portfolio assessment is to allow students to do work that represents what is important to them. Then one keeps a dossier showing the differences among students. The point is not to say that one child has reached point 11 in a track that is 30 feet long while another child has reached point 9. The students will be going in many different directions and criss-crossing and maybe not even covering the same territory.

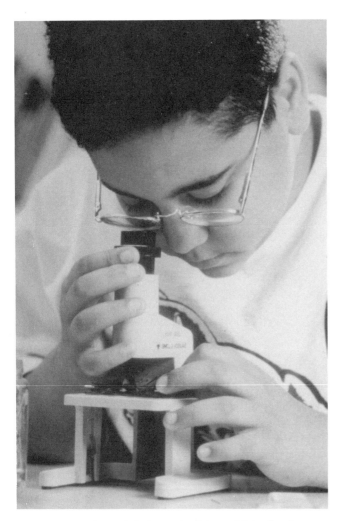

A student from the Rafael Hernandez Bilingual School in Boston examines a Pond Life specimen under a microscope. Photograph by Brian Smith/NASDC.

It is like the contrast that David Hawkins makes between climbing a ladder and living in trees. When you climb ladders, everyone follows the same track. But when you live within a tree, you can go out to many different branches, then come back in and go out on other branches. The ladder model only recognizes difference in terms of one student being higher than another. There are so many other differences among students to which schools need to pay attention.

I recently heard a teacher describe the observations she made of her students learning how to read. Every student had a different process. One student whose first language was not English spent his time copying children's stories. He copied and copied until he started to read them. Another student wrote the same six-word note over and over again. She wrote it in big letters and little letters, colored letters and black and white letters. Finally she started making single word changes in this little note. The students had very different ways of going about learning, but they all led to them being able to read at some point.

So what that suggests is to open up and create multiple avenues in our own minds as adults. The children have avenues and in some sense it's the adults' responsibilities to try to follow them?

Yes, it means opening up avenues in our own mind. And it's even more important to be willing to receive the avenues that the students are following. There are all kinds of fields in which there is a multiplicity of ways to approach things. In everything from mathematical algorithms to reading poetry, there is a multiplicity of perfectly adequate ways to encounter and approach the same materials.

One of the most startling examples of this is a discussion I had with teachers about division. One of the teachers asked, "What does it mean, anyway, to say twenty-four divided by eight?" Someone said that twenty-four divided by eight means you have twenty-four things and you make eight piles and you see how many end up in each pile. Someone else said, "No. That's not what it means. Twenty-four divided by eight means that you have twenty-four things and you put eight things in a pile and you see how many piles you get." They seemed to think that one of them was right and the other one was wrong. It's an excellent example of how two approaches can both be right. In many cases if a child does something other than what you expected, it's not "No," it is another "Yes." The more different yes's we have in a classroom, the more everybody learns.

How would you respond to a parent, teacher or administrator who is more concerned about the single right answer approach?

In arithmetic it is true that twenty-four divided by eight is three. Most parents and administrators wouldn't question that. But there are multiple ways to understand that one answer. We must believe in the integrity of the students' minds and the integrity of the subject matter. There is something about twenty-four divided by eight that will always end up with three. We don't have to be impatient that it's going to end up there. Impatience can rush a student into thinking it's important to say what people tell her to say and not what she believes in. It can make her lose confidence in her own ideas about the subject. It can make her feel incapable of finding things out for herself because someone had to tell her the answer.

How you feel about yourself has an enormous effect on how free you feel to think about the subject matter. No matter what domain makes people feel good about themselves, the domain which makes them feel uncomfortable is the one in which they think there is a right answer that they are incapable of getting.

There are a lot of people who feel very free working with poetry because they feel their ideas are valid. There are just as many people who feel put off by poetry because they think that a poem has only one right interpretation that they won't be able to figure out. It is the same in mathematics. Some people believe they can apply what they know to a problem and work through it in their own way. Others think there is only one way to approach math, and they won't be able to solve any problems if they don't know it. What blocks people is not the subject matter, but their belief that there is only one way to do something. When the subject matter is presented in a way that says "any way you can invent to understand this is valid," people feel they can do it and start to get excited about domains in ways they weren't before.

Would you say that most people have their own epistemologies in different areas, that in one domain there is much more freedom?

I don't think so. What I am trying to say is that you can make sense of any domain depending on how you approach it. Every person's mind can make a connection with a poem and a math problem. Often, it takes teachers to help them realize it and to present the poem or problem in a way that makes people think, "Well, I've got a way I could do this." For instance, I never present a poem with the question "What does this poem mean?" That's asking you to come up with some sentence that says better than the poet did what the poet means. So I present a poem and ask, "What do you notice?" Everybody can notice something—whether it is the rhyme scheme or the use of colors or punctuation. As soon as some people say something, people start to notice other things.

In everything from mathematical algorithms to reading poetry, there is a multiplicity of perfectly adequate ways to encounter and approach the same materials.

In your book you talk about the value of teachers observing a child's work over time—a sustained observation. Why do you think that's important?

What comes to mind right away is the reading teacher I mentioned earlier. If a visitor went to a reading class and a child was copying out of the book, the visitor wouldn't know what to make of it. Or if on the first day of school a child started copying from the book, the teacher might say, "That's not the way we do things around here." And that would lose the child's connection with reading. But by watching, letting the child do that, and seeing where his process goes, the teacher can follow what makes sense to a child and what's productive and fruitful for the child. What a teacher can notice over time is that what the child does is far deeper and has more continuity to it than it would seem in sporadic observation.

Teaching Discovery

by Nan Welch

The following is an excerpt from a letter to Dubuque superintendent Diana Lam.

I wanted to share again what a growing process this year has been. I am just completing an expedition that really gave me a clear picture of Expeditionary Learning. Our expedition was called *Discovery*, which we wrote around an existing second-grade unit, *Common Objects* (using magnets, gears and electricity). The expedition was not especially well written and was not something I was too excited to teach, mainly because I felt I did not have strengths or an abundance of knowledge in the areas of magnets, gears and electricity.

I plunged ahead with it . . . . the blind leading the blind, and I was amazed to see what transpired. My students soon led the way, as their curiosity about the concepts we were studying grew. Their questions became the blueprint for instruction. Soon I was relying on experts around us to further their quest for knowledge. A visit to Hempstead High School's automotive department provided us with a look at more gears than we ever imagined were in a car. A stop at the Morgan Clock Company kept our curiosity peaked as we observed gears working in a variety of clocks. One of our teachers at Lincoln is a bicycle expert and he gave up a planning time to explain the gears of a bike.

Students' questions became the blueprint for instruction.

Sixth graders from the Rafael Hernandez Bilingual School in Boston celebrate their first caving trip for the Rocks, Rivers and Caves learning expedition. Photograph by Scott Hartl/ Expeditionary Learning.

As we moved on to magnetism, Scott Gill provided a wonderful demonstration using magnets, which gave the students many experiments to duplicate on their own. As we studied electricity, our custodian, Jon Thill, led us through the boiler room on our quest to find fuse boxes. An Interstate Power employee came to our room to further educate us on electrical safety.

Suddenly, I stopped my belly-aching about the expedition and sat drinking in the success of knowing my students were learning and loving it. I began leaving myself notes all over the room that said: "Think—Discovery, Discovery, Discovery!" My students then shared their favorite concept from this expedition with a first grader, acting as a guide to his or her discovery. I am very confident that because of the expeditionary nature of this unit, my second graders grew far more in life-long learning than other second graders who were exposed to the traditional Common Objects unit.

◆ ◆ ◆

I was relying on experts to further students' quest for knowledge.

◆ ◆ ◆

I learned a number of things through this experience. First of all, the most effective expedition is one in which you have a burning desire to teach. (Ron Berger was so right!) Secondly, even though I didn't have that burning desire in this particular expedition, following the principles and providing my students with outside experts and real-life experiences allowed their growth to escalate in a manner that would not have happened in traditional curriculum; and I grew with them.

I have so far to grow in this whole process, but I feel at this point that there is no turning back. I am much more thoughtful in my teaching and, consequently, my students are blooming.

> **Reflections on the Discovery Expedition**
>
> My favorite thing in the *Discovery* expedition was the magnet expedition when we went down to a first grade. It was so fun to act like a teacher to a student for a day and come back and feel so good that you taught somebody younger than you something. It makes you feel so very happy.
>
> —*Mollie Thill*
> *Second Grader*

School Matters: Free Your Hands
Learning Is Doing at These Schools

by Diane Loupe

At 9:30 a.m., the Clairemont Elementary School playground is crowded, but not for recess. Parent volunteer Buddy Goodloe leads a class of students in the third, fourth and fifth grades in spreading a piece of plastic for an experiment on condensation.

Two students peer intently at fish in the school pond, while teacher Vivian Stephens and her students head for the school's nature trail.

The activities are all part of Expeditionary Learning, an education strategy being developed at schools in Decatur, Boston, New York City, Maine and Colorado and through a grant from the nonprofit, corporate-backed New American Schools Development Corporation.

For a couple of hours each day, instead of delivering staid, textbook-centered lectures, Clairemont teachers lead multi-grade groups of students in hands-on projects, field trips and other exercises designed to stimulate learning.

Teacher Barbara Lail, who spent a weekend in Maine learning about Expeditionary Learning, flips pages to an index of a plant guide her students use to identify plants and critters they've fished out of the school pond and woods. Using an index is a skill she once taught from a textbook, with a phony index.

Her students have used math to calculate the dissolved oxygen in the pond, language skills to write a report about the plants, and art skills to mount the plants onto a poster.

"If you're interested in it, you learn how to find knowledge," says Clairemont principal Judy Greene. "We teach how to find the knowledge."

Decatur City Schools became involved in the program last fall through the system's Outward Bound program, based at Decatur High School. All schools are using the technique, but Clairemont's program is among the most extensive.

Clairemont uses some student portfolios and self-grading, but also relies on more traditional teaching methods for such subjects as math. The program's impact on grades or standardized test scores hasn't been gauged.

Clairemont Elementary teacher Barbara Lail (third from right) looks under a log with pupils at the Decatur school during a nature expedition. Such activities are part of Expeditionary Learning, an educational strategy being developed at a few schools across the nation. Instead of listening to lectures, pupils get out of the classroom for a change of pace. Photograph by Joey Ivansco/ Atlanta Constitution.

Clairemont Elementary volunteer Buddy Goodloe checks vegetation with students in a pond behind the school. Photograph by Joey Ivansco/Atlanta Constitution.

Greene says the technique still has some bugs. Parents fret over whether students will still learn the information they need to know, and how to fairly assess what children have learned in expeditions.

And the jargony term "Expeditionary Learning" is often hard to explain.

Here's how fourth-grader Darius Jones defines it: "It's fun. It means more stuff to do."

Florence Edwards, an outgoing fifth-grader, thinks the technique is "just the funnest thing. I have read books my dad used as a child and I don't know why he didn't just take off. It seemed incredibly boring."

April 26, 1994, page C-2. Reprinted with permission from *The Atlanta Journal* and *The Atlanta Constitution*.

A Willingness to Learn

by Meg Campbell

♦ ♦ ♦

A willingness to learn is always preceded by a moment of humility, by acknowledgment that there is yet something left to learn, some deeper understanding available.

♦ ♦ ♦

Recently, I passed a store display of CDs and tapes called *Chant* (EMI Angel). It was Gregorian music sung by the Spanish Benedictine Monks of Santo Domingo de Silos. There was a raffle box, so I entered my name. Then I noticed the poster above the tapes: "Win a gargoyle." A grotesque 30-inch winged creature with its chin resting in its hands was part of the display. I hadn't wanted a gargoyle. I wanted to win a CD, but I shrugged and told myself I never win contests anyway.

♦ ♦ ♦

I knew nothing about gargoyles and what I had thought I had known was wrong.

♦ ♦ ♦

A few days later, I received a phone message saying I had won the gargoyle. Several days after that, I received a second phone call from the store. The woman insisted that I come to pick up the gargoyle or they would give it to "lots of other people" who wanted it. I thought gargoyles were demonic, certainly hideous, so I was resisting claiming my own. Still, I had won the gargoyle and I liked winning a prize, especially a prize others apparently valued. I didn't want to *lose* the gargoyle, even if I was unsure if I really wanted it. "Yes," I assured the woman. "I'll be over to pick it up."

"You'd better bring someone with you. It's cast iron and very heavy."

I began asking people what they knew about gargoyles. I knew nothing about gargoyles and what I had thought I had known was wrong. My questions were as raw as a five-year-old's. Are they bad? Why do they look so scary? Would you want one?

I learned gargoyles were placed on the roofs of medieval cathedrals and nineteenth-century Gothic public buildings to frighten away evil as well as carry rainwater away from the sides of the building. Gargoyles were sculpted as gutter spouts as well as protectors who keep bad spirits at bay and draw forth wisdom.

My gargoyle is now on a corner ledge in my office. When I look up from my desk, I see its tongue sticking out at me, its wide-open eyes and its wings. It feels to me as though I have a waterfall in that corner, so inexplicably calming is it for me to study its sandy, exaggerated features or just to know that it is there. Its oversized ears remind me what a powerful tool listening is for warding off danger and drawing out what is wise and good. Winning a gargoyle has aroused my curiosity to learn more about these mythical creatures, as I discover loveliness in what I had first not even wanted to see.

Looking back on this first year of implementation, I am amazed at and grateful for how far we have come. Evidence of the Expeditionary Learning design principles and components is in the culture, teaching and learning of design partner and "spirit" schools. I attribute this primarily to a deep willingness by educators to change, grow and learn as we hold ourselves and each other to the rigor and challenge of Expeditionary Learning design principles.

This willingness can be witnessed in every Expeditionary Learning school—in one school's patience and firmness in establishing five minutes of silence as part of a daily community meeting; in two teachers' willingness to take students on an overnight camping trip for the first time in twenty years of teaching. Another two teachers became passionate experts in the culture and history of New York City in 1934 as they prepared a learning expedition for their students, while a team in another city undertook the challenge of teaching several disciplines to a mixed-age group of students.

◆ ◆ ◆

> Its oversized ears remind me what a powerful tool listening is for warding off danger and drawing out what is wise and good.

◆ ◆ ◆

Gargoyle by Adrienne Campbell-Holt, an eighth grader at the Rafael Hernandez Bilingual School in Boston.

A willingness to learn is always preceded by a moment of humility, by acknowledgment that there is yet something left to learn, some deeper understanding available. Our ears, minds and hearts are open. This goes for all of us in virtually any situation, but especially when we are embarked on a mission of change and transformation. My gargoyle reminds me of that.

Walking Fine Lines

by Tammy Duehr and Nora Gill

Last summer, first-grade teachers Nora Gill, Tammy Duehr, Shari Flatt, Joan Kramer and Anne Roush designed a learning expedition around transportation for their students at the Table Mound Elementary School in Dubuque, Iowa. In the fall of 1993, they guided their students through the expedition with great success.

In their presentation of the expedition during the Boston Sharing Days in February 1994, Tammy Duehr and Nora Gill discussed their experiences with community experts, the practice of revision, and the delicate process of letting students discover their own wonderful ideas.

The following is a discussion with Emily Cousins, editor of The Web.

Tammy Duehr: We wrote the *Transportation* expedition last summer, but we did it a little differently than we had written it. At first we thought we would have the children choose one mode of transportation to study, then we decided they should have the chance to learn about all of them. We decided to break the expedition down into trucks, cars, planes, boats, and trains. We took different areas for about a week, and we tried to begin or end each part with a community expert.

We started by finding out what the students wanted to know. Instead of trying to answer all of these questions ourselves, we called in community experts. We would have a morning speaker, then small group work, a literature piece and an activity with that, a separate time for math, then the whole afternoon was focused on our model city project.

Nora Gill: I am the Chapter I teacher, so all the writing activities were scheduled for the hour block that I was available to come in and do guided writing with the Chapter I students.

How did your community experts work with the kids?

Tammy Duehr: We explained to them that they shouldn't come to present anything, just come prepared to answer questions. I reminded them that the kids are six years old. They want to know things like how heavy is the boat? How much does everything cost? When the kids found out that the first mode of transportation we went to see, a semi cab, cost $290,000, all of a sudden we were making a list of all the kinds of transportation and graphing prices to see what cost the most. We did the same for weights. The community people helped out with all this. We found some really great community people who went far beyond what they needed to do.

Nora Gill: Finding the time to make phone calls to arrange the visits was one of the difficulties of the expedition. Between five teachers, we had to figure out who's calling whom and arranging what. The flip side of that was that the five of us could help each other since the whole first grade—three classes—was doing the same expedition.

I think I have grown as a teacher by letting students discover on their own.

— *Tammy Duehr*
Table Mound Elementary School

Had the community people done this kind of thing before? Do you feel that they better understood the school, or were more interested in education?

Tammy Duehr: We had an engineer come in to speak about train safety. He lives in East Dubuque, Illinois, and he hears a lot about Expeditionary

Train by fourth grader Gordon Ryan for the Transportation learning expedition, Table Mound Elementary School, Dubuque, Iowa.

Learning. When he came to my classroom, he asked lots of questions. Recently, he returned to the school with two boxes of computer paper. When he came the first time, we had indoor recess, and he saw that the kids were drawing on unrecycled paper, so he said, "I wanted to drop this paper off, because we just throw it away and I thought you could use it." Then he stayed and asked the kids all about their expedition. He said he couldn't believe how much they could tell him about semis and airplanes. He said, "They know what kind of gas everything takes. I can't believe they can tell me how much everything weighs." I think the kids can explain what we do themselves. They are more powerful than we are.

❖ Pursuing Ideas

Tammy Duehr: Our major project for this expedition was building a model city. The model city's purpose was to show the interrelatedness of the modes of transportation. It fit into our social studies curriculum on cities and country. When we talked about model cities at Clark College in the summer, I was thinking of something really nice and small with every little thing perfect. I thought we could have ten little houses all in a row and miniature dogs.

The kids, however, were thinking huge painted boxes and planes on spirals flying in the air. They came up with things that I couldn't believe. At points I had to stop myself from saying, "No! This is not what I wanted!" and just let them go. I think they created something that is far better than anything I imagined.

The kids developed the problem-solving skills of planning ahead. We asked them, "What do you want to do tomorrow? If you want to do something with blue paint, you need to let me know, because I do not have blue paint in the room." We created a system where kids put a list in my mailbox of the things they needed for the next day. One day the list in my mailbox asked for a softball. I wondered what in the world they wanted a softball for, but I just got it for them. After a point I didn't ask any questions. The next day they made a water tower out of it.

There was one thing that I thought they did backwards, but I didn't say anything. First they made the map of the city, then immediately put the boxes on. I thought they should have put the grass on first. I told the other teachers, "I can't believe it; they are doing this wrong! How am I going to stop them from doing this? They are going to get to a point where they are frustrated, and I am going to have to pick up the pieces. It's going to be like I'm doing it all, so why don't I just tell them no." But I didn't say anything, even though it was hard not to.

They got the buildings up, and they still hadn't figured it out. The city looked done to them, but it didn't look done to me. I kept wondering how I could communicate to them that they needed grass without actually telling them. One day I was reading a book to them, and I pointed out the grass in the book, and said, "Isn't that nice grass?" and all of a sudden someone shouted, "We don't have any grass in our city!"

Now they had to figure out how to get the grass. At first they wanted me to figure it out. They'd ask me what I thought they should do, and I would say, "I don't know, whatever you want to do." They decided they would find some Easter grass, but there was nowhere to get Easter grass at Christmas, so one of the kids brought in green garland from her Christmas tree. I thought, this is going to be interesting, because pretty soon the grass is going to be higher than the buildings. I couldn't believe what they did. They took glue and squeezed it all over everything, then cut the garland and let the pieces fall, and made grass. It looked better than I could have done if I had tried.

◆ ◆ ◆

> Instead of trying to answer all the questions ourselves, we called in community experts.
>
> — *Tammy Duehr*
> *Table Mound Elementary School*

◆ ◆ ◆

Something similar happened with the flood wall. They wanted the flood wall to be taller than the highest building, but I thought, well, all right, but that's not how a flood wall should be. I tried to give them as much information as I could, but there is a point when you don't want to tell them everything. It's a fine line, because I also don't want them constructing something that doesn't make sense. Before they had glued on their flood wall, I told them they should take a trip down to the flood wall in town and have a look at it. They came back the next day and said, "It's not that tall; we walked on it." So then they decided to fold the box to make the wall shorter, and it worked out nicely.

One group used a cereal box for their hospital. We were using water-based paints so every time they tried to paint it white, the paint peeled off. I let them do that three times before I said, "Do you think we should figure out another way to do it?" They remembered that when they had problems with other boxes, they used masking tape to cover things up and redo them. So instead of getting a new box that didn't have a shiny finish, they put masking tape around the entire box, and painted it. And I thought, well, that's problem-solving. It was the long way, but they did it.

We often discussed the design principles, so at the end of the expedition I asked the students if they thought we had met all of the principles. When we got to Self-Discovery, they were confused. We've talked about it, but they were unsure and asked, "Did we do that?" So I said, "Well I think an example of Self-Discovery would be when you covered your box with masking tape. You discovered all by yourselves that the paint would not stick to the finish of the box." They all looked at me, and got very angry. "You mean you knew it wouldn't stick to the

Jason Webber, a student at Central Alternative High School in Dubuque, Iowa, researched Native American medicine for a learning expedition on Native American culture. Jason drew these dandelions and added the following text to accompany his drawing: "Dandelions, a common European weed, have appeared in nearly every lawn. Their roots contain a drug used in treating the liver. The leaves, very rich in vitamins, are prized for spring salads. The blossoms are excellent for teas and wines. The roots provide a delicious caffeine-free coffee."

box and you didn't tell us?" they demanded. I explained that I enjoyed watching them figure it out on their own. I think I have grown a lot as a professional teacher by letting them do some of their discovery on their own. They were really proud of the model cities.

One principle I was concerned about was Solitude and Reflection. When I think of solitude and reflection, I think of writing. I have children who can't read and write, and I wondered how I was going to get them to reflect. Someone reminded me that reflection also means thinking and internalizing. At the end of every day, we have a closing circle and we reflect. Shari Flatt came up with the great idea of posing questions that the kids did not have to answer out loud. Now, as soon as I say, "Circle up," they all sit down and close their eyes. They know they can't talk and they don't want to look at anybody because they are really thinking.

❖ Teaching

Nora Gill: For me the whole expedition was the mode through which I could teach the children to write. The reading and writing are tremendous at this point. I have never seen Chapter I students able to read and write this well.

The students did their own individual books after each mode of transportation. One Chapter I student was very needy in the beginning of the year, so I worked one-on-one with him for two months. When it came time to write his book, he started with four very short sentences, then he had three short sentences. As we went along he went to five sentences, and then to two paragraphs. The amazing thing is that he is able to read all of this. This child could not recognize words or letters or sounds at the beginning of the year.

Tammy Duehr: The drawings for the books came out really well also. We used a lot of the advice Ron Berger gave us last summer about revision. To tell you the truth, I thought he was nuts at first. I thought my kids would never want to do things over again. But they did; they really wanted to do the work over again.

Nora Gill: Shari Flatt and I were talking one day about how we could encourage children to draw their very best. Since neither one of us knew much about art, we talked to the art teacher and she said, "When it comes to drawing a semi or a bus or a truck, look for the overall basic shapes, like rectangles, circles or triangles." We reviewed those basic shapes with the children, and practiced drawing them. The drawings of the buses and semis turned out much better after that. We also encouraged them to draw in pencil for their first and second copies. Basic strategies like that made the drawings much better.

Tammy Duehr: We all decided from the beginning that the festival would be the last day, and when it came, the kids did not want to stop.

Nora Gill: They really enjoyed the expedition. When they came back into the room after recess, they would dive back into their cooperative groups and go right to work. You would never see a child dive into a worksheet without being told. Something has to be going right.

Outside-the-Classroom Experiment
A School Weaves Ideas from Outward Bound into Lessons

by Lynda Richardson

In a vacant classroom in Chelsea, after the rumble of schoolchildren had faded, five teachers collapsed into chairs and pondered aloud after another grueling day the big question that they all faced: how do you invent a place called school?

Six weeks into the academic year, the experimental School for the Physical City is open for 131 students in borrowed space, a fledging effort to transform the way that children are taught by using the Expeditionary Learning principles of Outward Bound. At least once a week the Brooklyn Bridge, Central Park, Ellis Island the city itself—becomes the classroom. Subjects like mathematics, science and history are brought to life and woven into academic lessons.

But as each day goes by the teachers who gather late in the afternoon are finding that there is much more to the creation of a new school than tacking on a name and opening the doors. Their days, although filled with exhilaration, frustration and signs of fluttery hope, are also a venture in expeditionary teaching.

"It's a matter of inventing it as we go along." said the principal, Mark Weiss, who manages to smile, partly because he has done this before when he helped create the Bronx Regional High School in 1978. "It's difficult what it takes to incubate a school. You have to start somewhere, and if you didn't push the edges of possibility you might not get started at all."

As the asbestos crisis and the actions of a new Schools Chancellor captured attention at the start of the school year, 31 new secondary schools have opened, a record, quietly conducting business out of the spotlight. Like the others, the School for the Physical City is part of an experiment begun under the former Schools Chancellor, Joseph A. Fernandez, to establish smaller, easier-to-manage schools with student bodies that would ultimately be one-third of the average at the 124 older high schools in the city.

At the School for the Physical City there are regular textbooks, homework and quizzes. There are the misery-inducing standardized tests, and credits required for a diploma, like in any other high school. But the teachers are trying to create a culture that goes beyond the standard fare to elevate achievement.

The school also tries to build a sense of community. The principal and the nine teachers conduct classes in specific subjects and are assigned to small groups of students called community circles. The groups go on explorations together and meet daily to discuss current events and personal issues. Each day the entire school gathers in a community meeting for five minutes of solitude and reflection.

The curriculum centers on the infrastructure of the city, and most classes are an hour and a half, instead of the usual 45 minutes. But the schedules are flexible to accommodate the expeditions. All students spend a full day outdoors at least once a week.

On a bright autumn morning a humanities teacher, Loretta Brady, and her students set out to chase shadows in a project to link math, history and language. With shiny aluminum rules, tape measures and backpacks, Ms. Brady's charges scrambled onto the A train and then the F to a cracked piece of asphalt on the Lower East Side to measure the height of buildings by observing their shadows.

The group moved a block away to learn more about proportions and ratios by measuring the shadows cast across the street by a tree and a building. They received a history lesson about the Federal-style buildings in the Henry Street Settlement area. They read a poem about shadows and then wrote a poem on their own.

October 31, 1993, p. 37, *The New York Times*. Copyright © 1993 by the New York Times Company. Reprinted by permission.

Outward Bound's ideals include "the having of wonderful ideas" and "the responsibility for learning." A park was transformed into a math class as students used yardsticks to measure buildings' shadows and determine heights. Photograph by Chester Higgins Jr./The New York Times.

"We learn by hooking up to what we already know," said Ms. Brady, 30, an alumna of Brown University who helped start another alternative school, the School for the Future, three years ago. "It seems less frightening. The whole gestalt of it has more impact.

❖ Old Wanamaker's Store

The School for the Physical City occupies six classrooms in Intermediate School 70 on West 17th Street, which also houses the regular neighborhood school and district offices. The school is to move to its own space in September, the old Wanamaker department store at 770 Broadway, at East Ninth Street in Greenwich Village.

In the school and the 30 others, with financial support from foundations, cultural institutions, unions, teachers, community groups and public agencies, educators see cause for optimism.

"It's almost like a Joycean epiphany," Superintendent Anthony J. Alvarado of Community School District 2 said. "You shouldn't look at it without recognizing the potential the larger system has to learn from what is going on here. When you look at them, what you recognize is, 'Holy cow!' Look at all the agencies, the people, the vision, the sense of purpose and expertise that are out in the city that have not been tapped in creative ways to support the human development of students."

The school is part of a partnership with the Cooper Union Infrastructure Institute; the New York City Mission Society, which is the oldest social-service agency in the city; and Outward Bound, which sponsors 12 schools around the country that use learning expeditions as a central focus.

❖ "We Need a Lot of Work"

There have been no hair-raising treks into the wilderness, but there was a fist-fight between a boy and a girl in the hallway. Some people at the school said the girl was winning.

Over time students are to embark on rigorous hikes and overnight trips offering the physical and mental challenges for which the Outward Bound program is famous. The students are to learn how to build a bridge over a stream and, perhaps, a building in the woods.

A humanities teacher, Edi Juricic, said he was not sure whether his students were ready for such endeavors. "We need a lot of work," said Mr. Juricic, who was in the Peace Corps in Micronesia and taught Outward Bound wilderness courses. "There needs to be self-discipline creating a great

❖ ❖ ❖

A school weaves ideas of Outward Bound into academic lessons.

❖ ❖ ❖

supportive community. I would like this class to be able to run without me."

The philosophy for teaching is as different as the form that the individual lessons take. For that, the teachers sitting wearily at the end of one day studied a poster that spelled out the Outward Bound principles, "the primacy of self-discovery, the having of wonderful ideas, responsibility for learning, intimacy and caring, collaboration and competition, diversity and inclusivity, solitude and reflection."

❖ Silence for Five Minutes

The students seem oblivious to all the planning. They have more immediate concerns. The heartthrobs have been identified. Baggy jeans and baseball caps are in. And there is the unavoidable, schoolwork.

Although each day begins with the five minutes of silence, the students, after all, are barely teenagers, if that, so there are a few snickers, squirming, an occasional outburst and many mystified looks.

A seventh grader who lives on Governors Island, Kieshelle Joseph, could not explain how the school works but said she likes it, anyway. "They teach you a lot of good stuff that you can use in life," said Kieshelle, who aspires to be a scientist or a teacher.

The School for the Physical City aims to transform how children learn, using the principles of Outward Bound. Steve Estime, center, works with a student, Francisco Bussetti.

"We seem to be a lot more together than at other schools. We share things. If you get something wrong everybody knows about it, and we try to solve it together."

Tony Ward, 12, who dreams of becoming an engineer, travels an hour and a half by subway from the Bronx. "I really like the idea of doing projects," he said in a shy voice.

His mother, Linda Smith, an executive assistant for a lingerie manufacturer, learned of the school last year when she and her son attended a high school fair at which the experimental schools set up recruiting booths.

"We were both excited," she said. "He likes math and science best, and it's a chance to learn about the city. If it's done properly, children can become scientists, engineers, and you know what? They can become politicians and win, because they will have inside-the-school knowledge, as well as outside."

The students, 73 in middle school and 58 in ninth grade, are a mixture of racial and ethnic backgrounds and academic levels. As in most of the other new schools, the students were selected from across the city, though children in District 2 have priority. The school, also like the others, will eventually build to the 12th grade. Enrollment will be limited to 700.

One chilly morning all the students boarded the C train to Central Park and spilled onto the Great Lawn for a trip that was part learning and part public relations. As schoolmates cheered, several ninth graders helped one another scale a 14-foot wood wall.

The trip featured appearances by Marvel Comics superheroes like Spiderman and X-Men colleagues, Wolverine, Magneto and Cyclops. The students received free sweatshirts.

As the students have their concerns, so do their parents, who are watching how school develops. One Friday afternoon a group of parents from Park Slope, Brooklyn, went to the school office. Mr. Weiss listened as one mother complained that her bright son was not being challenged by the math instruction. Another mother wanted to know what Mr. Weiss planned to do about disruptive youngsters. A father wanted to see the students engaged in the physical exertion that makes Outward Bound work. "When does it start?" he asked.

The answers are not always so easy for educators to give. But a science teacher who is trained in wilderness survival, Wayne Weiseman, said he felt instinctively that his students were headed in the right direction.

One day he and his students went to the Lower East Side to collect artifacts of urban life so that they could build mobiles. They returned with twigs, spent checkbooks and paper cups. As a boy rolled a spare tire, the teacher yelled out, "Can you tell me the physics that's happening here?"

"Friction," the students responded.

Before the end of the day, the junk floated above them on a classroom ceiling in a display of artistic talent.

"The symphony is starting to move together," Mr. Weiseman said. "Little by little it's beginning to happen."

Part Three

Educators as Learners

Professional Development Through Planning and Design
The Mini-Sabbatical and Summer Institute

by Leah Rugen

Expeditionary Learning Outward Bound is forging a vision and structure for staff development which is rooted in the notion that through intensive collaboration, personal reflection, and study, teachers can greatly stretch their professional abilities and reshape their classrooms and schools. When Expeditionary Learning faculties undertake the One-Day Community Exploration (an initial staff development exercise focused on building knowledge of community as a learning resource) and later, the Mini-Sabbatical or Summer Institute, they are embarking on a learning expedition of their own. These staff development experiences bind together social and intellectual experience, and closely reflect Expeditionary Learning's design principles. In fact, they represent an intensive exploration of the Expeditionary Learning design through the process of designing curriculum, schedule, and the structure of relationships.

In the first year, following the One-day Community Exploration and other introductory experiences, Expeditionary Learning faculties began their most intensive phase of professional development and preparation for implementing Expeditionary Learning in their schools. They worked together in teams, learning to collaborate out of a sense of real purpose. Mini-sabbaticals and summer institutes are five- to ten-day structured experiences which focus on the design and planning of Expeditionary Learning curricula, schedule, and relationships. Because of the challenge and commitment required of teachers, the collaborative nature of the work, and the focus on building relationships and community, such institutes become very personal experiences of professional growth and learning.

Mini-sabbaticals involved teachers being released from their classes for the length of the experience, while substitutes or administrators taught their classes. In summer institutes, teachers received honoraria to devote ten days of their summer to a similar process of intensive, structured planning and design. Extending the notion of teacher-as-learner to teacher-as-constructor of knowledge, the mini-sabbaticals and summer institutes call upon and challenge teachers' professional knowledge and experience. By asserting that it is teachers, in collaboration with colleagues, who will best develop learning expeditions (the fundamental building block of Expeditionary Learning curriculum), Expeditionary Learning affirms their critical leadership role. This is frequently a new and challenging role

Expeditionary Learning's planning institutes insist that the only way to grasp a learning expedition is to create a plan in collaboration with colleagues.

for teachers accustomed to rigid state and local requirements, and top-down curriculum development through textbooks and teachers' guides. Expeditionary Learning developed the mini-sabbatical and summer institute models in order to effectively support, challenge, and coach teachers in assuming this creative role. The two models depend on the close interweaving of professional development, curriculum development, and collaboration.

Like most ground-breaking ideas, this model of professional development is quite simple and rooted in precedent. A parallel can be found in the way professors in higher education design their courses, creating syllabi and soliciting peers' suggestions. Similarly, the National Writing Project teaches the writing process by immersing teachers in writing groups and their own writing, and hospitals plunge interns into supervised clinical rotations. In each of these examples, peer review and critique are essential parts of the process, ensuring accountability and the meeting of high standards. Expeditionary Learning's planning institutes insist that the only way to grasp a learning expedition is to create one in collaboration with colleagues, submit it for peer review, and then implement it with students.

With the institutes and other models of staff development, Expeditionary Learning is trying to deepen and extend collaboration and peer review. Many aspects of Expeditionary Learning's approach are unique. The connection to Outward Bound provides a powerful emphasis on creation of community and careful attention to the process of developing relationships. Likewise, Outward Bound's tradition of challenge and quality work lends the institutes a sense of purpose and high expectations. The explicit use of the ten design principles provokes thought and provides a strong common ground. Finally, each staff development experience is structured to model and put in practice the Expeditionary Learning design.

❖ Building a Culture of Professionalism and Collaboration

The environment of the planning institute closely mirrored the Expeditionary Learning classroom,

Architecture Summit blueprint by Linda Thacker, a teacher at Winston Middle School, Baltimore.

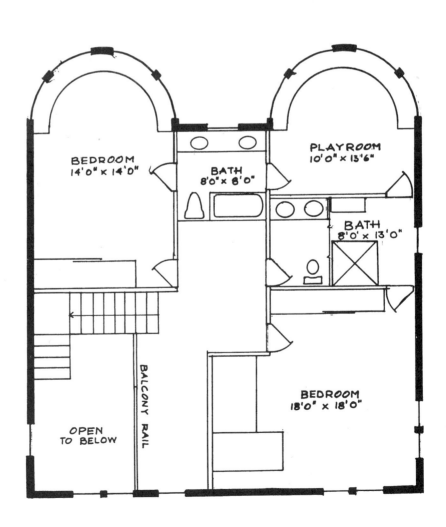

although, significantly, many institutes took place outside of schools—on college campuses and in a children's museum. Certain critical ingredients seemed to be vital to anyone's learning process. Complementing the physical environment was the emphasis on creating a supportive and collegial emotional environment. Taken together they formed the basis for a new professional culture.

For each institute, rooms were arranged to promote productive exchange. A permanent circle of chairs for every participant provided the forum for daily community meetings and discussions. In their work groups, participants sat around tables and had access to computers. Some people were able to use a word processing program for the first time. There were ample supplies and materials, and teachers were encouraged to bring in additional resources as the ideas for learning expeditions emerged. As the week progressed, the rooms filled with books, journals, and supplies contributed by colleagues. Since much of the time was spent in small planning groups, space was arranged to allow them to work effectively and to encourage communication between groups. Generally, one facilitator was responsible for a group of 20-25 teachers, mirroring a realistic teacher-student ratio (this does not preclude using additional facilitators as needed and available). The facilitator moved throughout the groups, providing ideas and facilitation as needed. It is worth noting these simple details, since in many schools productive work space for teachers is non-existent, preventing effective collaboration and exchange of ideas.

Rituals from Outward Bound and Project Adventure were woven into the routine of each day, stressing the value of the individual and the importance and effectiveness of the team. As people came in teams from schools, and would be implementing Expeditionary Learning together in the fall, these rituals had the potential to be part of an ongoing and sustaining practice. Each day often began with a cooperative game or problem-solving initiative stressing communication and teamwork. Brief readings, initially chosen by facilitators and then picked up by participants, punctuated days with insight, humor, and critical perspective. As in a learning expedition, it was important for groups of teachers to get out of the classroom periodically, spending time doing research in the community, engaging in physical activity, or allowing for solitude and reflection. Journals were used as a means of reflection, observation, and thinking, and became useful tools in the planning process.

By asserting that it is teachers, in collaboration with colleagues, who will best develop learning expeditions, Expeditionary Learning affirms their critical leadership role.

Some groups spent a portion of a day working on a "Full Value Contract" (developed by Project Adventure), which is a group agreement. During this process, individuals expressed their commitment and ability to contribute to the group in concrete terms, while the group as a whole considered how it would function and what values would govern its process. Each of these rituals or tools for learning and communication helped to build the teams, and at the same time, became a model of what teachers might use in their classrooms.

Probably the most important aspect of a professional culture involves an openness to critique, exchange of ideas, and revision. Certain structures built into the institutes encourage these qualities. Critique and feedback are difficult for adults as well as children and adolescents. If one is supported and acknowledged as an individual, one is better able to make use of constructive criticism. For this reason, many facilitators adopted the use of a "recognition board" on which participants posted notes and observations acknowledging individuals' specific contributions to the group. Regular community meetings in which participants could discuss issues and ideas, and critique sessions in which they began to comment upon each other's work, supported and deepened this process. In "Gallery Reviews," teachers posted their works-in-progress on newsprint hung around the room. Colleagues then circulated and wrote ideas, questions, and suggestions, which then might be discussed in individual conferences or in the whole group.

The institutes culminated in full or half-day presentations of plans for learning expeditions, which often proved to be the intellectual and social equivalent of a peak ascent for many teachers. It was a new and nervewracking experience to submit one's professional ideas for review and critique, and to hold honest and explicit discussions of standards.

❖ The Week's Story: Structure and Flow

An outline of the basic structure of the planning institute includes the following stages: an overview of Expeditionary Learning and reflecting on the design principles; community building and group goal setting; forming working groups to plan learning expeditions; and creating plans and presentations for colleagues. Of course, each stage involves much more detail—the brainstorming process to arrive at themes for learning expeditions, the discussion around defining good projects and purposeful fieldwork, and the research and investigation involved in finding good resources.

It is important to note that it has been very effective to involve teachers and local leadership in the planning of institutes. Advance planning and communication create greater investment in the process and enable participants to come prepared with themes, ideas for resources, and questions.

If the whole institute were compressed to fit into a five-day period, it might look roughly like the following outline. Obviously this whole process can and should be expanded depending on the time available to the group.

❖ Sample Week-Long Institute

Monday: Facilitators present an outline of the week, an overview of Expeditionary Learning using the design tree and principles, and a framework for planning. Important rituals are introduced—the morning community meeting, recognition board, journal writing, etc. Facilitators take care to help the groups get to know each other and incorporate physical activity at key intervals. They engage participants in a discussion of their goals and expectations for the week, and an initial meeting of working groups. Often Monday will end with groups posting their themes and initial ideas for comments from the whole group (ideally teams come with their themes already selected and an initial collection of resources).

Tuesday: After an opening morning meeting in which participants share ideas and resources, working groups are formed and the planning process begins in earnest. The groups initially focus on determining the theme and guiding questions for the learning expedition, agreeing upon the learning goals which will have priority, and the outline of the projects and core tasks which will make up the core of the expedition. The day might end with another whole group meeting with reports back from small groups.

Wednesday: Following the same basic structure as Tuesday, the working groups may decide they need time for individual research and collection of resources. This day, at the midpoint of the institute, may end in a more detailed whole group review of the plans in progress.

Thursday: Planning reaches its peak of intensity as groups scramble to come to agreement and hone the outlines of their expeditions as much as possible. They work on deciding what and how to present to their colleagues tomorrow.

Friday: The morning will include time to continue working on plans and an informal presentation to colleagues. Most of the day will involve formal presentation of learning expedition outlines and whole group critique sessions. The presentations do not assume that learning expedition plans are completed—only that after a week of serious planning, research, and resource collection, they are ready for substantive peer review and questioning. For many people, this is the first time they have submitted their work as teachers to peer review and critique, making even informal presentations powerful and challenging. The institute concludes with celebration.

Such an outline, however, does not capture the intensity or *narrative* flow of the institute.[1] In fact, the planning institute is more like an expedition than

---

1. Joseph McDonald calls teaching a "narrative activity" in his essay "Dilemmas of Planning Backwards" (Coalition of Essential Schools, 1991). He explores this idea further in his book *Teaching: Making Sense of an Uncertain Craft* (New York: Teachers College Press, 1992).

a course or workshop. As with an expedition, the teachers are assembled for a concrete and compelling purpose, and because many have never before worked collaboratively or thought about teaching and learning in quite these terms, the environment and experience are almost as unfamiliar as the wilderness. As a result, the week is full of creative tensions, highs and lows, and periods of crisis which belie its calm and ordinary surroundings. It is an emotional as well as an intellectual experience.

As with most education, teachers' professional development experiences have by and large been individual and distant from the school's daily reality. In the Expeditionary Learning planning institutes, people were being asked to work in-depth preparing a theme for study, to construct a learning experience that was interdisciplinary and project-based, and to work closely with colleagues and expose their thoughts and efforts to review and critique. All of their planning had serious implications for their school's structure, schedule, use of space, and definition of roles. It is no wonder there was typically a crisis of confidence midway through the institute.

❖ The Learning Expedition Plan: Reflections on the Planning Process

Although the process of learning and engaging with colleagues was profoundly important, equally important was the fact that the institutes resulted in a concrete and useful product—the plan for a long-term (four- to eight-week) learning expedition and the assembly of an initial bank of resources. The plan needed to address learning goals, theme and guiding questions, basic time frame, student tasks and projects, fieldwork, and learning resources.

Of course there are many different styles and methods of effective planning, and it is difficult to find an approach which balances the need for structure and organization with the need to be responsive and flexible. It is certain that one commits to a general direction and mode of travel when setting out on an expedition. However, every teacher has had the experience of suddenly realizing that a plan is not working, or that something much more compelling and useful has emerged. Following the expedition metaphor, these changes can be compared to changes en route that happen either in response to danger or injury, or in pursuit of tantalizing options. Academic learning expeditions need to have both this flexibility and this commitment to certain parameters and direction.

Part of the commitment and direction in planning was an explicit discussion of what teachers would expect students to know and be able to do as a result of the learning expedition. Again, balance was extremely important. Planning teams needed to avoid becoming bogged down in endless discussion of language or creation of elaborate lists. At the

Teachers Samidh Guha, Patrice Lambert and Bob Johnson design sculptures at the Facing History and Ourselves Summit. Photograph by Scott Hartl/Expeditionary Learning.

same time they needed to grapple seriously with setting goals for learning and determining what that learning would actually look like.

At the beginning of the institutes, facilitators laid out a variety of options and guidelines for creating learning expedition guides (plans), along with the expectation that everyone would create a plan which, in their view, made them as prepared as possible to teach the learning expedition in the fall. Another expectation was that teams of teachers would present their plans to colleagues at the end of the institute, adding another layer of consequence and purpose.

Typically, planning teams began by brainstorming and agreeing upon a theme and guiding questions, then discussing possible projects, and learning goals. After a significant collection of ideas and resources was gathered, they began to look at time and a possible sequence for the expedition. Of course, in actual fact, the process is not linear and involves much circling back to revisit and rethink goals, question project ideas, and in some instances start afresh with a stronger idea.

What we have only begun to do is evaluate how these plans were actually translated into action. How much did teachers and students diverge from them? How useful were they in practice? Following this essay is an example of a learning expedition guide, along with the students' final project which resulted from the expedition.

❖ The Facilitator's Role

Like the Expeditionary Learning teacher, the leaders or facilitators of planning institutes played a complex role that blended organization, coaching, presentation, and facilitation of discussion. Bringing a combination of teaching, Outward Bound, and other educational experiences, they led and coached small groups of teachers through an examination of practice and through the creation of learning expeditions (and of new relationships with colleagues and students). Co-creators rather than "curriculum experts," they attempted to help teachers define and then stretch their definitions of learning expeditions. The facilitator's ability to lead critique and debriefing sessions was critical to the success of the process. The small working groups needed support, and those which had direct facilitation tended to be more productive. Although a variety of experiences can prepare one to play this role, it is essential that institute facilitators have a sophisticated grasp of educational issues, deep understanding of Expeditionary Learning, and significant experience working with teachers and leading groups.

They must find a comfortable midpoint between providing concrete support and allowing teachers to find their own answers to problems and questions. Because the institutes are emotional as well as intellectual experiences, facilitators often have to help the group to manage and resolve conflict, and be a sensitive sounding board for individuals' fears and doubts.

Some of the specific strategies employed by facilitators included presenting and engaging participants in discussion of the design principles, introducing specific learning activities and planning strategies, recommending and discussing relevant articles, and highlighting examples of effective teaching and learning.

❖ Conclusion: Variations on a Theme, Deepening Our Practice

What this essay has not really touched on is the degree of local variation and ownership that must be in place in creating planning institutes. For some sites, the notion of a mini-sabbatical in which teachers were released from their classes for a full week was a powerfully effective structure. For others, because of the unreliability of substitute coverage, it was not a feasible option. Mini-sabbaticals and institutes which fully involved members of schools and districts in advance planning were naturally the most successful.

Outward Bound's tradition of challenge and quality work lends the institutes a sense of purpose and high expectations.

The ongoing planning and collaboration happening at all of the sites is ultimately more significant than the institutes and more difficult. It is the work of building, reflecting, and changing that can occur only in the context of implementation. It is more difficult because it is coming in the midst of the action, and it involves the constant struggle to find common planning time and then to use it well.

As we look toward the coming opportunities to work with teachers, we have the chance to deepen our practice. Thoughtful discussions of students' work and teachers' practice should become the core preparation for planning new learning expeditions. We will continue to look for ways to build the culture of critique and revision within Expeditionary Learning.

Rafael Hernandez Bilingual School teacher Arlene Agosto de Kane works with a fourth grader during the school's learning expedition on Pond Life. Photograph by Brian Smith/NASDC.

Dubuque Teachers Map a New Course

by Mike Krapfl

After months of abstraction and confusion, here are some real answers about Expeditionary Learning. To Becky Campbell, Bev Graves and Nicole Lyon of Dubuque's Bryant School, Expeditionary Learning was a chance for second graders to preserve and value their family history.

The three teachers were among 30 who met at Loras College this past week to develop units of Expeditionary Learning for their classrooms. They presented their ideas Friday afternoon.

Listening in were about 50 colleagues, principals, administrators, parents and even family members.

Campbell, Graves and Lyon carefully explained how they'll teach their unit.

They'll ask students to collect a family treasure, interview a grandparent or senior citizen, invite that person to lunch, draw up a family tree, research the countries their families came from, examine Dubuque's history at the Woodward Riverboat Museum and share all that they learned with their classmates.

The students would spend most of every school day for three weeks working on the expedition. It would include just about every subject a second grader studies.

This wasn't dreamy stuff the teachers were talking about.

They had lesson plans drawn. They had checked and double-checked the curriculum. They had evaluated their own experiences as teachers. They had thought about how they'd grade the students' work. They had done so much writing, Campbell had ink smeared on her fingers.

They had a plan.

After putting that plan into a 20-page report, Campbell and her colleagues said they're convinced Expeditionary Learning will work.

"This will be very good for the kids," Campbell said. "If it wasn't going to be good for the kids I would have known on the first day."

Scott Gill was there explaining what these teachers have been doing.

Gill, a math and science specialist for Dubuque schools, stood in the middle of a room buzzing with work.

In a patient and thorough way, Gill explained that the teachers have been divided into small groups and asked to plan a three-week expedition for next year.

"They're finding new ways to get kids interested in what they need to learn," he said.

During the next three weeks, all 120 teachers at the four schools trying Expeditionary Learning—Bryant, Lincoln, Table Mound and Central Alternative—will get their chance to plan an expedition.

While the teachers are doing a mini-sabbatical, substitutes will teach their classes. The cost of the substitutes is covered by the district's $200,000 grant to plan Expeditionary Learning.

Most teachers at last week's session said they had been dropping by their schools to see how their classes were going.

They said they hated to miss a week with their students. "But it's going to be worth it," said C. J. Klenske, a fifth-grade teacher at Lincoln. "We've developed so much enthusiasm and camaraderie this week."

Something happened this week that's never happened before.

Nicole Lyon, the physical education teacher at Bryant School, worked at a computer. Halfway through her mini-sabbatical, she was learning fast.

Lyon—whose hair has turned white but who still goes by Nicki—showed off some of her computer diagrams.

"It's absolutely the first time I've used a computer," she said. "I'm 52 and I thought I'd get out of working on computers."

February 28, 1993; pp. 1A-3A, *Dubuque Telegraph Herald*.
Published with permission of the *Telegraph Herald*.

She held up her work and beamed.
"I'm proud of that," she said.

Tables were a mess of industry and creativity.

Stacked on one end were books about rivers, pond life, prairies and grasslands. There was also a book titled *Thoreau Revisited.* On the other end of the table were brochures describing Dubuque County's Heritage Trail. Next to that was a brochure listing every single thing fifth graders are supposed to learn in Dubuque's public schools.

Between the books and brochures were three Lincoln teachers: C. J. Klenske and Nancy Wright, who teach fifth grade, and Jean Gagliano, who teaches hearing-impaired students.

Klenske was busy writing the text of the team's expedition into a spiral notebook. Wright and Gagliano were filling up a teacher's planning chart.

"Did we get the protozoa in there?" asked Wright, who said she likes teaching kids about protozoa.

As it turned out, they hadn't found space for the microscopic animals in their science unit. But they would.

Their expedition is all about cycles, they said. That's life cycles, season cycles and even bicycles.

Using the Heritage Trail, the teachers plan to teach fifth graders everything they're supposed to know about science. They'll take trips to the trail throughout the year, including some on bicycle, to see, touch and smell the various cycles of nature.

"Put this down as a possible idea," Wright said. "Visit a science lab at one of the colleges."

Talk about your strange teaching ideas.

At one point, all 30 teachers were lined up in a small circle. They were packed in tight, their hands on the shoulders of the person in front.

The teachers watched Scott Hartl, who taught the use of hands-on methods in Schenectady, N.Y., and now works for Expeditionary Learning in Boston. He had been leading the teachers all week.

At a signal from Hartl, all the teachers leaned back. And there they were, resting on their neighbors' kneecaps.

It seemed silly, but the exercise carried a powerful message: by working together, trusting one another and solving problems along the way, they can accomplish something.

The teachers greeted their accomplishment with applause, cheers and abashed smiles.

Suddenly, a professional crisis arose.

Shirley Deppe, a teacher at Central Alternative High School, was so frustrated with Expeditionary Learning she needed a pep talk from her colleagues.

What is Expeditionary Learning? she asked midweek. Who will give me the answers?

Deppe's customary smile had turned to a frown; it was time for her to do some thinking.

On Friday, just after all the teachers had presented their work, Deppe was smiling again.

"I think it was OK," she said of her team's expedition. "No, it was better than OK. From where we started on Monday and where we ended up there was a tremendous amount of growth."

She and her colleagues came up with an expedition to teach high school seniors about housing. The unit includes a trip into the city to find housing appropriate for, say, the income level of a community college graduate.

What made things better for Deppe?

"I realized that they weren't going to give me answers," she said. "It's really us here—the Dubuque teachers—who will make it work. We are defining Expeditionary Learning."

A River, a Raft, and a Summit

by Melissa Rodgers

Margarita Muñiz, principal of the Rafael Hernandez Bilingual K-8 school in Boston, spent the first week in March 1993 white-water rafting down the Colorado River in the Canyonlands National Park. She joined twenty-five other principals and teachers and staff from Expeditionary Learning Outward Bound in a five-day river expedition conducted by the Colorado Outward Bound School. The expedition allowed educators to explore firsthand the principles of Expeditionary Learning.

Margarita Muñiz had never been camping. A successful, high-powered, urban principal, she speaks eloquently of the experience of facing, for the first time, the unexpected challenges of nature. "It was decided that we would all climb the same cliff—the Doll House. For me, it was very physically demanding; on a personal level, I felt worried about holding people up." Everyone made it to the top of the cliff, with those who walked more slowly leading the group to set the pace. Connecting this experience with her work in the public schools, Margarita spoke about tracking, and about Expeditionary Learning's principle of inclusivity. "We were going up the cliff with the conscious decision that everyone was going to make it," she says. "It was the group's acceptance and decision that made it important for me to reach the goal—I would not have challenged myself that way without the group. We need these inclusion activities within our schools. Not everyone can do everything, but we need to find challenging things that everyone can do."

Nancy Bradley, principal of the Table Mound Elementary School in Dubuque, Iowa, talks about the instructors' role in giving the group a fair assurance of success as novice rafters steered their boats through the rapids. "You knew the whole time that you'd be successful or fail on your own. But the instructors were there. You knew you'd never experience real failure." Nancy Bradley wants teachers to think about how they too can assure success for all of their students.

For many, the white-water rafting and the hike up the canyon have also become metaphors for risk taking and challenge. Barbara Volpe, director of the School Renewal Project at the Public Education Coalition in Denver, says that one of the most common phrases among the Denver group is now "academic cliffs." She speaks about the connection between physical and intellectual risk taking. "If you take a situation that is high stakes—powerful because it is life threatening—like getting through the rapids at Satan's Gut, and you set it up properly, then kids can do it. Some may take a different route or take longer, but all the kids can do it.

> We were going up the cliff with the conscious decision that everyone was going to make it. We need these inclusion activities within our schools.
>
> — *Margarita Muñiz*
> *Rafael Hernandez Bilingual School*

Then you can transfer the risk taking and the moral courage to an intellectual situation. For some kids, writing a research paper or solving a geometric theorem feels the same as facing a big rapid. But their successes in the physical world can serve as metaphors for succeeding in the intellectual world." As Margarita Muñiz notes, "It is in the challenge and the effort that the most important lessons are learned." Expeditionary Learning's endeavor is to challenge all children, and to get all children to the top of the cliff.

On March 10, the group faced a challenge of a different sort. While scouting the rapids ahead, Scott Gill, instructional facilitator for the Dubuque, Iowa, Public Schools, came across a man—John Thomas—who had been stranded by the river since

Steve Rippe of the Voyageur Outward Bound School leads a portage out of the boundary waters during an Outward Bound wilderness course for Dubuque, Iowa, teachers. Photograph by Mike Krapfl/Dubuque Telegraph Herald.

February 20. Having survived on a diet of mice, lizards and water, the man had suffered severe weather-related injuries and was near death. Patrice Lambert, a nurse from Dubuque, cared for Thomas while Outward Bound's Peter Bailey, Scott Draper and Joe Nold set off forty miles down the river—some of the time in the dark—to call for help. Everyone else stayed by Thomas's side, tending to him and watching the bonfire that marked the site for rescue helicopters.

"It was probably one of the most dramatic examples of service that one can imagine," says Expeditionary Learning's Mieko Kamii. "This critical situation created a possibility of acting, of rising to the occasion, of putting aside personal desires in order to respond to an emergency. It gave the group a remarkable opportunity to experience in common not only the drama of the rescue, of having a helicopter land in the middle of the night, of seeing three of its members set off on a very risky journey, but also the collaboration—forming a line to pass the Dunnage bags from the river to the campsite, for example."

Collaboration is one of Expeditionary Learning's key principles. Leah Rugen, who works at the New York City Outward Bound Center, says that she was "blown away" by the experience. "The rescue was a peak experience," she says, "particularly certain elements of it—the fire-watch, group journaling—there were a variety of ways for people to get involved and feel a part of it. We all took part."

Other, less dramatic moments provided opportunities for learning and discovery. "There was a moment during the hike up the mountain that was like a Socratic seminar," Leah Rugen says. "Joe Nold led this questioning about geology, sitting among rock formations. It struck me as a graphic illustration of how learning can happen anywhere, and happens most powerfully when it ties into a personal experience—looking at the rocks and feeling moved." Barbara Volpe also recalls that moment fondly, as well as the time when her Outward Bound instructor discussed the slope of the stream and the physics of water currents as her crew navigated the rapids. She says, "Adding the intellectual dimension in that setting was icing on the cake."

The night of the rescue, watches kept the fire going to mark the site for the rescue helicopter. Here is an excerpt from the Firewatch Journal.

4:39 AM, March 8, 1993

The aftermath...and the afterglow! When the helicopter arrived, the whole group turned out to watch or help as needed. Scott Draper returned with the helicopter and shared his, Joe's and Peter's challenging eight-hour run of the canyon. We are all so glad they are safe, that John has been evacuated . . . The others capture a few moments of sleep before what promises to be a long and challenging journey.

Tom O'Neill, principal of the Lewenberg Middle School in Boston, remarks on the teaching that the Outward Bound instructors modeled throughout the expedition. "I appreciated their technical skills, but mostly found it astounding how literate they were," he says. "Being in the canyon with someone who could quote poetry, whole sections of books, all referring to nature, to our particular situation—that was a powerful experience." Tom O'Neill talks about how the instructors served as learning guides while the group hiked up the Doll House. "They approached everything so calmly. I was looking at the formations of sandstone, but they pointed out the things I would not have seen on my own: 'There's coral there; there's an old sea shell.'" The instructors used the depth of their knowledge to inform and enrich—not supplant—the group's own discoveries.

> **This journal entry was written at the end of the trip on the bus ride back to Grand Junction, Colorado.**
>
> *Who was the hero? Is it John for the courage to be alone for so long? I haven't been alone for more than a few hours, ever. Is it Patrice and Scott? With confidence and skill they showed much strength. Is it Scott, Peter, and Joe? Rapids at night, determination to do right. But do heros dance by the firelight? Was it those who stayed behind to work and worry, those who carried watch through the night and huddled around the fire with John? Or maybe those who carried on the details of this newly formed community?*

Nancy Bradley says: "They forced us to look at a totally different way of learning. I experienced the absolutely finest teaching I've ever experienced."

The human dimension of the expedition resonates strongly for the participants. "I met some wonderful people," Margarita Muñiz says, "for example the principals in Boston. We know who we are but we had never really shared." For Leah Rugen, the sense of belonging to a boat crew was important in creating bonds. "In the small group you develop an intimate experience that is different from the large group—you develop an identity over time." She thinks that this is an important lesson for teachers.

Intimacy also grew out of experiences of shared silence and reflection. Structuring solitude and reflection into the expedition was challenging with such a large group, but important. Leah Rugen particularly remembers a "moon moment" when, at Jerry Pieh's suggestion, the group sat together in silence to watch the moon. Tom O'Neill also remembers this moment: "We stood and watched the moon come up over the mountain one night. The whole idea of it was moving, powerful—the brilliant sky at night." Solitude and reflection are essential for Expeditionary Learning, he thinks. "We don't take enough time for solitude—particularly those of us from the inner city—to think about what we are doing every day. I call it 'the tyranny of the urgent.' You don't have time for reflection. I think that the river expedition pointed out in a most profound way the need for solitude and reflection. This was my first experience like that."

The principle of forming a relationship with the natural world was powerfully present throughout the expedition. Margarita Muñiz recalls: "Being so close to nature and experiencing its grandeur, I kept thinking about what Mies Van Der Rohe said: 'God is in the details.' Going up a canyon wall, looking at the fossils and minerals embedded in the stones, at the erosion that carved the sandstone cliffs, that's what kept running through my head."

The guides forced us to look at a totally different way of learning. I experienced the absolutely finest teaching I've ever experienced.

— *Nancy Bradley*
Table Mound Elementary School

For many, the expedition has metaphorical connections to their jobs in public education. Barbara Volpe says, "I came back to a frustrating, difficult meeting and thought, 'relax, this is like Satan's Gut. You can get through this.' It was a metaphor for persevering and using your head when you get anxious." Learning transferred from the physical expedition to a new situation—in Barbara Volpe's words: "confidence, patience, resolve and a willingness not to let anything get in the way."

Northbound on an Expedition

by Mike Krapfl

❖ Adventure in Lake Country Offers Lesson in Teamwork

Day 1

Hellos and introductions were hard and short at 6 a.m. We were all tired and there was plenty of anxiety about the trip ahead. We—a group of 15 Dubuque teachers, parents and community members—were headed north to Minnesota's Boundary Waters Wilderness Area. There, by canoeing and carrying our gear and ourselves through the Northwoods, we were supposed to learn all about Outward Bound and its project, Expeditionary Learning.

But we weren't thinking about learning that first day.

We were worried about what we'd heard from the first of three Dubuque groups to make the expedition: the mosquitoes were terrible, the black flies were worse, the instructors were demanding, the course was impossibly rigorous, the tents were small, you better have just the right gear (but of course we didn't). In short, the talk said we were about to embark on a nightmare of a teacher workshop.

So we were all a little edgy as we climbed into the two school vans. We all had our own thoughts—and some small talk—for company. But that would change soon enough. We divided into two groups, or brigades, and started to live and work with the company of our group. Before the day was over, we slept and snored together in tents designed for people who were much smaller than most of us.

Above our heads that first night—above the "Home Place" of the Voyageur Outward Bound School on the Kawishiwi River near Ely, Minn.—was a mother lode of silver stars.

Day 2

We tramped through the woods, carrying 40-pound sacks of gear on our backs. We were in the middle of a long hike into lake country when our expedition turned hard. It was warm. We sweated under the weight of the packs. The trail was rough, wet and rocky. Given half a chance, half of our brigade would have abandoned ship right then—and we hadn't even tried to carry one of the 80-pound canoes.

This was a portage. It's how you skirt bad spots or get from one lake to another on a canoe trip. It didn't take our group very long to figure out that it didn't like to portage. Wanita Kueter stopped for a rest. So did Dianne Andersen. The word rigor started getting used, as in, "Portages are just too rigorous." Rigor, as in academic rigor, happens to be one of Expeditionary Learning's favorite words.

> **Reading from the Voyageur *Readings Book*, picked out at that night's camp:**
>
> *"And there at the camp we had around us the elemental world of water and light and earth and air. We felt the presences of the wild creatures, the river, the trees, the stars. Though we had our troubles, we had them in true perspective. The universe, as we could see any night, is unimaginably large, and mostly dark. We knew we needed to be together more than we needed to be apart."*
>
> —Wendell Berry

"[Students] must have tasks that required perseverance, fitness, craftsmanship, imagination, self-discipline and significant achievement," says an Expeditionary Learning brochure. "A primary job of the educator is to help students overcome their fear

August 1, 1993; p. 1E, *Dubuque Telegraph Herald*. Published with permission of the *Telegraph Herald*.

and discover they have more in them than they think."

◆ ◆ ◆

> Be tough,
> Yet gentle,
> Humble, yet bold,
> Swayed always
> by beauty
> and truth.

— *Bob Pieh,
Founding Director
Minnesota (now Voyageur) Outward Bound School*

◆ ◆ ◆

Our brigade, the Cree Brigade, wasn't ready to make that discovery. The weight of canoes on shoulders was too painfully fresh.

When we got to water, we were left to figure out paddling for ourselves. Self-discovery, we learned, is another tenet of Expeditionary Learning.

At the end of the day, after teaching ourselves basic strokes, we made a tidy camp near a bay of the Kawishiwi River.

We started a fire spiced with cedar twigs and cooked a vegetable stew. The slammer, or latrine, was behind us and out of the way. In the Boundary Waters, people are only allowed to camp at such designated sites.

> **Journal entry (on the road somewhere in Wisconsin):**
>
> *"It's culture shock. A new group brings out the silences in me...(farther north)...The trees have changed and so has my mood. Being in a group, which is rare for me, is feeling more comfortable. Together we've survived mechanical trouble, a three-hour delay and a song by Steve Heer (a school social worker). It's pine country now. It's good to see a change."*
>
> *—MK*

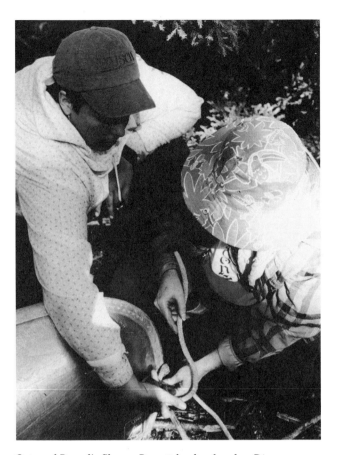

Outward Bound's Sharon Bassett lends a hand as Dianne Andersen learns to tie a knot. Photograph by Mike Krapfl/Dubuque Telegraph Herald.

After eating, we sat on the rocks, talking about the day, complaining about the rigor, waiting for the mosquitoes to chase us into tents.

Day 3

Our instructors—Sharon Bassett, 27, of Cambridge, Mass., and Steve Rippe, 32, of Minneapolis, Minn.—got a wonderful idea.

Sure enough, that's another principle of Expeditionary Learning. Expeditionary Learning wants to "foster a community where students' and adults' ideas are respected," says its literature.

The instructors' idea was certainly respected. Let's take advantage of this tail wind, they said. All we had to do, they explained, was pull the big tarp from the gear bag and make a sail.

We gathered the canoes side by side and held them together. What we made, essentially, was one big raft. Marge Clark and Kathy Sheth tied the tarp to their paddles and hoisted it into the wind. Sue Whitty secured the tarp's bottom. Within minutes we were scooting across Gabbro Lake.

> **Journal entry (from the solo):**
>
> *"I'm watching an eagle fly. It looks so easy—their flapless soaring. But watch the wings. They're always moving, always adjusting; using the flow, but not necessarily going with it. I like that."*
>
> —MK

Bassett, who likes to break into song, flashed a huge smile. Rippe, who likes to break into nature talks, was grinning. The rest of the Cree Brigade was holding tight.

The Outward Bound instructors aren't really instructors. Except for Rippe's impromptu talks about owl eyes and other natural wonders, there's very little formal teaching. There's lots of guiding, lots of question-answering and lots of role-modeling.

It was up to us, for example, to ask: "How do you make a left turn from the left side of the canoe without sticking the paddle in the water like a rudder and wasting all our momentum?"

The response was quick. Rippe and Bassett showed us the "J-stroke" and a few other fancy maneuvers.

We were sailing fast as we left Gabbro Lake and skimmed into Bald Eagle Lake. We passed a small island and decided to shoot for the next campsite. Still together, we turned past a rocky point and headed out of the wind toward shore. Somehow, we managed to land together. That took a lot of teamwork and just a little luck.

Somewhere, out on the Boundary Waters, we had become a team.

Day 4

David Olson was out there alone.

It was breakfast time and most of the group was grabbing bowlfuls of granola and powdered milk.

A few minutes later we had all picked a spot on shore, or on a nearby island, to do what Outward Bound calls a solo.

A solo, explained Bassett and Rippe, is a chance to think and write about the outdoors, about the expedition, about your classroom, about your life.

Students must have tasks that require perseverance, fitness, craftsmanship, imagination, self-discipline and significant achievement. A primary job of the educator is to help students overcome their fear and discover they have more in them than they think.

— *From a brochure about Expeditionary Learning*

Time alone is another of the Expeditionary Learning principles. It falls under the heading of solitude and reflection. "Solitude, reflection and silence replenish our energies and open our minds," says the literature.

Olson, who had gone on an Outward Bound trip in Utah, already knew about the solo. He knew he wanted a long one, so he'd asked if he could solo overnight.

The instructors said sure, but he had to take responsibility for finding a good campsite, for building a shelter from rain and bugs, for keeping

> **Journal entry:**
>
> *"I now know what a portage is. It, for one thing, is a sweaty, difficult challenge. Wendy Miller and I portaged the first canoe in. The trick, of course, is to balance the thing on your shoulders. It gets easier fairly quickly, but it is awkward. It's even an awkward sight. It's like a 17-foot aluminum slug is making its way through the Northwoods, over logs, up hills, down rocks and through the mud. The paddling, thankfully, is much easier. We all, however, have lots to learn."*
>
> —MK

> **A reading from Voyageur's *Readings Book*, recited before dinner:**
>
> *"I would be forced shivering into a new, unfamiliar world, where I had to forge new friends and a home for myself, and although such experiences are painful and awkward at first, I know...that they are the best things to make one grow—always biting off just a bit more than you chewed before and finding to your amazement that you can, when it comes right down to it, do that too!"*
>
> —*Sylvia Plath*

himself safe and sound. They were there to help; but it was his project to do.

As it turned out, the solo was the expedition's highlight for most of the brigade. The portages were the lowlight. They weren't even deemed necessary evils. To most of the brigade, the portages were just a sweaty hell.

Just before dinner, after a three-hour solo and a long portage, we circled up for a talk. Dianne Andersen couldn't stop smiling about the solo. "What a wonderful solo," she said.

> **Journal entry:**
>
> *"After a nice ride though moose country—we didn't see any though 'we sounded like moose coming in,' Steve said—we began our last portage. It was a beautiful one. The canoe was steady enough on the shoulders so I could enjoy the view. And what a view: a bridge over the rushing Snake River, a meadow filled with daisies, wolf scat on the trail and some long, flat places where you put down your guard and stumble on a small stone."*
>
> —*MK*

Somebody in the group, from somewhere in the dark, added another thought: "What a wonderful portage."

Day 5

Wanita Kueter was suspended on a little cable between two white pine 60 feet off the ground.

She was taking the test of a high ropes obstacle course.

The course is wrapped around a stand of very old and very tall pines. The course, at first, looks scary. Crazy.

But Kueter, who's had problems with her shoulder all week, was pressing on, making her way across the thin cable.

She wore a tight harness around her waist that was connected to two safety cords. They, in turn, were connected to cables along the course.

She went up a ladder, across two parallel logs, up a cable bridge, around and around a tree. All the while, brigade members shouted encouragement.

Finally, after a few more careful steps, she made it to the swing. It is not your typical back yard swing. It's 60 feet in the air. You start from the top.

Kueter, who's tried skydiving, eased herself off the platform. She fell straight down. The swing caught, leveled and threw her back into the air.

Keuter grinned the rest of the evening. So did the rest of the brigade. Everyone reached a goal on the ropes.

It was a time to be proud of self. And it was a time to be proud of Cree Brigade.

School Visits

by Meg Campbell

Anthropologists note that it is in observing others that we develop a keener sense of our own uniqueness. Teachers comparing and contrasting their own practices and struggles say that they gain a deeper appreciation of their own strengths and areas for growth as a result of school visits. The private sector calls this "benchmarking," finding out and learning from others' best practices. We think it a simple idea whose time has come.

Our approach to professional development is shaped by our belief and design principle that learning happens best in intimate and caring settings that foster communication and reflection. The purpose of professional development is to support adults as expeditionary learners themselves, and often this is effectively accomplished by creating the circumstances for meaningful one-on-one and small group candid exchanges to occur. We have therefore resisted the impulse to organize a national conference or convention of Expeditionary Learning educators, choosing instead to host a series of smaller Sharing Days in five cities.

These Sharing Days are predicated upon the value of teacher experience and wisdom. They allow for teachers from other sites to spend Friday visiting Expeditionary Learning schools and, on Saturday, for visiting teachers to share their progress in implementation with host city teachers. Sharing Days also give both host city and visiting teachers the opportunity to hear from other educators. Ron Berger, a Shutesbury, Massachusetts, elementary teacher has noted that he has learned and continues to learn more from visiting other schools than from any other method of professional development. Traditionally teachers seldom have the opportunity to visit other schools within their own district, let alone in another state or region. Yet when teachers spend time in each other's classrooms, they find themselves revitalized. They discover new ideas when they see how their colleagues facilitate student critique sessions or create time for solitude and reflection. They also feel validated when they see their work as part of a larger community of teaching and learning.

School visits by teachers afford the host school a particularly interested audience for student work, which in turn prompts self-reflection by host faculty and students. What is our best work? What have we really learned? Where are we struggling? Since our Sharing Days visits also are structured in small groups, visiting teachers optimally have the chance to observe learning expeditions in progress and talk teacher-to-teacher with the expedition guides. Both the visitors and the hosts benefit from sharing their perspectives.

The purpose of professional development is to support adults as expeditionary learners themselves.

Time for discussion, reflection and sharing is equally scarce. For this reason, on Saturday, Sharing Days visits are dedicated to teachers talking with each other about their work. Common themes emerge. For example, Tammy Duehr, a Dubuque first-grade teacher, reflected on how her commitment to the principle of self-discovery causes tension within her as she balances between choosing when to offer her own knowledge and ideas and when to let the first-grade students make discoveries on their own; Christine Cziko, a secondary teacher at the School for the Physical City in New York, observed that she faces the same tension when teaching her urban ninth graders.

If we really believe that experience is a powerful teacher, then orchestrating opportunities for teachers to share and learn from one another's successes and failures makes good sense. It is not glitzy, but it works.

A Principal Reflects on the First Semester

by David Olson

Central Alternative High School in Dubuque, Iowa, has existed for over twenty years. It has made the slow steady progress of many midwestern alternative schools, beginning as an after school tutorial program and gradually expanding to offer its own diploma about fourteen years ago. The school has always prided itself on using "family" as a symbol for all that should be good and right in education.

When I came to Central as principal four years ago, I found the school was lacking a clear vision. The school was in a maintenance mode, but the staff knew it and was trying to reclaim a direction. Staff members attended stimulating conferences and brought back wonderful ideas, but we needed a way to pull it all together. We needed our own real map.

We found it in the fall of 1992 when we learned about Expeditionary Learning Outward Bound. The Expeditionary Learning design seemed to fit with all the pieces we had created so far. We decided to transform our whole school, and spent the spring and summer venturing into a number of new forms of staff development. We attended mini-sabbaticals and summer institutes, worked with Project Adventure, Facing History and Ourselves, and Educators for Social Responsibility, and trekked through the North Woods of Minnesota on Outward Bound expeditions. When we almost reached the point of overload, the school year began and we were off in a new structure of reorganized curriculum, teams of teachers, block scheduling, and many other changes that we only later realized must occur.

Things have felt different from the start. Higher expectations for academics have been placed on students, with continuing support through our school-based youth services initiatives. Each student has received an Expeditionary Learning journal to record thoughts and ideas. Group initiatives used as metaphors for life appear as part of group work. Community meetings launch each day. Many of our old traditions, like a school-wide Thanksgiving dinner, a yearbook, and casual conversation in the hall, seem to feel awkward until we learn to assess what needs to stay and how to reshape it.

◆ ◆ ◆

It is so hard to be a learner; we return to feeling like students.

*— David Olson
Central Alternative High School*

◆ ◆ ◆

Nearing the end of the first semester as an Expeditionary Learning high school, the staff is tired! We have all worked long, hard hours. No one has escaped the impact or effects of change. Some

A drawing of David Olson, principal of Central Alternative High School, Dubuque, by two Central students: drawing by Tabatha Adams, pen and ink by Lisa Benson.

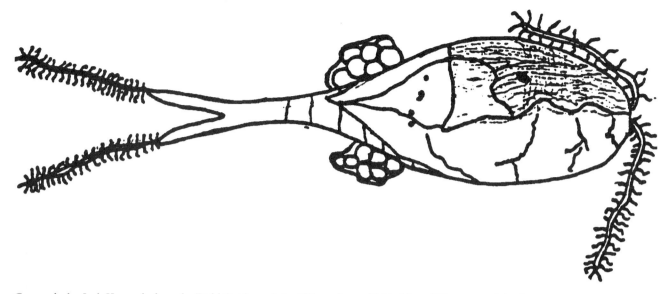

Copepods, by Josh Heacock, from the Field Guide made by fifth graders at Table Mound Elementary School in Dubuque, Iowa.

students are still complaining about how different everything is from last year. Parents ask questions they never asked before. We have more ownership than ever before (which sounds great, but it includes a tremendous fear of failing). We are realizing that some of our mistakes might be OK if we make some changes for next semester. It is so hard to be a learner—we return to feeling like students.

As teachers are giving good-bye hugs to each other before leaving for holiday vacation, there is a remark that this will be the longest that staff has been apart in almost a year. One team makes quick plans to meet after Christmas, before the New Year, to organize the next learning expedition.

It is now two days after Christmas, a quiet snowy Monday morning. The custodian beat me in, salted the steps, and even put on a pot of coffee. It is so quiet in the empty school. I walked around pondering if the school really looks like an Expeditionary Learning school. Have we made changes to raise student achievement? How will I support the staff to know we're succeeding?

Then to my wondering eyes should appear...a student! Yes, he found the door open and a computer he could use to write that community survey project he just had to finish. All morning Nate stayed, calling his teacher at home, reading the drafts over the phone, making changes, and calling again. My phone rang and Char, a former student (who dropped out), said, "David, you're there. When do I sign up to come back next semester? I really need an education."

◆ ◆ ◆

Higher expectations for academics have been placed on students, with continuing support through our school-based youth services initiatives.

◆ ◆ ◆

Is the hard work of transforming a school worth it? Why don't I know instantly? The real proof will come after several years of implementation, but Nate is enough proof for now.

A Conversation with Expeditionary Learning Principals

Meg Campbell (Expeditionary Learning Outward Bound): Let's start this conference call by looking at how your role has changed now that you are working within an Expeditionary Learning school.

David Olson (Central Alternative High School, Dubuque, Iowa): One of the changes I see is that administrators need to be a lot more supportive. Dramatic school change sometimes rattles the confidence of teachers. As the teachers have taken ownership of Expeditionary Learning, they sometimes have less confidence about the new things they are trying. When something works, they feel great, but pieces of it don't always work, so more than ever, they need me to be supportive, nurturing, and responsive.

Mark Weiss (School for the Physical City, New York): I agree. I've been a teacher for 27 years and for 13 years I was the principal of Bronx Regional High School, an alternative school in the South Bronx in New York City which I founded. I have always felt that I loved kids and the office staff and related well to them, but somehow I had a gap with teachers. I wasn't a teacher of teachers, because I felt like a colleague of teachers. I always want to maintain that posture in some way, but at the same time, we have an obligation as leaders to invest a lot in the teachers, who then teach the kids.

I've been trying consciously to pull back from kids and listen more to teachers. I want to spend my energy listening to teachers better and helping them be the people they want to be in the classroom and in the school. It's been a struggle; it's something I have to work on. For example, I tend to sit in my office and let the kids interrupt a teacher because kids are so important to me. "Oh you need a basketball. Oh there's a flood in the bathroom." Suddenly, teachers are finding that I am not responsive, and kids are finding they can interrupt me any time they want. There has to be some balance. So I am working on it.

Meg Campbell: And where are you getting your energy? Who's nurturing the nurturer?

Mark Weiss: The dream. I look for those places where we are succeeding, and try to draw energy from that. And I always watch the kids. It's great to see the kids return from team days [the days students do fieldwork in the city]. I love to see a group of kids come back from the Cathedral of St. John the Divine and know they had a top-notch day, that they experienced something important.

> I think Expeditionary Learning helps you become a better administrator, because it helps you focus more on what's going on in the classroom.
>
> — *Nora Pou*
> *Blackstone Elementary School*

Nora Pou (Blackstone Elementary School, Boston): I am being molded as an administrator by Expeditionary Learning, since this is my second year as a school administrator. I think Expeditionary Learning helps you become a better administrator, because it helps you focus more on what's going on in the classroom. As a school administrator, your priorities are to make sure the students learn.

Meg Campbell: What about Mark and Nora's point about a shift to being a teacher of teachers? Is that how you had already perceived yourself? Do you find you are spending more time with teachers developing curricula?

Margarita Muñiz (Rafael Hernandez School, Boston): What has changed in my perception is where I might have said, "I don't think this is a good idea," I now sit back and say, "OK, this is the way I feel about it, but if you guys feel very strongly about going in another direction, that's fine."

For example, I think it was very courageous when the teachers mixed the sixth, seventh, and eighth graders together. That was a big step onto new ground. They were taking on a new expedition, a new way of working together, a new role in terms of the curriculum, and a different student grouping. I thought it was a lot to take on, but they wanted to do it, so I said fine, go ahead. I supported them throughout the expedition. There was a learning curve for all of us involved in that expedition.

Bill Colom (Blackstone Elementary School, Boston): One of the biggest challenges in a large school like the Blackstone is having the non-Expeditionary Learning staff members accept the new role of the Expeditionary Learning teachers. The Expeditionary Learning teachers have extended blocks of time in their schedule and more planning time because they took on the challenge of implementing Expeditionary Learning while the others did not. You have to support your entire staff.

Meg Campbell: I think Bill is making the very valid point that this design is a lot easier to do in a whole school than in part of a school.

David Olson: I think it is easier to do it in the whole school, but even if you are doing it whole-school, you really have to recognize all the different places where people are. Some people are so much further along than other people. At various times all of those roles seem to change.

Meg Campbell: You talked about having to be more nurturing, and more emotionally available to the staff. Nora said that she feels her role as an administrator is now much more focused on the classroom. Have you have felt a similar shift, David?

David Olson: I think it depends on the day, because some days I am very removed from the classroom. The reason I say that is because I am doing a lot of management for the teachers. Teachers are making more and more decisions in the classroom. Therefore, they don't want to have anything to do with the decisions that infringe on the classroom. The teachers used to be very interested in how every penny in the budget was spent, and we made a lot of decisions about the budget as a group. Now they have so many decisions about what and how they are teaching, that they just want me to take care of it.

Mark Weiss: Is that good?

David Olson: Is it good? No, it would be great to have some help and some input on those decisions. But they are just too busy with other decisions right now. So on some days it feels like I am doing more management than classroom things. On other days, I am very involved in what is happening in the classroom. Those are the better days.

A draft sketch of Nora Pou, assistant principal at the Blackstone Elementary School in Boston, by fourth grader Alberto Vargas.

Mark Weiss: I get pulled in those directions too. You'd like to be in classrooms with kids and teachers trying to figure out how to engage kids in meaningful learning, because that's how we will break the mold. But we have to make strategic choices about what is needed in order to keep the school going in the direction we want it to go.

David Olson: One of the strong ways that I am able to nurture teachers—and it seems almost a required way—is by participating with them in a lot of the staff development. That's when—how did you put it, Mark?—you are a colleague of the teachers. I like the colleague of teachers role when I am participating in a Project Adventure workshop or a mini-sabbatical, and we work really hard together. That's been a positive part of the whole thing, and a good way for me to nurture.

Meg Campbell: The other question I put out for everybody is, as the leaders in the school, what evidence are you finding schoolwide of the Expeditionary Learning design principles? Are there ways you are changing the culture of the school? Are you focusing on one particular principle?

Mark Weiss: I have been trying to analyze that; to what extent and how are we doing Expeditionary Learning? I think it snuck up on me. I see it in the regular, consistent access to the city that our kids have had. I am looking at the Primacy of Self-Discovery and the Having of Wonderful Ideas as being the fruit of weeks and weeks and weeks of youngsters going out into the city at least one full day a week. Often, they go out more than that, since teachers can take their students out whenever they want to.

When the weather was good, I went out every day with my Community Circle. Community Circles are an advisory system, in which every youngster is in a Community Circle and each one of us is an advisor to students over the whole time they are at the school. Whenever it was nice out and we felt like we wanted to be out there in the streets of New York, my Community Circle went outside and bonded with each other and got to know the city. Our Community Circle now knows that part of the city incredibly well, and all the other parts of the city they have explored.

I didn't know that it would have that effect. I kept wondering, "So what is one day a week? What does it mean?" But think about what it would be like if you did it with your own kids. Say you went out for a full day every week to another and another and another place, and you studied it, and you had a team day packet. All of a sudden, the richness of that learning and the richness of your relationship would be incredible.

One of the strong ways that I am able to nurture teachers—and it seems almost a required way—is by participating with them in a lot of the staff development.

— *David Olson*
Central Alternative High School

The community meetings that occur every morning are another expression of the design principles. Sometimes they are rough and ragged, but I don't think there is anyone who would not want to have them. The meeting includes five minutes of silence, and sometimes that too is a little ragged, but at the same time, I think there is a feeling that the silence is part of this culture. We are proud of a school that can be quiet for five minutes in the course of a hectic New York City day.

Margarita Muñiz: What struck me most in the Egleston Square project was the students' Responsibility for Learning. Here is a quote from a student, Aisha: "We learned that it was very important to ask what people in the neighborhood wanted. It is much easier to build something that the community supports." The students learned that you really have to work through the community to be able to get somewhere with your ideas. Reuben John, another student, said, "Our construction went pretty fast because we did our research, and because everyone worked together. Everyone had to do their jobs for it to be a success."

As a staff, we have been experiencing the Primacy of Self-Discovery. We are discovering within ourselves what it takes to work together, to share ideas, to cooperate and change midstream. All of that has to happen when we develop learning expeditions.

Nora Pou: At the Blackstone we are still struggling to find evidence of those principles schoolwide. They are more evident within the classroom, more in some classrooms than others. It has to do with the type of exposure teachers have had to how the principles are carried out in the school setting. Our teachers need staff development, and to be able to visit other classrooms and see by themselves what each one of those principles means.

David Olson: I think we have changed a lot. The principles are evident all over the place. Students have a lot more responsibility and a lot more pride in the work they are producing than they ever had before. We have a bulletin board in the main office for Students' Best Work. The amount of time the students spend trying to make something good enough to put on the main office bulletin board is something different for us. We changed the traditional A, B, C, D, F grading system to an A, B, and a Not Yet. This has really encouraged students to work harder and the quality has improved. We never used to display student work of the quality that we now do.

The design principles are also evident in our weekly staff meetings. I have eliminated any sort of information that can be written down, so we have time for sharing, talking, and doing initiatives. Sometimes we have silence together. I think this time is essential. At the beginning of every staff meeting, we have something called Maiden Voyages in which everyone has a chance to share something new they saw a student or staff member do during the past week. That's been very uplifting because we really have been trying a lot of new and different things, and it's important that we have the time to tell each other about them.

Margarita Muñiz: Here is a closing reading: *"Caminante no hay camino/se hace el camino al andar."* This is by Antonio Machado, and roughly translated it means: "Walker, there is no road. You must make your own road as you go." All of us are breaking ground in many ways and we need to support each other as much as possible.

The White Aster, by Jennifer Lampe, from the Field Guide made by fifth graders for their learning expedition on pond life at Table Mound Elementary School in Dubuque, Iowa.

Part Four

The School Community

Student Agreement for Participation in the Rocky Mountain School of Expeditionary Learning

In their continued commitment to building an Expeditionary Learning school culture, members of the Rocky Mountain School of Expeditionary Learning (RMSEL) in Denver have developed a Student Agreement for Participation based on the Expeditionary Learning design principles.

The agreement, written by RMSEL business manager Susan Keene with the assistance of the staff, parents, community members, and students on the school governance board, grew out of discussions about the school's expectations of student behavior. The RMSEL board believes that clearly articulated standards of behavior can help guide students' participation in their community. Each student will meet with a teacher and his or her parent(s) to discuss the agreement, giving the students the opportunity to gain a clear understanding of what it means to be a member of the RMSEL community.

I, _____, understand that the Rocky Mountain School of Expeditionary Learning has been founded on and is directed by ten specific principles of design. In accordance with these principles, the following is a list of expectations for my behavior and performance at RMSEL that constitutes a contractual agreement between myself and the school.

As a student of RMSEL, I am committed to the following:

❖ The Primacy of Self-Discovery

Learning happens best with emotion, challenge, and the requisite support. People discover their abilities, values, "grand passions," and responsibilities in situations that offer adventure and the unexpected. They must have tasks that require perseverance, fitness, craftsmanship, imagination, self-discipline, and significant achievement. A primary job of the educator is to help students overcome their fear and discover they have more in them than they think.

I am excited about the prospect of discovering my abilities, values, and "grand passions" and am committed to providing the perseverance, fitness, craftsmanship, imagination, self-discipline, and significant achievement necessary to do so.

❖ The Having of Wonderful Ideas

Teach so as to build on children's curiosity about the world by creating learning situations that provide matter to think about, time to experiment, and time to make sense of what is observed. Foster a community where students' and adults' ideas are respected.

I promise to persistently work toward achieving rigorous standards of academic and character excellence, even if that means I perform a task over and over and over until I attain this goal.

I agree to share my ideas with classmates, teachers, and other RMSEL community members whenever appropriate and in turn, I agree to respect the ideas and suggestions of classmates, teachers, and RMSEL community members that are shared with me.

❖ The Responsibility for Learning

Learning is both a personal, individually specific process of discovery and a social activity. Each of us learns within and for ourselves and as a part of a group. Every aspect of a school must encourage children, young people, and adults to become increasingly responsible for directing their own personal and collective learning.

With the help of my teachers, parents, and other mentors, I agree to take on more responsibility for directing my own personal learning and, as appropriate, that of my RMSEL community.

I will respect the natural world and commit to taking responsibility for caring for the environment.

❖ Intimacy and Caring

Learning is fostered best in small groups where there is trust, sustained caring, and mutual respect among all members of the learning community. Keep schools and learning groups small. Be sure there is a caring adult looking after the progress of each child. Arrange for the older students to mentor the younger ones.

I promise to conduct myself in such a way as to be considered a trustworthy, reliable, concerned, caring, and respected member of the RMSEL community. I will act in accordance with the RMSEL Code of Conduct. I will consider myself a role model for other students in the school and, as such, I agree to work with younger students to assist them with their development and education as appropriate.

❖ Success and Failure

All students must be assured a fair measure of success in learning in order to nurture the confidence and capacity to take risks and rise to increasingly difficult challenges. But it is also important to experience failure, to overcome negative inclinations, to prevail against adversity, and to learn to turn disabilities into opportunities.

I am committed to achieving academic success. I will work hard, take risks, and overcome challenges. In the event some of my efforts fail, I promise to work hard to prevail against adversity and to learn to turn disabilities into opportunities.

❖ Collaboration and Competition

Teach so as to join individual and group development so that the value of friendship, trust, and group endeavor is made manifest. Encourage students to compete, not against each other, but with their own personal best and with rigorous standards of excellence.

I am committed to academic and character achievement that exceeds what I would describe as my own personal best. I promise to persistently work toward achieving rigorous standards of academic and character excellence as prescribed by the school, even if that means I perform a task over and over and over until I attain this goal. In addition, I promise to be a productive member of any group with which I work.

❖ Diversity and Inclusivity

Diversity and inclusivity in all groups dramatically increase richness of ideas, creative power, problem-solving ability, and acceptance of others. Encourage students to investigate, value, and draw upon their own different histories, talents, and resources together with those of other communities and cultures. Keep the schools and learning groups heterogeneous.

I will learn more about my own personal history and culture as well as the histories and cultures of my fellow RMSEL community members and will demonstrate nothing but the highest respect for people of all walks of life in everything I do.

❖ The Natural World

A direct and respectful relationship with the natural world refreshes the human spirit and reveals the important lessons of recurring cycles and cause and effect. Students learn to become stewards of the earth and of the generations to come.

I will respect the natural world and commit to taking responsibility for caring for the environment.

❖ Solitude and Reflection

Solitude, reflection, and silence replenish our energies and open our minds. Be sure students have time alone to explore their own thoughts, make their own connections, and create their own ideas. Then give them opportunities to exchange their reflections with each other and with adults.

I will use time for solitude and reflection productively to explore my thoughts and to create ideas that I will exchange with other students and with adults.

❖ Service and Compassion

We are crew, not passengers, and are strengthened by acts of consequential service to others. One of a school's primary functions is to prepare its students with the attitudes and skills they need in order to learn from and be of service to others.

I believe that we are crew and not passengers in life. I will demonstrate this belief by participating in service projects so that I can learn from and be of service to others.

I have read and understand the list of expectations and agree to participate in the RMSEL program in accordance with these expectations. I understand that failure to do so will result in counseling sessions with my teacher(s) and parent(s) and will impact my evaluations at RMSEL.

_____
Student Signature

_____
Parent Signature

❖ Parental Commitment to This Agreement

As parent of this RMSEL student, I agree to assist my child in maintaining the level of participation outlined in the Student Agreement and agree to support the staff and school in this effort. In addition, I agree to:

- support the pursuit of education in my home;
- see to it that my child attends school every day except in the case of illness or emergency;
- participate in two to four parent/teacher conferences a year;
- volunteer to assist the school in whatever way is practical for me.

I have seen the RMSEL Code of Conduct and understand that RMSEL is bound by and operates strictly in accordance with Colorado State Law regarding student behavior.

_____
Parent Signature

Two students from the Rafael Hernandez Bilingual School in Boston take notes in their natural history journals for the fourth-grade learning expedition on pond life. Photograph by Brian Smith/NASDC.

Circles
"Where Everyone Knows You Really Well"

by Meg Campbell

The tradition and ritual of forming a circle, practiced in Outward Bound and Project Adventure courses and in Expeditionary Learning classrooms and schools, has its roots in the human discovery that a circle is the most efficient way for a group to ensure that every member is equidistant from the source of heat and warmth. When everyone's face is in full view, both communication and the sense of personal safety are enhanced. Gathering in a circle offers an opportunity to pause, reflect, debrief and listen, and to share ideas, silence, readings, favorite books, opinions, initiatives and the natural world.

A successful community circle is much more than an advisory group. The bonds are deeper and the range of activities is broader both because enough time is set aside and because the adult guide brings to the circle a strong sense of utilizing this ritual to strengthen community, communication, character and intellect.

Circles strengthen the sense of individuals growing with the support of community. The understanding that Expeditionary Learning joins character development and intellectual growth and achievement is evident in how community circles are structured. At the School for the Physical City (SPC) in New York City, for example, 140 students (grades 6-9) and the entire staff begin each day with a community meeting convened by principal Mark Weiss. Space in their temporary location this year is at a premium, and the community meeting therefore must take place in a crowded room that otherwise is two adjoining classrooms with a partition. Nevertheless, each community meeting begins with five minutes of shared silence. Poet and teacher Kathleen Norris in *Dakota: A Spiritual Geography* (Ticknor and Fields, 1993) writes about the power of "making silence" with her elementary students. SPC

A second grader in Dubuque, Iowa, helps a first grader tie his shoes. One goal of Expeditionary Learning is to teach students to be of service to others. Photograph by David Guralnick/Dubuque Telegraph Herald

consciously and strategically uses this daily silence as a way to set the tone for the entire community of the purposefulness and depth of the day ahead.

Four days a week, SPC students also meet for forty-five minutes in smaller community circles of approximately twelve students. (The fifth day is a full day of fieldwork related to the learning expedition underway.)

Two days a week, every community circle becomes a reading circle. "The having of wonderful ideas" is cultivated through development of the habit of reflecting upon the reading every community member has chosen to pursue (beyond assigned reading). One community circle staffs the mobile book cart which is filled with challenging, quality trade books which are available for perusal during morning breaks. Given space constraints, two or more community circles are facilitated simultaneously in every classroom, as well as the office and corridor. Nevertheless, these circles have become the building blocks for the larger school community. "It's where everyone knows you really well," one freshman explained to me.

◆ ◆ ◆

A successful community circle is much more than an advisory group.

◆ ◆ ◆

Community circles in every classroom have contributed significantly toward shaping the Expeditionary Learning culture. At Table Mound Elementary in Dubuque, Iowa, community circles are held during the morning. One kindergarten group begins and ends each day in a circle, including music and singing. Readings for these young students include reflections and discussions on what courage and perseverance mean and students share their experiences and strong opinions. As their first learning expedition, *Books, Book, Books*, was concluding, students shared what aspect they found most enjoyable. This discussion was undertaken with the assistance of a ball of yarn, so that as the students took turns stating their ideas, they then passed the yarn to another student and thereby created their own web. This ensured in a concrete way that every student had the opportunity to be heard. A community circle of Table Mound second graders included a discussion, with notes taken on large paper by one of the students, on what the design principles mean to each of them. "Collaboration and Competition" means that "we don't laugh when someone falls down."

Many teachers have commented on the new skills required to facilitate community circles effectively and their sense that the circles are getting stronger over time. Teachers have also noted the value that the structure, flexibility and continuity of community circles provides. Any community is made up of smaller groups of people. Community circles recognize this fact and are one way the design principle of Intimacy and Caring is integrated into the rhythm of every week.

Valerie Hartung drew this Kiowa teepee for a learning expedition on Native American culture at Central Alternative High School in Dubuque, Iowa.

The One-Day Community Exploration
An Expeditionary Learning Professional Development Experience

by Leah Rugen

Overview

Professional development and the role of the teacher form the keystone of Expeditionary Learning. We believe that each professional development experience must embody Expeditionary Learning's ten design principles and closely mirror the kind of active and deeply reflective learning we plan for students. By becoming learners themselves, teachers internalize the ideas and practices of Expeditionary Learning.

The One-Day Community Exploration was a natural initial building block in our professional development sequence, because it immediately put the ten design principles into action and gave them a living context. By working in small groups to conduct investigations of a community, teachers engaged in the kind of learning they would be planning for students. Because they had a concrete task and were actually out in the community, ideas and questions about how to implement this kind of learning with students flowed freely.

Expeditionary Learning seeks to challenge and change the view that learning happens best in silent, passive classrooms. We believe that movement and engagement with the outside world—human society and nature—provoke intellectual thought and stimulate learning. A teacher from Dubuque captured this view when she described her husband's weariness after a day of being lectured to for "in-service" in contrast to her energy and ideas after a day of physical and intellectual exploration in the community.

In the following narrative, I will outline the basic structure for the Community Exploration, provide illustrations from two of the sites (Dubuque and New York), discuss issues of logistics and planning, and comment on the role of the facilitators or instructors.

> We believe that movement and engagement with the outside world—human society and nature—provoke intellectual thought and stimulate learning.

◆ ◆ ◆

Structure of the Day

❖ Framing Expeditionary Learning and the Community Exploration

As with any learning experience or investigation, it is important to create the context and overall purpose for the Community Exploration. Participants are not simply going on a neighborhood tour to collect facts, information, and impressions (though this can be an important outcome). They are engaging deeply with the design principles. They are investigating key questions: What is Expeditionary Learning? How can I implement it with my students? What is the nature of community and what constitutes a valuable community resource? As in a student's learning expedition, the investigation of these questions has a clear purpose—the creation of a concrete product such as a community resource guide or an initial plan of a learning experience for students.

Depending on the time available, and the number of participants and facilitators, there is a range of possibilities for an opening sequence of small group activities (exercises and problem-solving initiatives) and discussion to open a process of getting to know each other's thinking and experience, and build common understanding of Expeditionary Learning. For example, a silent walk across the Brooklyn Bridge presented as a "mini-solo" powerfully introduced the value of solitude and reflection, as well as the ways in which one can experience a place through the senses.

A logical step in this investigation of Expeditionary Learning is to introduce and discuss all of the design principles, asking people to engage actively with them. In New York, facilitators conducted a blindfold walk from a busy street corner to the waterfront in lower Manhattan overlooking the Statue of Liberty. After a moment of silence to soak in the view and the experience, the group discussed the walk in terms of the design principles. Which ones were most in evidence? How? The resulting discussion was rich in ideas and provocative questions (such as whether a blindfold walk was a very positive metaphor for learning!).

❖ Goal Setting and Planning in Small Groups

Once the context and broad purpose have been established, it is time to launch into the substance of the day—the community exploration. Facilitators review the parameters and guidelines (including safety considerations), and invite participants to speak of their own expectations and goals. Each small group sets out in its own direction committed to rejoin the others at a specific time and place to present their ideas and pool resources.

In Dubuque, each small group was given a resource packet, including a map with an area circled, defining the territory for the exploration. Every group had the same concrete task—that of identifying and investigating potential community resources within the defined area. Each participant was asked to take responsibility for a design principle and for making sure it was attended to and discussed throughout the day. After an initial planning period the groups took off for the community finding that "every time we went to a place it made us think of something else."

◆ ◆ ◆

An unassuming man in a park turned out to be a fount of local history and information.

◆ ◆ ◆

Similarly, in New York, the group of teachers was given a resource packet and asked to confine their exploration to a specific community or neighborhood. Because they were attempting to create a "mini-expedition" for themselves, in addition to gathering resources, the groups spent quite a lot of time planning—refining questions to shape their exploration, and discussing which thinking skills and methods of inquiry they would try to use throughout the day.

❖ The Exploration

Given five or six hours, a map, a plan, and very limited money for lunch and supplies, what can be accomplished? Participants were both surprised by how much they learned and discovered during such a short time and made well aware of how much work and thought was still needed. One teacher wrote in her journal that although she was exhausted at the end of the exploration, she knew "we've just touched the beginning."

Throughout the day ideas and assumptions were challenged and expanded. A Dubuque teacher felt that her thinking of what defines an educational resource was changed when her group ran into an unassuming man in a park who turned out to be a fount of local history and information. Whereas they had been thinking primarily of businesses and professions as resources, now they began to consider people in the street, shopkeepers, and elderly people in the park as sources of information and stories. Unaccustomed to discussing their work as teachers with strangers, they were surprised by the level of interest expressed by the people they interviewed. In turn, community members were pleased and excited to be asked for their ideas, and were delighted by the thought of being resources for students' learning expeditions. Their response is even more significant than it seems on the surface. It points to the ways in which Expeditionary Learning widens and strengthens the community of learners, breaking down traditional barriers.

A group of New York teachers concentrated on an in-depth examination of one city block in the Lower East Side. They looked at and discussed the various signs and symbols found on doorways, walls, and sidewalks; and interviewed residents to discover their definitions of community and whether they believed their neighborhood fit the definition. As another group spent the day probing the Brooklyn

Bridge and surrounding neighborhoods, they experimented with different learning strategies. Drawing the bridge made them notice and ask questions about details of structure and design. Interviewing strangers prompted them to examine biases and assumptions. How does one learn or acquire "true" information?

❖ Final Presentations and Discussions: Putting Learning in Context and Deciding the Next Step

The final presentations and discussion have the potential to be the most important part of the Community Exploration day. Here, teachers have the opportunity to crystallize their understanding, build on each other's learning, and raise challenging questions. It is important not to let this time be squeezed out by the demands and opportunities of the exploration. Having the goal of producing a final, usable product also greatly adds to the value of the experience. In Dubuque, creating and performing skits was the means by which small groups discussed what they had learned and communicated their learning to the larger audience. The goal of producing a resource book provided a still more tangible result of the day. Their success in creating this book gave them optimism and increased commitment to Expeditionary Learning: "It was realistic and concrete, and we saw it can be done."

❖ Planning Issues: Framework and Content, Safety and Logistics, the Role of the Facilitators

Although the teachers themselves quickly take over and manage their own experience, laying the groundwork through careful planning is a critically important part of the success of the experience. Again, depending on the configuration of the group of teachers, facilitators may decide to involve participants in the initial planning and design. Because they were planning for the faculties of four schools, the Dubuque facilitators did all of the initial groundwork. In fact, they kept the plans veiled in secrecy, and the element of surprise added to teachers' realization that the day would not be a typical in-service experience. In New York, working with a small group of teachers enabled the facilitators to involve them in the planning—enhancing the personal impact and value of the day as a team-building experience. The two examples we have included in this narrative underscore the flexibility of the Community Exploration as a professional development activity. In Dubuque, the day was planned for 150 teachers—in New York, for ten.

The specific planning issues are simple but critical. Facilitators should conduct their own investigation and survey of the communities to be explored, and determine what information and resources to provide participants. Some facilitators have chosen

Drawing of a subway entrance by Michael McDonald for the learning expedition Our City, Ourselves at the School for the Physical City in New York.

to set up an initial site visit or interview. This is probably not necessary for adults, and may detract from their independent experience, but it does model the kind of careful organization and legwork one needs to carry out in planning student expeditions. A critical component of the day is the small group size and configuration. The small groups that will be engaged in conducting the exploration should be no larger than ten. If planning for a large group of teachers, organizers should consider whether they wish to use the groups to build existing teams, or to introduce people who do not typically work together. Some of the other necessary planning details include determining the sequence of activities and questions which will best frame the experience; planning the final task and shape of the final discussions and presentations; and, of course, handling logistical details such as sites for the opening and closing and a budget for transportation, lunch, and supplies.

◆ ◆ ◆

> The small groups that will be engaged in conducting the exploration should be no larger than ten.

◆ ◆ ◆

It is also important to outline a process and build an awareness of safety considerations. Do not assume that adults will act safely naturally. Neighborhoods, streets, and parks, particularly in urban areas, are unfamiliar learning environments for groups. And people in groups tend to get lulled into a false sense of security. Providing guidelines and discussion of safety issues also models a vital part of planning learning expeditions for students.

Finally, throughout the day, the role of the facilitators is to provide context, raise important questions, highlight and summarize participants' insights, and provide the organizing structure of the experience. Naturally, it is important that facilitators have considerable school experience, understanding of Expeditionary Learning, and the ability to adapt to the needs of the group. In effect, the role of facilitator is to model the kind of teaching—guiding, coaching, and supporting—that we are asking teachers to practice through Expeditionary Learning.

Conclusion

The One-Day Community Exploration outlined is only a beginning step in an ongoing process of professional development and renewal. Its deceptively simple structure gets at many of the key questions and ideas of Expeditionary Learning. As one can expect, there are many natural tensions which emerge from this kind of process, particularly within transforming schools and districts. Teachers are being asked to give up some familiar practices, embrace new ones, and open their classroom doors to the community. The support and structures which follow this kind of initial experience are critical in ensuring that Expeditionary Learning takes root and grows.

Service: Crew, Not Passengers

by Emily Cousins

Kurt Hahn, the founder of Outward Bound, said, "You can preach at [students], that is the hook without the worm; you can order them to volunteer: that is dishonest; you can call on them, *'you are needed,'* and that appeal hardly ever fails." Expeditionary Learning students are realizing that their communities do need them, and that they need their communities to deepen, broaden, and give purpose to their learning.

While Expeditionary Learning draws from a tradition of project-based learning, it extends that tradition by explicitly embedding service in the curriculum of learning expeditions, as well as in the entire culture of the school.

Service in learning expeditions deepens the definition of what it means to be a student to include giving of one's best self and best work to others. A service ethic affirms that every person has something valuable and unique to give. It also acknowledges that all students have something to learn from the process of developing significant service projects, mastering the skills necessary to carry them out, seeing their actions enrich their communities, and reflecting upon their service experiences.

❖ Learning from the Community

Service anchors students' learning in the real world, because how students perform service and what they do have real consequences and impact. Last fall, middle school students from the Rafael Hernandez School in Boston designed uses for vacant lots in their neighborhood as part of the learning expedition on structures. These students became accountable not only for the professional expectations of urban design, but also to the needs and desires of community members.

The major project of the *Structures* learning expedition was designing and building models for communal uses of a vacant, inner city lot. Rather than assume what the community wanted on the lot, the students asked the community members directly. Students were split into small, multi-age groups, and each group surveyed 100 community members. The students' designs had to be possible and realistic. They went to City Hall to research zoning ordinances and to the Harvard Graduate School of Design to see how architectural models are made. They talked to architects about scale and to gardeners about landscape design.

Service anchors students' learning in the real world, because how students perform service and what they do have real consequences and impact.

Many of the Hernandez students live near the vacant lots. Thinking of alternative uses for the lots touched their own lives as well as the people they surveyed. Paolo Marrero, a seventh grader who lives near the school, explains, "A lot of the kids around here play where there is broken glass and garbage, or near drug houses. They don't have anywhere else to play. What we found out is that lots of people want a community center so kids have a safe place to play. So what we did was we thought about what the people who live here want. We put together what they wanted and what we wanted in the community center."

Maria Campanario Araica, director of instruction, believes this kind of problem-solving was one of the most important lessons of the learning expedition. "When one group was deciding between a garden or a playground, they had to consider the needs of the community. They decided that if they made a playground, it wouldn't be fair to the older people, so they made a garden instead." Students learned to collaborate and to keep focused on the community at the same time.

The process through which the students went is the same one that professional urban planners use. Boston Urban Gardeners (BUGS) has a contract with the Public Facilities Department to design an alternate use for one of the lots the Hernandez students surveyed. Greg Murphy, one of the designers from BUGS, saw the students present their work and was very impressed. "The students did their share of community outreach," comments Murphy. "From our experience, we know that a design for the lot will work only if the community is involved and a sense of ownership grows. The kids realized that. They were right about that."

BUGS was so pleased with the students' work that they used it as the starting point for their own work. "The residents told us that the Hernandez kids had been working in the community. The first thing we did was go to the Hernandez with a landscape architect. We wanted to kick off our process by learning from what they had done. We also wanted to acknowledge that what they did was work that professionals do out in the world. We wanted them to know that people value what they did."

Realizing that people value their work is a tremendous boost to children's self-esteem. At the end of their long efforts, these students receive not just a letter grade, but the appreciation of their community and the professional world. They've gained experience with interviewing strangers, calling city officials, and evaluating data. But most important, they have learned that they have the ability to think through problems in their neighborhood and come up with solutions that the greater community supports.

Soon, BUGS will convert one of the lots into a public garden. Murphy says that the BUGS design includes much of what the students' designs did. There will be planting beds that he hopes the students will use. "The community is very pleased with what the students have done. They hope the Hernandez will continue to play a role in the garden."

❖ Filling a Need

Service teaches students how to identify a need and take the steps necessary to address it. Many of the students at Jack Elementary School live in the Kennedy Park housing project in the Munjoy Hill

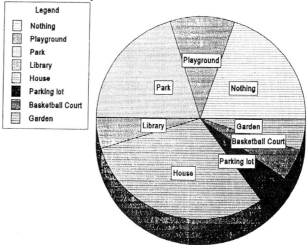

Middle school students from the Rafael Hernandez Bilingual School in Boston generated this pie chart for their Structures learning expedition after asking 100 community members what they would like in vacant lots in the neighborhood.

section of Portland, Maine. As part of a fourth- and fifth-grade learning expedition on Munjoy Hill, Bill Keefer from the Portland Housing Authority came and asked the students what they would like to see in their neighborhood.

Student Scott Profenno knew what the neighborhood needed. "I think we should have a bike shop. Kids need a cheap place to get their bikes fixed." Most of the children in the community ride bikes, but few of them have the money for repairs. Broken bikes pile up in disuse instead of getting fixed. All of the students agreed with Scott, and the idea for the Kids' Quick Fix Bike Shop was born.

"I knew we had to figure out a way to make the shop work," explains special education teacher Karen White. "The students wouldn't let me not do it." White had known all along that she wanted service to be a part of her learning expedition. She had asked the students to draw maps of the Kennedy Park project, but they showed little interest. When the idea for the bike shop came up, she encouraged them to pursue their own idea. Service can never be entirely scripted and it most often contains an element of surprise. White was willing to risk the unexpected because she knew her students' interest would sustain the project.

The students began their project by applying for and receiving a grant of $50 from the Portland Partnership of businesses and schools. The Portland Housing Authority agreed to let the students use the

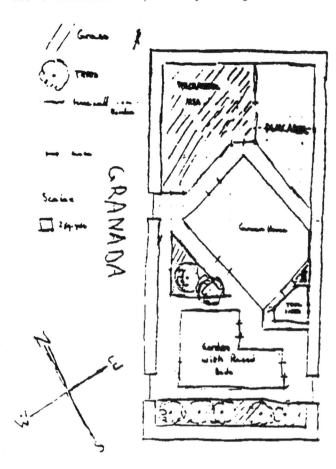

A site map for an alternate use of a neighborhood vacant lot by Peter Kunz, a sixth grader at the Rafael Hernández Bilingual School in Boston, for the Structures learning expedition.

basement of their Kennedy Park offices for the bike shop. White had explained to the students that they could run the shop as long as they has adult supervision while it was open, so the students found parents who were willing to supervise two afternoons a week. They also found parents who were willing to help by donating paint, cabinets, and time for cleaning. Keefer believes this parent support was essential: "Parent involvement is often the missing link, but parents were really interested in helping with the bike shop. Now the kids will be able to keep the shop open all summer, because the parents are going to supervise them."

Making the bike shop a success took more than simply finding a space and some money. The students had to learn how to repair the bikes and how to manage a business. Scott Profenno, the student who had suggested the bike shop, is particularly adept at fixing bikes. "This project showed the advantages of multi-year teaching," observes White. "I had Scott last year. He truly had a great deal of difficulty in the area of reading and writing, but he is a master mechanic. Knowing this and knowing his parents, I knew we would be able to pull off the bike repair shop with his help."

Not only was Scott able to teach the other students about making repairs, but he also learned new skills of his own. "Last year," White explains, "writing three sentences would have been a struggle for Scott. Now he has written a great fictional book about himself winning the Tour de France."

The process the students went through is the same one that professional urban planners use.

In addition to learning from Scott, the students invited speakers to come and teach them about bikes. They called Portland bike shops to ask if repair people would give them lessons and demonstrations. They had people come to talk about bike safety. The man who created the Portland Bike Trail organization offered to talk to the students and donate bike maps. While the students were learning the repair skills, they were practicing them two afternoons a week in the shop.

White felt strongly about incorporating the service project into the whole expedition. Since the students were so excited by the bike shop, they were eager to learn the skills they needed to make it run well. They quickly learned words like "lubricant" and "disengage" for their spelling tests. They prepared for phone calls to bike shops by carefully writing out scripts. Through Junior Achievement, the class had worked with a man from a local bank. When the students began working on the shop budget, they said, "Why don't we ask him if he'll come and help us." The banker returned and recommended they open a checking account. "Now," White says, "our math centers around filling out deposit slips and balancing our checkbook."

Not only did the bike shop shape the curriculum, but it also informed the culture of the class. Through the shop, the students experienced the satisfaction of attending to community needs. Student Tina

Graham observes, "It's a good experience to create things for the community. We help the neighbors by having a bike shop they can afford." Another student, Violet Richards, adds, "If someone can't afford it, we lower the prices." These important lessons of responsibility and compassion transfer to the interactions the students have with each other. Many of them noted that they liked learning from one another. Tina Graham speaks for many of the students when she says, "It's fun working with each other because we get closer. We don't have many fights anymore."

Not only is White thrilled with the progress of the student work, she is also pleased with the way the students have grown through their service. "This has been their project through and through," she believes. "There has been a great difference in their self-esteem, and the way they feel about themselves. They know they have done something. I really feel like they believe there is nothing they can't do." Whether it's a group of children providing a service for their peers or a young boy writing his first book about winning the Tour de France, the students certainly have shown their ability to make change.

Drawing by Christina Roman, a ninth grader at the School for the Physical City in New York, for the learning expedition Our City, Ourselves.

Students Open Shop to Keep Broken-Down Bicycles on the Road

by Edie Lau

The Kids' Quick Fix Bike Shop gives real-life experiences to Jack Elementary School students.

The bicycle Laurie Charles got from her aunt the other day is a Miami Miss, a lavender one-speed with fat white tires—really lovely, except for one thing. The chain was rusted hard.

A few weeks ago, that bike might have joined other bikes in her household, broken and abandoned. But those days are over.

The Kids' Quick Fix Bike Shop has arrived.

Students in Karen White's class from Jack Elementary School on Munjoy Hill are running their own bicycle repair shop, catering to kids like themselves who don't have the money to pay professional bike mechanics. Eight-year-old Laurie Charles was just that kind of customer. She got a new chain—and the resulting freedom on wheels—on Monday for a cool $1.50.

◆ ◆ ◆

Our bikes are breaking, and no one can fix 'em.

—*Heather Charles, 12*

◆ ◆ ◆

The bike shop opened April 15, after five months of planning. White, a special education teacher, can hardly believe it's real. She thought the students would have lost interest long ago.

"I was kind of hoping!" she admitted.

Instead, she has found her class of 13 fourth- and fifth-graders irrepressible. In three days of business, they have had three jobs. They are diligently keeping records of their inventory, organizing tools and sweeping up the shop. They're learning to budget. On spelling tests, they're tackling words such as lubricant, caliper, clockwise, screwdriver and disengage.

White said the students are inspired to complete assignments that are related to the bike shop. Twelve-year-old Scott Profenno, for example, recently wrote six pages about winning the Tour de France. Before the bike-shop project greased his imagination, Scott would struggle to write a single page about anything.

The whole thing began in November, when Bill Keefer from Portland Housing Authority talked to the class about Kennedy Park, a low-income housing complex that is home to many Jack students.

Keefer, resident initiatives coordinator, told the students his job is to make public housing better for

Violet Richards logs in her arrival at the Kids' Quick Fix Bike Shop, where students keep records of their inventory and learn to budget. Photograph by Doug Jones/Portland Newspapers.

April 26, 1994, pp. 1B-2B, *Portland Press Herald*.

its residents. He asked, "What would make it better for you?"

Scott piped up. The kids in the neighborhood need a cheap bicycle repair shop, he said, because they can't afford the commercial shops.

One thought led to another, and next thing you know, Keefer had arranged space for the kids in housing authority property at 51 Mayo Street. Cleaning and painting the grimy storage basement fell to the students and their parents. Parents also donated cabinets and tools. The students learned to write letters and make phone calls to solicit donations. They got $100 in grants, and opened a real checking account.

Sally Walker, an employee of Back Bay Bicycle, showed White's class how to do simple repairs to make such bikes safer and more comfortable.

The ambitious project is possible because Jack participates in something called Expeditionary Learning, White said, which stresses teaching students with real-life experiences rather than textbooks.

In Kennedy Park, real-life bikes have seats that point up, instead of lying flat. Brakes don't work, so the riders drag their feet on the ground to stop. Some flaws can't be skirted at all. Heather Charles, 12, said she and her little sister, Laurie, have been through several bicycles. "Our bikes are breaking, and no one can fix 'em. We just throw them away."

Kids all over the neighborhood have collections of broken bikes, Heather said. "Most of them put them down in the cellar, and forget about 'em."

Now they can remember.

Kids' Bike Shop

Jack Elementary students running the Kids' Quick Fix Bike Shop at 51 Mayo St., Portland, intend to stay open even after school ends for the year. Parent volunteers supervise.

Prices are set spontaneously by the young workers. The students are volunteers for now; they may pay themselves later, if the shop is successful.

The class wrote this description of their shop.

1. The kinds of bikes we fix are: Fuji bikes, BMX bikes, Huffy bikes. All of the bikes you can think of, we fix.
2. Things we fix on a bike are: seatpost, seat, chains, gears, freewheels, rear brakes, flat tire, handlebars.
3. Open two days a week, 3:30 to 5:30 p.m. Mondays and Wednesdays.
4. We sell reconditioned bikes.
5. Reasonable prices and friendly service.

Dennis Coffin, Scott Profenno and Violet Richards put a new chain on a customer's bicycle at their shop on Mayo Street. A Back Bay Bicycle employee showed the students how to do simple repairs. Photograph by Doug Jones/Portland Newspapers.

A Letter in Praise of a Fourth-Grade Condor Expert

by Walter Peterson

The following is a letter to Dubuque School Board president Merle Gaber from Walter Peterson, chancellor of University of Dubuque. Peterson writes about the tremendous interest and excitement he saw exhibited by Bryant fourth grader Andrew Stratton as Andrew researched condors for his All Creatures Great and Functional *learning expedition.*

Teacher Cyndie Nelson explains that a "light bulb went on for Andrew when he started studying condors. He's turned on now, and the work he has done has been fantastic. He can tell you everything there is to know about condors." Nelson adds that teachers learn a great deal through expeditions as well. "I know more about condors now than I ever thought I would!" she says.

April 5, 1994

Dear Merle,

I wish to recount the most recent experience that Barbara and I have had with Expeditionary Learning, and it has most certainly been exciting. Andrew Stratton, a fourth grader at Bryant School, through Expeditionary Learning has become interested in the California condor. His teacher, Cyndie Nelson, knew that our son is with the Fish and Wild Life Services in the mountains of Southern California as part of the team of six working with the condor release program.

Ms. Nelson put Andrew in touch with us and we are delighted. When he came to our home he was already well informed and very well read on the California condor. I have never seen a fourth grader so excited about any project. We have provided him with everything from a video tape, to pictures, to written materials that our son continues to send, varieties of posters and the like. When Barbara gave him a condor T-shirt, he nearly burst into tears. Barbara and I look forward to attending the special session this spring when these projects are on display.

Would that I had been exposed to Expeditionary Learning when I was in the fourth grade with a teacher as exciting and stimulating as Cyndie Nelson.

I trust that we will have the opportunity to work with many other students who are involved in the program. I commend the School Board for its support of Superintendent Lam and Expeditionary Learning. It is the most stimulating program that has come to Dubuque in many, many years.

Sincerely,
Walter Peterson,
Chancellor, University of Dubuque

Drawing of a condor by fourth grader Andrew Stratton for the All Creatures Great and Functional *learning expedition at Bryant Elementary School in Dubuque, Iowa.*

What's New in the Wires
A Closer Look at Electronic Mail

by Melissa Rodgers

I am Amy Coffman. I am 18 years old. I am attending school at PRVTC (Portland Regional Vocational Technical Center) in the early childhood occupations. I am doing an expedition on multi-age classrooms. Anything you could give me would be helpful. Please send mail back to Tom Lafavore.

Amy Coffman's message appeared on Expeditionary Learning's electronic mail (e-mail) network on January 7, 1994. The message was posted to the network's News conference, a bulletin board that every person who has an e-mail account with Expeditionary Learning can access for updates, anecdotes, ideas and information about the Expeditionary Learning schools and the Cambridge office. Amy's message is one of many examples of how e-mail supports the implementation of Expeditionary Learning in schools and how it has begun to permeate school culture. E-mail widens the circle of our conversations and deepens the level of our discussions. More than an efficient means of exchanging information, e-mail is a powerful instrument for generating provoking dialogues among Expeditionary Learning partners.

On January 18, 1994, Amika DiGennaro, an Expeditionary Learning teacher at the Blackstone Elementary School in Boston, replied:

Hi Amy! ... I'm currently a 5th grade teacher in Boston. I've taught multi-age/grade classes several times (most recently last year).... I think it's great for several reasons. First, there is always about half the class who can help the new kids feel comfortable. Also, just working with the same students for more than one year helps a teacher establish solid relationships with families and really get to know a child well. I also think it helps create a "family" feel to classrooms, which has a positive impact on cooperative learning skills and support from classmates. Have you had an opportunity to work in a multi-age setting yourself? What sparked your interest in this subject? Good luck with your project! Amika.

> Using e-mail is like thinking aloud. It is closer to how the brain works than many other modes of communication.
>
> —Meg Campbell

This type of exchange, between a student in Portland and a teacher in Boston, would probably never have occurred without e-mail. Contrary to the widely held belief that electronic communication will dehumanize exchanges, e-mail fosters extensive and frequent communication among Expeditionary Learning partners all over the country. Phil Gonring, a lead teacher at the Rocky Mountain School of Expeditionary Learning in Denver, reflects, "When confronted with e-mail, my first thought was that it would be a depersonalized mode of communication. But in fact I am a lot more comfortable with other people in the Expeditionary Learning community because of it. It is so hard to communicate otherwise—we play telephone tag and don't have the time to write letters. With e-mail you can engage in some back-and-forth, get an idea out and back from another site in the course of an hour."

Phil Gonring had never used e-mail before the fall of 1993. Susan Keene, the business manager at his school, helped him get online. "I found it very easy, quite convenient, and a lot of fun," Gonring says. In this respect, he is representative of the Expeditionary Learning community; most of us have had no prior experience with e-mail. And most of us were rapidly enthralled. Over 150 teachers, administrators, Outward Bound staff, partner organizations and Expeditionary Learning staff now have individual e-mail accounts on the Expeditionary Learning servers (e-mail Post Offices) in Cambridge and

Portland. There are plans to network these two servers to site-based ones in Dubuque, Denver and New York as well. The modems that transfer electronic messages are in use all day.

❖ Building Community

We rely increasingly on e-mail because it enhances communication by allowing us to disseminate information rapidly and efficiently. Because it saves time, e-mail truncates distance between the Expeditionary Learning sites. Phil Gonring says, "Communication is the single most important part of relationship building, so e-mail is a great tool for community building. Since I have been on e-mail, I definitely feel in closer connection with people who are not in Denver. We share information about what is going on in our schools. We also share personal information—check in. It does not always have to be business; the personal exchanges are just as important."

> **There is no reason why every teacher cannot have an e-mail account on a computer in the staff development library.**
>
> *—Diana Lam*

Dubuque's superintendent Diana Lam agrees, noting the importance of interpersonal connections to support rapid and bold institutional change. Like Phil Gonring, she points to the shortcomings of the telephone for ventures such as Expeditionary Learning that have a national scope and depend greatly on frequent communication between different time zones. "E-mail is the fastest way to communicate," she says. "When communication happens quickly, action is more likely to follow."

Collaboration is a pillar of Expeditionary Learning—a principle that applies to our organizational model as well as to our teaching practices; e-mail is one of the mechanisms that we employ to create a culture of collaboration. Diana Lam confirms, "If one of the design principles of Expeditionary Learning is collaboration, I think that e-mail has certainly fostered it. It has allowed principals who are going through similar experiences to be connected with each other. Once teachers have full access to e-mail, we will see Expeditionary Learning become an even richer collaboration."

❖ Exchanging Information

Some of the most interesting e-mail exchanges are the conversations between teachers that appear on the News bulletin board. Tom Lafavore, a teacher at PRVTC who administrates the Portland server, concurs: "There is a fantastic amount of information that can be passed back and forth," he says. "Organizationally and in terms of curriculum, e-mail has tremendous potential for designing and creating expeditions and touching base with everyone in the country."

Margarita Muñiz, principal of the Rafael Hernandez School in Boston, recently sent the following message to News:

"We are developing an expedition using waterwheels and the mill work done at the turn of the century in the New England area. We are looking for possible sources of information, firsthand accounts, or any other material related to this topic. We have National Geographic *resources already, but are especially looking for anything in Spanish related to immigrants at the turn of the century, child labor laws, etc. Gracias por su ayuda."*

Expeditionary Learning's Meg Campbell responded promptly with a suggested bibliography, and resourceful e-mail correspondent Amika DiGennaro offered ideas about programs and sites:

"Call the National Park Service folks at the Tsongas Industrial Park in Lowell. They're a great resource because they're free, will come to Boston with hands-on programs, and have a museum tour and tour of mills. ... The Children's Museum does a great workshop on making waterwheels. Good luck with your project—sounds like fun!"

Nora Pou, assistant principal at the Blackstone, hopes that more teachers will get online soon. "I think that the key would be for teachers to visit each other first," she says; "then they could say in person, 'Please feel free to contact me and ask for any ideas.' Teachers need to have exchanges with others who are going through the same process of change."

◆ ◆ ◆

E-mail widens the circle of our conversation and deepens our discussions.

◆ ◆ ◆

In fact, the quest for ideas and input has spurred Expeditionary Learning teachers to join the e-mail network. Tom Lafavore explains that specific questions have prompted teachers to use e-mail more than encouragement from the principal's office. "The teachers who have gotten online are the ones who have sought information," he says. "One teacher was seeking information on the Victorian Christmas—he wanted me to ask for ideas over e-mail, and I said, 'Why don't you just get online?' So he made an appointment." Teachers who use e-mail grow accustomed to its capacities and turn to it regularly.

Teachers and administrators within one school also communicate through e-mail. Within the Cambridge office, the Expeditionary Learning staff relies almost exclusively on e-mail for planning, news, and updates. Meg Campbell says, "My image of e-mail is fireflies—you see them when they blink but they fly around even when they are not blinking. E-mail messages are ideas that blink for others even when I am not online."

❖ Generating Ideas

The very magnitude of Expeditionary Learning that makes e-mail necessary is a source of strength for the project. Because Expeditionary Learning schools exist in cities throughout the United States, those of us who use e-mail bring disparate points of view and experiences to our conversations. Every time teachers and administrators communicate with other parts of the country through e-mail, they cut through the culture gaps that separate schools. Grappling with a range of experiences and ideas is also an opportunity to learn.

In the fall of 1993, many Expeditionary Learning teachers developed Full Value Contracts (a term coined by Project Adventure, Inc.) with students. Tom Lafavore posted a message to News expressing an interest in examples of Full Value Contracts. David Olson, principal of Central Alternative High School in Dubuque, wrote back with his thoughts about what makes a Full Value Contract successful:

"1. Do not share the actual contracts with others. Groups need to formulate from scratch what they need to function together.

2. The process, not the product, is most important; but the product needs to exist to validate the process.

3. The power is in the circle. The circle should have empty chairs removed and should be tight. The best method of recording is chartpaper on an easel which is physically placed as a 'member of the group.' ..."

David Olson's detailed account brought the conversation about Full Value Contracts to a level of depth that would be difficult to attain without e-mail. Meg Campbell likens using e-mail to thinking aloud. "E-mail is closer to how the brain works than other modes of communication," she says. "It is akin to quick thought processes—easy and instantaneous."

❖ Pushing Limits

So why is every Expeditionary Learning teacher not on e-mail? Tom Lafavore says, "In some schools teachers are wary of e-mail because it is new technology. Some teachers are already struggling with computers and this is an added dimension."

Fear of new technology is one reason but rarely the determining factor that keeps teachers from getting online. Phil Gonring believes that "the teachers at the Rocky Mountain School of Expeditionary Learning are not afraid of technology. We are all concerned with saving time and understand that technology is a way to do it."

Interestingly, time is also the greatest deterrent to teachers' learning how to use e-mail. Phil Gonring adds that "getting all the teachers online will require them to come in and sit with Susan Keene and go through the system. The only obstacle to this is time."

Tom Lafavore affirms this view. "The schedule is such that teachers do not have time to use e-mail," he states plainly. In addition, school schedules, as they stand, do not include time for an on-site person to provide technical support for beginners.

Third, Tom Lafavore points to the shortcomings of the revamped phone systems that many schools have adopted. The new networks are digital and do not support modems, which require analog lines. "Our current phone system is set up for networking efficiently within a school but not with the outside world," Tom Lafavore says.

A fourth obstacle to widespread use of e-mail is its location in the school building—which relates directly to the time concern. Will Pidden, a teacher at King Middle School in Portland, says that if he had a computer with a modem on his desk, he could access e-mail between classes. Currently, he must go down the hall to use e-mail, which does not fit into the reality of school activity. Tom Lafavore agrees: "The downside to e-mail at PRVTC is its location. It is not in an easy access room and is not convenient so it is underutilized. It should be in a convenient, open place—a small teachers' room, a library. Every teacher should somehow have access to e-mail." But Diana Lam thinks that this is possible without greatly reallocating resources. "Perhaps we cannot have a computer for each teacher," she says, "but there is no reason why every teacher cannot have an account on a computer in the staff development library."

Nora Pou thinks the question is primarily one of habit and routine. The Blackstone has installed the e-mail software and a modem on one of the computers in the staff room. But, she says, "I need to make a habit of going there. It is a new thing to get into your routine and it takes time to get used to a new tool."

❖ Horizons

We would like to both increase the pool of people with whom we can communicate through e-mail and diversify the ways in which we use e-mail in the schools. Expeditionary Learning's e-mail system is self-contained and designed to serve the Expeditionary Learning community, but networks such as the Internet allow people to access information and communicate electronically with others around the world. The server in the Cambridge office has a dial-in connection to the Internet, which means that anyone with an account on the Cambridge server can send messages to and receive mail from the Internet. In fact, we will soon be using our system to communicate with the eight other New American Schools design teams as well as with NASDC.

New ways of using electronic communication in the schools might include getting students online too. Phil Gonring has high hopes for this. "I have a vision that eventually our students will communicate with students at other sites and we will have joint projects," he says. "A student in New York could ask for information that exists only in Denver, and Denver students could carry out the research. That is what I hope to see on the horizon." Commercial services—including some that use the Internet—make this possible. Diana Lam observes, "In Dubuque, we have students connected through the National Geographic Kids' Network that promotes distance learning. They work with students around the country comparing data. If we are connected to e-mail, we can access the world. That's what we want."

Students at Jack Elementary School in Portland, Maine, work with computers. Photograph by Scott Hartl/Expeditionary Learning.

Respecting Parents

by Emily Cousins

Expeditionary Learning schools are exploring different ways to strengthen the connections between parents and teachers. Learning expeditions make explicit the focus of student inquiry so parents know exactly how they can contribute to the teaching process. Teachers draw upon parents' expertise and participation to add essential human, cultural, and natural resources to learning expeditions. Some schools are reinterpreting the use of parent nights, others are benefiting from the recent success of Family Centers. All of the schools are broadening the role of parents so they become more active partners in student learning. In the process, the design principles of Diversity and Inclusivity, Collaboration, and Intimacy and Caring are expanding to encompass the whole school community.

❖ *Broadening the Scope*

Expeditionary Learning teachers have found that approaching parent involvement without preconceived notions has allowed unexpected resources to surface. Learning expeditions have encouraged them to tap into parent expertise they did not even know was available.

When Hernandez Middle School teachers in Boston were planning their *Structures* expedition, they knew it would be helpful to call parent Eben Kunz, a practicing architect. Kunz offered the teachers invaluable assistance in converting measurements to scale and building models. What the teachers did not realize at first was that parent Bertrand Daniels, the owner of a small limousine business, also had training in drafting techniques.

Daniels became interested in the expedition when he started helping his daughter Quania design alternate uses for a vacant lot. He called her teacher, Brian LaFerriere, to learn more. "Brian said that all the subjects—math, science, English, language—were all applied to the work with the vacant lots," Daniels recalled. "That's what made me interested. I had studied drafting so I knew I could help. I offered Brian some suggestions and he invited me in to see how things were going."

Daniels spent an afternoon working with his daughter's group, passing on some drafting techniques and encouraging students to think about their models. "I've helped Quania with her work at home before," he explained, "but this was the first time I wanted to go to school. The school makes you feel really welcome. They suggest it's a good idea for parents to go to the school. They say, 'Come up anytime,' and you feel comfortable when you get there. That's the feeling a parent should have."

Because he understood what the students were working on, Daniels was able to step forward with his skills and contribute to student learning in a meaningful way. Throughout the expedition, Daniels continued to offer his drafting experience to the students. "I tried to make what I know about drafting understandable to Quania so that she could learn it and tell the other students in her group. I saw that the other kids learned from her, and she learned from them. She's interested and I am interested. I think that's great."

The Jack Family Center opens school doors to parents who might not have felt included in the past.

❖ *Learning Firsthand*

The Expeditionary Learning staff development model is based on the idea that it is best for teachers to learn through the same method that they will use to teach their students. Parents also benefit from experiencing Expeditionary Learning firsthand. At a recent Middle School Curriculum Night at the School for the Physical City in New York, math teacher Debbie Semple changed this standard parent-teacher forum to one where parents learned about math the way their children do.

When parents arrived in Semple's class, they were asked to sit in groups of four or five. Instead of a traditional presentation, Semple passed around copies of Pascal's Triangle, a triangular array of numbers that generates multiple number patterns, and asked the parents to complete the first pattern. A little surprised, parents turned to their task and began discussing ideas and haggling over theories. As they were hard at work, Semple told them, "I am trying to get you to think in the way that I am trying to get your children to think. We are asking students to investigate, because math is now about problem-solving and communicating. I usually have students work in groups of four so they can face each other."

When everyone had finished the pattern, Semple asked a member of each group to explain his or her answer. Though everyone had found the same answer, each group came upon it in a different way. "People have different ways of thinking," Semple explained. "This type of problem is a way to tap into different styles. I always ask students to explain their work so we can discover how they think."

Excitement began to build in the classroom, as parents spotted more number patterns and Semple named and explained them. "That's a pattern of symmetry, and that's a pattern of negative numbers," she said, and oh's and ah's erupted around the room. "That's a pattern of binomials," Semple declared, and suddenly the parents went from a simple number pattern into an algebra lesson.

Parents went away from this Curriculum Night with a richer understanding of the way their children learn in an Expeditionary Learning school. This kind of firsthand experience is helpful when parents are making decisions about the workings of the school. The School for the Physical City, with the assistance of its partners, including the New York Mission Society, hopes to offer parents many opportunities to understand better the process of Expeditionary Learning.

❖ Opening the Doors

Some parents may feel less than comfortable in schools because of negative associations with their own school experiences. These parents may have a great deal to offer their school communities, but they may not always find a way to enter. The Jack

A Dubuque, Iowa, parent participates in a low ropes initiative. Photograph by Dave Kettering/Dubuque Telegraph Herald.

Elementary School in Portland, Maine, has found a way to open the doors to parents who might not have felt included in the past. Jack has created a Family Center that successfully welcomes parents by addressing their needs and offering them ways to contribute to the school.

Then principal Myrt Collins and current principal Kathy Marshack started the Family Center a few years ago with the belief that Jack students would succeed only if their parents took an active role in their education. They knew that in order to include parents who might have had negative school experiences, they would have to make the Jack School a very welcoming place.

The Family Center at Jack Elementary School is indeed a welcoming environment. Housed in a converted classroom, the Center has comfortable couches and chairs, shelves of children's books, and craft materials all around the room. The walls are covered with lively children's art and posters that offer parenting advice: "Words that help: I love you. You are Special. I'm proud of you." "Children may forget what you say, but they'll never forget how you make them feel." One wall is covered with human services information, from food stamps to flu shots to baby-sitters.

Thirty to forty parents come to the Center each day to sit and talk or to attend programs. Center activities are organized by full-time coordinator Kathy Sabbath, whose position is supported by Chapter I funds. "The programs we offer," said Sabbath, "come out of listening to what the parents want for themselves." Many of the parents wanted to take GED classes, but the only ones offered were far across town, so Jack offered classes right at the school. "We need parents in school to help children read," remarked Sabbath. "Well, some parents need help with reading before they can help their children. We decided to start from the beginning."

Other programs include parenting classes and shared parent and toddler time. Many programs connect the parents directly with the curricular life of the school. Parents can learn how to do desktop publishing so they can print student books. There are meetings to explain the new report cards and the Jack reading program. And the most important element, according to Sabbath, is the free child care provided by other parents for all of these events. Lillian Moore, a foster grandparent who is a backbone of the child care assistance, welcomes the opportunity to spend time with children. "I love it," she proclaimed. "It gives me something I like to do."

Crystal Boulier is a frequent visitor at the Family Center. She has one child at Jack and one who will attend next year, and she attests that she has been to "every program Kathy has." What Boulier finds so helpful is that her GED, computer, parenting, and exercise classes as well as her teacher conferences are all in one place. Since she is at the school on a regular basis, she has been able to help teachers by becoming a room parent. She calls other parents to tell them important information, thereby creating extra planning time for teachers. "Most parents don't feel a part of their kids' education," Boulier commented. "But I know the teachers. I know what goes on here. I feel a part of my daughter's education."

By reorganizing existing resources, from the use of the room to the use of the Chapter I funds, Jack has created a vital link between parents and school. Now that parents are a presence in the school, they are often called upon to take part in making decisions. When the administration was reviewing designs for landscaping work around the school, they came to the Family Center to ask for parent input. One parent suggested putting a picnic table at the point on the grounds that overlooks the harbor. Sabbath agreed: "I always like to go there to talk with parents. It would be good to have somewhere to sit."

A diagram of the milkweed plant, by Seth Bourgeous, from the Field Guide made by fifth graders at Table Mound Elementary School in Dubuque, Iowa.

Rocky Mountain School of Expeditionary Learning student Tahesha Jackson looks out the window of the shuttle during an urban exploration in Denver. Photograph by Cyrus McCrimmon/Rocky Mountain News.

School Opens Bid for New Learning Paths

by Janet Bingham

On a green lawn beneath a shining sun, nearly all of the 215 students of Colorado's new Expeditionary Learning School stood shoulder to shoulder in a circle.

But wait. Six kindergartners were shrinking shyly into the shadows outside the group.

"Come on you guys! We need you too," coaxed ninth-grader Valerie Black-Mallon, 14, expanding the circle to bring the bashful 5-year-olds into their very first "learning expedition."

It was opening day at the new school, run in Denver by four metro-area school districts and designed to pioneer a "break-the-mold" approach to education. By focusing on learning through active hands-on experience, the school intends to help students stretch their limits of performance in the same way that Outward Bound challenges participants in rock climbing or white water rafting expeditions.

More than 2,800 students from Denver, Cherry Creek, Douglas County and Littleton applied for 215 available places ranging from kindergarten through ninth grade. The winning students, chosen by lottery, were getting to know each other for the first time yesterday.

Their first learning expedition was an exercise in trust-building, cooperation and mutual support called the "lap-sit."

With the shortest people in front, tallest in back, everyone turned in the same direction, put their hands on the shoulders of the person in front of them, and at a single command, proceeded to lean back gently, trusting that the persons behind would provide laps for them to sit on.

For a moment it worked. A cheer went up, then squeals and laughter as someone toppled over and everyone behind collapsed like dominoes onto the ground.

Valerie grinned triumphantly at six 5-year-olds who were now all giggling in her lap. The ice was broken. But Valerie also knew the bigger lesson. "Everyone needs to support each other," she said.

On wilderness expeditions, Outward Bound students learn to work together so they can accomplish things they didn't think they could do alone, said Dale Whyte, Colorado Outward Bound program director. In the same way, she said, students at the Expeditionary Learning School will learn to work together to reach their full potential.

Students and teachers together will create three- or four-week "expeditions"—journeys into the unknown world of learning—building each journey around a theme. "We're not talking about disjointed field trips, but a common thread around which students will learn math, science and English," said Whyte. While there will be field trips, many of the expeditions will be intellectual.

As an example, she said, in reading about the "Black Death," the bubonic plague epidemic that swept Europe in the fourteenth century, students might come up with all kinds of questions about what caused it, how it spread, how many people died. They might decide to create a fourteenth century medieval village, drawing on their own research to create characters and house plans. They might interview a medieval historian. They might interview a public health epidemiologist to learn about epidemics today. They might do research at the University of Colorado Health Sciences Center.

The enormous number of applications shows that many people are looking for a different approach to education, said Barbara Volpe, project director for the Public Education Coalition. The coalition is helping the school get started with grant money from the New American Schools Development Corporation.

Most operating money comes from the school districts, with each student bringing the same money that any other student in that district gets from the state—about $4,400 a year. Parents have also agreed to pay a $315 per year transportation fee to cover the high cost of bringing students from four districts.

September 8, 1993, p. 2B, *The Denver Post*.
Reprinted with permission from *The Denver Post* and Janet Bingham.

The school is in once-vacant Southmoor School in southeast Denver.

Parents yesterday were excited. "We were looking for a different structure," said Cherry Creek parent Vic Derks, father of Chris, 8. "We like the way children will be learning through experience."

"We're ready to try a new way of thinking about education," said Denver parent Frank Biondolillo, father of Aaron, 5. "They won't be so tied to the classroom. They'll be learning through experiences in the community."

Valerie, who chose the school over Cherry Creek High, likes the family and community atmosphere of a small school with students of all different ages. "I can learn things from working with the little kids—they see the world so differently—and they can learn from me. With lots of teamwork, with all of us working together, it will be great."

Students at the new Expeditionary Learning School in Denver, which opened September 8, 1993, learn a lesson in trust. The kids in the big circle lean back, confident those behind them will provide a seat. The school is operated by four metro area districts. Photograph by John Prieto/The Denver Post.

Part Five

Rethinking Time

Slaying the Time Giant
A Discussion with Harold Howe II

by Emily Cousins and Melissa Rodgers

In Classical Greek literature, there is a giant named Procrustes. Procrustes had an iron bedstead where he put travelers who asked to stay the night. If they were too long for the bed, he cut off their feet. If they were too short, he stretched them until they fit.

According to Harvard professor Harold Howe II, former United States Commissioner of Education and member of our Council of Senior Advisors, time is the iron bedstead of American public schools. We cram students into forty-five-minute periods, five days a week, regardless of how long it takes to fully understand and explore a topic. "We think of time as a given," Howe asserts. "People think of changing the curriculum. They think of changing the pedagogy, but they don't think about the time factor, which is really fundamental to dealing with both these things."

This way of thinking takes its roots in nineteenth-century economic structures that determined the length of the school year. Howe explains that "the budding public school system had to make treaties with the farmers about when the children could go to school. Over time they came up with 180 days and that has become almost sacrosanct, like the forty-five-minute period. I expect that in a modern society like this one, we ought to have more time in school for kids." Howe is wary, however, of simply tacking on more time if the time is not used well. "I honestly don't think it makes a difference if you extend the school year but you don't change what you are doing with it. To do more of the same unimaginative instruction is not very much of a gain.

"I came across a wonderful saying in something written by Kim Marshall," Howe continues: "Tell me and I forget. Show me and I remember. Involve me and I understand." But forty-five minute blocks leave little time for understanding and little room for authentic teaching and learning. Moving from class to class, taking attendance and checking homework repeatedly encroach upon class time. This in turn shapes the pedagogical choices of teachers who, given time constraints, often resort to lecturing. It also creates a culture of low standards where getting something done supplants the push for deep learning. As Howe says, this type of teaching and learning "has become so normal that it is hard to budge it. People are accustomed to it, because *something* is learned. They are accustomed to being satisfied with what is learned."

People think of changing the curriculum or changing the pedagogy, but they don't think about the time factor, which is really fundamental to dealing with both these things.

— *Harold Howe II*
Former U.S. Commissioner of Education

To enable teachers to move beyond these practices, the schedule must flex to foster children's natural ways of learning. Howe believes that "a school model has to have some capacity to promote both group work and individual attention. The current model does not do that. The assumption is that everyone will learn the same thing in the same way in the same length of time and that's crazy! Nothing else we do as humans suggests that."

Coupling new perceptions of time with innovative teaching methods, however, creates opportunities for powerful learning. The most meaningful learning happens when students are directly involved in what they are studying, and this requires extended periods of time. Howe illustrates this with an example of an eighth-grade social studies teacher who designed a project about the textile history in nearby Lawrence and Lowell, Massachusetts.

Students looked at the impact of the cotton gin on northern industry, the workings of the labor market, the background of immigrant workers, and the development of labor unions. Students visited the old mills; they went to Ellis Island in New York; they wrote plays about the labor struggle; they did extensive research in local libraries; and they built a model of the weaving room of an old factory. "That kind of process, seeing real things, talking to people and doing their research creates an excitement, a sense of participation in a learning process. You simply can't do this in a forty-five minute period."

The forty-five minute period also discourages the kind of collaborative work that is central to Expeditionary Learning and that Howe believes is an essential learning medium. Howe cites a recent study of Harvard undergraduates in which students were asked about their most valuable learning experiences at Harvard. The majority of students said they learned more from each other than from the faculty. They found that study groups, collaborative projects, and informal discussions fostered the most rewarding learning experiences. Collaboration takes time. While we do not question the validity of these college-level findings, we rarely extend their conclusions to K-12 education. Howe says: "The same thing happens with little kids in the classroom. The students in a kindergarten classroom were once asked to figure out if the rug in that room would fit in the next room. They got together and wondered how to do this. They said, 'Well, we can lie down along the edge of the rug and see how long it is.' So they had six or eight kids lie down in a row and

The assumption is that everyone will learn the same thing in the same way in the same length of time and that's crazy!

— *Harold Howe II*
Former U.S. Commissioner of Education

Middle School students from the Rafael Hernandez Bilingual School in Boston experiment with a ball during a hands-on science project. Photograph by Brian Smith/ NASDC.

discovered that this rug was eight and a half kids long. Then they went into the other room and found out that the room was only seven kids long and the rug would not fit. This is an experience they won't forget. It taught them about the nature of measurement. It hitched the process of learning those things to something that was real."

Clearly, teachers who want to make a shift from the traditional factory-oriented classroom to the Expeditionary Learning one are going to need time. They will need not only time with their students, but also time for development and planning. Yet once again, conceptions of time make it difficult for teachers to have these opportunities. "If you ask the people who serve on school boards in the United States what they think teachers ought to do with their time, you almost always get the answer that teachers should be spending all their time with students. Whereas in many Asian schools, teachers spend only a portion of their time with students and the rest of their time with each other or alone planning projects that allow students to participate in the learning process."

Once we make the connection between the depth of student involvement and the restructuring of time, Howe believes "we can dream up all kinds of possibilities of how a schedule might look." Expeditionary Learning is one of these possibilities. With its emphasis on student-driven learning, rigorous interdisciplinary curriculum, and extensive staff development, "Expeditionary Learning cries out for a different kind of thinking about time." Howe declares that "we are not going to be able to do Expeditionary Learning with the way that time is now distributed." If, however, we let the needs of our varied students and teachers shape the way we look at time, we will create schedules that replace outdated models of the past with innovative designs for the future.

Fourth graders from Jack Elementary School in Portland, Maine, discuss their project for a learning expedition on newspapers. Photograph by Scott Hartl/Expeditionary Learning.

Inventing New Wheels
Redesigning School Schedules for Expeditionary Learning

by Emily Cousins

"We fixate," says Diana Lam, superintendent of Dubuque Schools and Expeditionary Learning senior project advisor, "on the idea that we have to teach a little bit of everything at the same time." Lam notes that our long-held model for organizing school time is but one configuration and not necessarily the most effective one. "We can still teach the same amount, but organize it a little differently. What if I spend the first trimester on an expedition with a strong humanities focus, and the second trimester on a science expedition. We would still meet local requirements, but we would have used time differently."

Expeditionary Learning holds that time has to be used differently than it has been in conventional, bell-oriented schedules. "If you were to try to find a way to destroy the opportunity to learn, you would use the present schedule of most public high schools," observes Professor Harold Howe II. Expeditionary Learning schools depart completely from conventional scheduling structures. There will be no bells in Expeditionary Learning schools, and the clock will not be the driving force behind the curriculum. Instead, the schedule will be flexible to meet the needs of teachers and students. Learning expeditions will provide teachers with creative ways to share and divide time. Extended blocks of uninterrupted time will allow students to explore topics in great depth.

As Expeditionary Learning schools design new schedules, common themes and lessons emerge. Most obvious is the fact that scheduling is a very difficult process. There are no patent answers, since each schedule must be tailored to the specific needs of individual schools. Teachers and administrators must ensure that new scheduling designs benefit the students in their schools.

Principals and teachers have also discovered that it is easier to create a schedule for small groups of students who work with the same teachers for an extended period of time. Expeditionary Learning schools group their students in crews of twenty-five students subdivided into watches of eight to ten students. Watches and crews build relationships with teachers, who can orchestrate the way they use their time. Small groups, which foster intimacy, caring, and collaboration, also facilitate scheduling; it is more efficient to set up an open schedule within which small groups move freely than it is to have a fixed schedule where everyone moves at the same time. Time is not wasted or constrained by a universal schedule, and each group can pursue its own projects.

Mark Weiss, principal of the School for the Physical City, An Expeditionary Learning Center, has discovered that designing a schedule for a new school is a long, evolving process. The school opens in September with eight teachers and 120 students in grades 6-7 and 9-10. Students will work in small groups with at least one teacher. The school will also meet regularly as a whole group to build a larger community. The school uses the physical city as a thematic starting point, with the urban infrastructure serving as a giant laboratory for students to learn history, demographics, physics, math, literature, economics, and art.

◆ ◆ ◆

> *If you were to try to find a way to destroy the opportunity to learn, you would use the present schedule of most public high schools.*
>
> — *Harold Howe II*
> *Former U.S. Commissioner of Education*

Since students will be spending a lot of time in the field, the schedule must remain flexible. The teachers have decided to map out a general schedule that allows teachers to plan their days and weeks according to the needs of specific expeditions. One week, teachers may plan to bring a group of students to the Brooklyn Bridge every day, while the next week they may be in the classroom focused on a humanities segment of their expedition. The schedule will expand and contract to suit the expeditions.

The teachers have decided that there should also be constants in the schedule. Leah Rugen of New York City Outward Bound says that there will be "things that will punctuate the week and the year with regularity. There will be a lot of flux, so we need things that will give the schedule a backbone." Suggestions include community meetings each morning and presentation/celebration time every Friday afternoon. Teachers are also considering a daily reading circle in which students and teachers discuss books that they have read together.

Weiss thinks that there is a need for another type of constant which he calls "cognitive scaffolding." While the teachers want to keep the schedule flexible, Weiss asserts that "we are not so open ended that we don't commit to academic rigor or find time for such things as math. We think that students will need support structures." Since each expedition will not cover every field, and since each student will start expeditions with different skills, the schedule must comprise tutorials, academic support, specialized courses, and intensive seminars.

The schedule must also include time for staff development. "There's a concept out there," Weiss says, "that staff development is somehow separate from what goes on in the life of the school." The teachers at the School for the Physical City want to reintegrate development into the daily routine. To foster this, they hope to have planning time every day. Weiss wants to have planned time for staff development, but he also wants to make room for the unplanned moments. "I believe that the work people do in order to make a school is, in fact, staff development. We may find that in the middle of the year we will need to know more about assessment, or more about a certain area of the curriculum." He also acknowledges that venturing into uncharted territory is difficult. "There is a certain level of discomfort in reinventing what we know needs to be reinvented," he says. The schedule will have to ensure a great deal of staff support, time for reflection, and opportunities for collaboration.

We can still teach the same amount, but organize it a little differently.

—*Diana Lam*

David Olson, principal of the Central Alternative High School in Dubuque, is working with his staff to transform the traditional schedule their school has followed for years. Central High School has 168 students, many of whom are considered "at risk" and are in dropout prevention programs. In the past, teachers at Central High tried team teaching and interdisciplinary projects, but they found themselves severely constrained by the forty-five minute classes, eight periods a day. Now, to accommodate Expeditionary Learning, they have completely redesigned the schedule.

In the new schedule, on Monday through Thursday, teams of teachers work with small groups of students during a four-and-three-quarter-hour block. This is called Learning Community time. Regarding the name, Olson explains that "as an alternative school, we often use a family analogy. While family seems to take in social and emotional needs, we liked Learning Community because it also builds in more of an academic or lifelong learning focus." The afternoons include structured time for solitude and reflection, specialized seminars, and group instruction. On Fridays, there is a three-hour Learning Community time with afternoons devoted to student presentations and service activities.

Since students will be spending a lot of time in the field, the schedule must remain flexible.

Each team decides how to schedule the daily blocks. Olson explains that "at first, there was a mental block on the teachers' part; they thought that if there were forty students and three teachers that they would be with all of those students all the time in the same classroom. But it's not going to be like that." The extended block is wide open, allowing teachers numerous possibilities for working with students. "I gave an example in which one teacher was working with three students, one was working with twenty, and on was working with twelve, depending on what kind of instruction they were doing." This kind of grouping gives daily scheduling much more flexibility and creativity.

Olson believes that the most important element in the new schedule is the staff development time. "To implement Expeditionary Learning," Olson says, "staff development has to be daily. That is why I have built in a forty-five-minute block of planning time in the morning and a sixty-minute block at the end of the day." The teachers will plan the course of their expeditions before they start, but daily regrouping will help the teachers meet the students' changing needs.

The daily planning time will also help teachers adjust to the new demands of Expeditionary Learning. Olson realizes that the new schedule requires a big shift for teachers in how they use time with their students. "I think there is a long process of getting used to it. I've been talking to the staff about scheduling since January." To encourage the staff to consider scheduling possibilities, Olson has been presenting different ideas. "I try to take them way out on the edge, and then they come back to a middle ground." One model about which Olson asked them to think was the staff preparing and eating lunch with the students every day. This was an obvious violation of the teacher contract. Yet it encouraged the teachers to think about the possibility, and they soon began to say that they might like to eat lunch with the students once every two weeks. "In scheduling," Olson says, "I ask them to consider things I don't even think are possible, just to get them thinking about it. As a result, they begin to have their own creative ideas."

Drawing by Massimilian Cipullo, a student at the School for the Physical City in New York, for the Our City, Ourselves learning expedition.

"My January Happens in October"
A Look at Multi-Year Teaching

by Meg Campbell and Emily Cousins

Teachers and students working together over multi-year cycles is one of the key components of Expeditionary Learning. It has been used successfully in a number of schools across America, including the Waldorf School, where students stay with the same teacher for eight years. It has also been very successful at the Koln-Holweide School in Cologne, Germany, where students and teachers stay together for grades 5-10.

The idea holds tremendous appeal for parents, who note, for example, that they would not want to change their children's pediatrician each year, and for students who welcome stronger relationships with teachers who know them well. Another appeal of multi-year teaching is that it can be implemented without additional cost to the district or school.

Successful multi-year teaching requires a significant paradigm shift on the part of teachers who no longer view themselves primarily as a "second-grade teacher" or as "tenth-grade biology teachers." Several Expeditionary Learning Teacher Advisory Board members are currently involved in multi-year teaching. In recent interviews, every one told us this was an excellent way to teach. Susan Sanchez, a teacher at the Memorial Spalding School in Newton Center, Massachusetts, explained, "If you put children first, if you understand your job to be the education of children, to help them learn and for them to teach you, having a child twice allows you to do just that and more."

Here are some of the elements that make multi-year teaching so successful and rewarding.

❖ **Fosters a Climate of Trust and Friendship**

One of the most significant advantages of multi-year teaching is the level of trust that is built over time. Instead of experiencing the confusion of adjustment every year, students become familiar with one teacher and one peer group. Lynn Talamini-Hervey, an elementary teacher in Peacham, Vermont, said her students know her so well they can say, "Look at her face; she wants you to stop doing that." Students become accustomed to working with classmates with many styles of learning. Instead of being pressured to compete, they are encouraged to respect and help one another.

◆ ◆ ◆

The idea holds tremendous appeal for parents, who note, for example, that they would not want to change their children's pediatrician each year.

◆ ◆ ◆

This kind of consistency is helpful for all students, especially those who may need extra support. Alma Wright teaches at the William Trotter School in Roxbury, Massachusetts. Many of her students have numerous baby-sitters and attend day care centers. She believes that multi-year teaching provides needed continuity and stability. "They know when they go home at the end of the year that they will be coming back to the same teacher. And it is not the anxiety of 'what's my teacher going to be like? What classroom am I going to be in?' which a lot of young children have."

When teachers and students remain together for an extended period of time, they can work together to create a constructive social environment. Ms. Sanchez explained that in multi-year settings, "social interactions, good or bad, are ironed out. If there is a clique, you can deal with it. But if that clique keeps getting hidden and remixed every year, you don't deal with it as well." Ms. Wright noted that

"I have a few students who are not really on grade level who probably could be disruptive because they just can't follow along, but I pair them up with a second grader so when they really have problems I can say to the second grader, 'Would you help him along,' or 'Will you help me keep her on task.' I found that to be very helpful because it gives the second graders some responsibility and it gives the first grader an older sibling to help them out."

❖ Increases Student Achievement and Depth of Study

The cycle of multi-year teaching allows teachers and students to get deeply involved in learning projects. Paul Thompson of the Blackstone Elementary School in Boston asked, "You know how in January students start taking off academically? In the second year, my January happens in October. After a few weeks of getting reacquainted, we get right down to work." Projects can get to deeper levels, since all the students share a base knowledge and experience from the previous year. In their first year, Mr. Thompson's students learned about whale migration. In their second year together, they studied whales again on a more sophisticated level.

Many multi-year classrooms are also multi-grade, and Ms. Talamini-Hervey found that "learning happens at a more rapid rate in mixed-age groups." Because multi-year teachers are so familiar with their students' abilities, they can set appropriately challenging standards for them. Older students are expected to use their skills to tackle increasingly difficult projects. Younger students are expected to learn from the quality of the older students' work. In a multi-year classroom, students learn not only by being exposed to various content areas, but also by being in an environment that encourages every student to do what is challenging and rigorous for him or herself.

❖ Fosters Students' Character Development

Since students in a multi-year environment work with a wide range of ages and abilities, they begin to accept and nurture one another. Ms. Talamini-Hervey explained, "If someone can't do something, it is accepted that they are just not on that level yet. Students aren't allowed to say 'You can't do this because you are too young.' They don't call each other 'baby.' If someone is crying, it is because they are upset, not because they are a 'baby.'"

This kind of acceptance and trust encourages children to reach out, take risks, and discover abilities they might not even have known they had. Ms. Talamini-Hervey gave the example of a learning-disabled third grader who was exhilarated by helping a first grader learn to read. Ms. Wright said that collaborative learning in her classroom "allows students who might in no other way become a leader to say 'I know something this child doesn't know and I can show them how to do it.'" Over an extended period of time, this kind of confidence and personal achievement can open the doors to academic growth.

❖ Encourages Teacher Renewal and Accountability for Student Performance

Teachers who have never done multi-year teaching are often concerned about the work load, yet none of the experienced teachers with whom we spoke found this to be a problem. Rather, they saw the challenge of keeping their students engaged over a long period of time as a means of staying refreshed and interested. Ms. Sanchez said, "I knew I couldn't do certain things the same way, because the newness was lost. And I wanted to keep those kids who figured they knew it already coming back. I wanted to keep open a new level of enthusiasm. Did I have to do that? Probably, for my own sanity. I have to change in order to like things."

Teachers said their investment in their students increases over time. Their commitment grows out of the relationships they establish with the students and out of the awareness that they are responsible for a considerable amount of their students' education. Not only does this encourage teachers to strive for more from themselves, but it also encourages them to collaborate and support one another. Every teacher with whom we spoke appreciated the added assistance and sharing of ideas that occur among teachers in multi-year schools.

❖ Strengthens Parent/Teacher Communication

Just as multi-year teaching strengthens the relationship between teacher and student, it also strengthens communication between teacher and parent. Teachers said they felt more comfortable talking to parents about their children since their observations came from a significant and extended relationship with the children. In turn, parents respected the teachers' comments because they realized how well the teachers knew their children.

◆ ◆ ◆

> Projects can get to deeper levels, since all the students share a base knowledge and experience from the previous year.

◆ ◆ ◆

❖ Encourages Multiple Routes to Knowledge

The teachers with whom we spoke said the longer they work with the same children, the better they understand the students' learning styles. The teacher can then shape and focus the curriculum so that it allows for multiple routes to knowledge and is appropriate for all students. The special attention given to multiple learning styles gives more children the opportunity to succeed. Teachers can slow down the pace for learning-disabled students or increase the challenge for gifted students.

Ms. Talamini-Hervey asked her first and second graders to solve a math problem by taking it apart and dramatizing it. The student who got the right answer was a first grader who normally wouldn't have understood the problem, but because she was a visual learner, she figured out the problem as soon as she saw it acted out. This kind of success gives students the confidence they need to face greater challenges.

The awareness of individual learning styles is especially important in cases where students have special needs. Paul Thompson gave the example of a special needs student he has had for three years. Paul said in another environment, the student would have easily fallen through the cracks, but since Paul had the time to understand the way he learns, his needs are now being met.

Drawing by Andrew Stratton, a fourth grader at Bryant Elementary School in Dubuque, Iowa, for the All Creatures Great and Functional learning expedition.

Part Six
Standards and Assessment

Beginning the Conversation
Assessment in Learning Expeditions

by Mieko Kamii and Marie Keem

This article is intended as a point of departure for an extended conversation on assessment in the context of Expeditionary Learning. The approach we want to develop is one that generates information which is useful to both students and teachers; that directs students toward improved performance and further learning; and that assists teachers in making instructional decisions supportive of students' growth.

Assessments should be opportunities to think and to learn as well as to demonstrate acquisition of significant knowledge and skills (Wolf, 1990). They should be conceived of as guided learning activities whose goals are to assist students and teachers in developing deeper understandings of what good works are. Assessments provide students with direction in how they might achieve such measures of excellence as writing powerful essays, and solving and explaining solutions to complex quantitative problems. This stands in sharp contrast to the view of assessment as a "test" or post hoc event whose primary purpose is to rank students along a continuum.

Meaningful assessments of student work involve critique and discussion, revision, and reflection by both students and teachers. It is in the context of "critique sessions" that students and teachers have a chance to talk about the strengths and weaknesses of particular pieces of work: Which aspects of the story, lab report, solution, or drawing were strong, effective, informative, pleasing; what parts seemed troublesome, confusing, misleading?

As discussions of strengths and weaknesses progress, performance standards—what makes for quality work—become evident to all conversational participants: What was it about the story that kept you attentive (and where did you get confused)? Which parts of the lab report would you would like to reproduce (and which seemed unnecessary)? Why was that solution to the math problem clever (and what parts of the explanation were muddled)? What makes the drawing feel well balanced (and which elements are puzzling)?

Discussions such as these, focused on specific performances or pieces of work, enable students to become analytical about their own and others' work and to build an understanding of criteria and standards.

A key element of this approach to assessment is revision. Students must be given opportunities to compose drafts, give and receive feedback on them, and then revise their works so that they may reconsider, experiment, try new ideas, and progress toward the high standards set by the community.

Assessments should be opportunities to think and to learn as well as to demonstrate acquisition of significant knowledge and skills.

Finally, a rich approach to assessment involves reflection, the capacity to distance oneself from one's own work, to evaluate the responses offered by others, and to take responsibility for the decisions about where to take the work next and when it is finished. Teachers, too, must give themselves opportunities to reflect on how students are meeting, exceeding,

Note: The ideas outlined in this paper draw on presentations made at a recent conference on assessment sponsored by Performance Assessment Collaboratives for Education (PACE) at Harvard University.

References: Wolf, D. P. (1990). "Assessment as an Episode of Learning." In R. Bennet and W. Ward (Eds.). *Construction vs. Choice in Cognitive Measurement.* Hillside, NJ: Lawrence Earlbaum.

or falling short of expectations in specific areas to make instructional decisions and to compose periodic summary evaluations.

Here we wish to propose building an assessment system composed of four types or levels of activity: incidental/observational, ongoing, culminating, and external processes of evaluation.

❖ Incidental/Observational Assessment

One of the hallmarks of experienced teachers is that they instinctively watch to see who among their students understands or is having difficulty with whatever problem is being discussed, and what sorts of help—procedural or conceptual—specific students might need. For example, a teacher might ask his or her students for explanations of how they arrived at their solutions to a math problem and listen to students' accounts of a historical event. He or she might also confer with students about who they are as readers, as writers, as mathematicians, as historians, as artists, as athletes, and so forth. In this way teachers get a sense of the distribution of skills and attributes among their students.

> Students discuss the many characteristics of good work and go on to identify specific examples of them.

However, we need to go beyond "everyday awareness" by refining observational skills and recording what children are doing, asking, and feeling, in addition to how they are responding to various tasks and situations. This is vitally important in tailoring expeditions to meet students' specific learning needs. In this sense, assessment is an important learning experience for teachers.

Example 1

A teacher with highly developed observational skills shared the following example of notes she made on a kindergarten student, Dan. The teacher documented Dan's progress in a variety of areas over the entire school year and used her notes as the basis for discussions with Dan's parents and with his teacher for the next year. The following is an excerpt from her notes about Dan's progress in literacy.

Literacy

9-92 Dan writes his first name, using mostly capital letters.

11-92 Dan can identify most of the upper case letters and some of the lower case letters (h,t,l,m,f,s). Through Dan's journal writing I can see that he is putting sounds and letters together.

He surprised me when he spelled the word "bat" for me during his first selection from his journal for his portfolio. I was thrilled when he talked so freely about his work. I can tell that he prefers small group settings at this time.

1-93 Dan chose a book to enter into his journal. He loved the idea of being the author and illustrator. He is writing his name using fewer capital letters but still reverts back sometimes. I think the title of Dan's book showed a lot of creativity.

Dan thoroughly enjoyed the unit on Ezra Jack Keats and even chose a picture of Willie, a character in Keats' book, to include in his journal.

3-93 Dan recognizes all letters and knows beginning letter sounds. He can use inventive spelling but rarely takes the time unless he is asked a specific question. Dan now shares stories and other treasures in small or large groups.

5-93 Dan now completes sentences with minimal assistance. He enjoys stories and will supply a missing word. Dan did a great job on beginning and ending sounds on his last portfolio entry from his journal.

He wrote his letters for me. There were some reversals and a few omissions. I believe he got tired at the end because there were errors that he usually does not make.

These records of initial evaluation and progress are culled from many situations and reflect deep understanding of what Dan was working on and why certain acquisitions represented progress. Finally, they provide a clear sense of Dan's development and emerging skills, as well as insight into how a portfolio or journal might serve to record growth across particular content areas.

Two students from the Rafael Hernandez Bilingual School in Boston observe the specimen that they gathered for their learning expedition on pond life. Photograph by Brian Smith/NASDC.

❖ Ongoing Assessment

Ongoing assessment is an arrangement of pauses in the forward momentum of the expedition so that students and teachers can get their bearings. It is intended to help students see their own progress and receive feedback on their work from the teacher and other students. Ongoing assessment is different from incidental/observational assessment in that the students are actively engaged in the assessment process, the discussion is focused on specific aspects of the activities and interactions in the classroom, and there is discussion of standards.

A variety of activities can be used for ongoing assessment: short essays done as homework and then shared with the group; a planned project designed to involve individual and group work; or one of many other possibilities. Their nature as assessments stems from several characteristics. First, there is explicit discussion of standards. Students discuss the many characteristics of good work and go on to identify specific examples of them. Second, students evaluate their own work and the work of others relative to the standards, pointing out to one another where a given work might be revised. Third, there is discussion of expectations and whether a student has met, exceeded, or fallen short of them.

Example 2

W. Leo Snow's middle school expedition, *Crossing Cultural Bridges: The Search for Tsali on the Trail of Tears* (found in Expeditionary Learning's *Book of Exemplars*) provides an example of opportunities for ongoing assessment. As part of a year of discovery which included trips to interview various authorities, examine authentic artifacts, and contemplate the terrain through which both soldiers and Native Americans had tramped, each student wrote a "novella." These were continuing letters surrounding the student's imaginary role during the removal of the Cherokee from North Carolina to Oklahoma in the 1830s. The students enriched and extended their knowledge by writing themselves into the history they were studying. Each shared his or her work with the class.

This is an example of an activity that has rich assessment possibilities. Settings of this kind are an opportunity for students to engage in serious discussion, to think about what they know (and don't know), to revise their writing, and to critique their own and other students' work. Implicit in this examination and reconsideration of work is refinement and consolidation of students' knowledge of the historical situation and events. An entry from one novella is given below. To turn this activity into an assessment, the teacher would establish a classroom culture of constructive critique and revision in which one would look for the kinds of observations and questions which follow the entry.

Chapter 6

Dear Wind In Her Hair,
Hi! Have you heard the news about Tsali and his family? If you haven't I'll tell you.
One day William Holland Thomas met up with Tsali somehow, and told him (Tsali) that he might as well forget trying to hide from the soldiers and just give himself up.
Well, that's when I come in. I was in the woods gathering food, for the next couple of days, and I came to camp to simply rest. When I saw we had company, I turned arond [sic] and ran as fast as I could back towards the mountains where Euchella lived. I know I would be safe there if only Euchella would except [sic] me.
Well, I went to Clingman's Dome and nobody was there, so I claimed the cave as my own. To this day I still dwell there. My only fear is that one day one of Euchella's Indians will come back and find me there. Hope your life is going well. Write back soon, okay?
Love, Falling Leaf

Positive observations: (1) This entry uses a lot of historical detail. (2) The author is able to mentally put himself or herself into the situation, thereby helping the reader imagine being in that time and place.

Questions/critique: (1) To what extent does the author understand the historical detail to which she or he refers? (2) A person actually writing this letter would have more to say about Euchella and Thomas because they were key figures. Their names were loaded with significance and no doubt conjured up many associations, thoughts, and feelings that the student could have accessed through the same kind of historical imagining that is evident in the third paragraph.

❖ Culminating Assessment

Culminating assessments are opportunities for re-examination and closure which build on learnings acquired through incidental/observational and ongoing assessments. As the expedition crescendos to its final moment, there is a need to match that finale with a grand review and demonstration of accomplishment. Students need to evaluate where they stand with respect to the different domains explored, making connections across disciplines and possibly with contemporary concerns in the local, national, and world communities.

The purpose of assessment is to help students understand the standards of quality performances, appreciate the many faces of excellence, and develop ways to improve their work.

This activity is intended to serve both those inside and outside the classroom. Revisiting the activities of the expedition highlights milestones for those intimately involved in the process and sends a solid message about achievement to parents, administrators, and the community at large.

Example 3

We present another aspect of W. Leo Snow's work and highlight its possibilities for culminating assessment. Mr. Snow's students produced and sold a magazine entitled *Cherokee Life*. It contained reports on important personalities and events relevant to the removal of the Cherokee along with summaries of several trips and interviews which took place during the expedition. To fund the magazine, the students sold advertising space, designing the ads themselves.

The production of *Cherokee Life* was an activity ripe for employment as a culminating assessment. Without a doubt, the students had to revisit many aspects across the entire learning experience. If we could sit in on one of the many production/editing meetings as outside observers, we would hope to see the students actually reading each other's work critically and offering positive comments and suggestions with reference to all of the knowledge that the expedition uncovered. These kinds of activities would offer evidence that serious assessment, with multiple references to criteria and standards, was integral to the culminating activity.

Guiding students through a process of review creates a foundation for returning to the lessons of the whole expedition and using them as the basis for assessment. The students could brainstorm a list of the topics and ways of thinking which they had explored. If the list were placed on the wall, its constant presence in the students' meetings would provide a tangible and readily available thinking tool to use as a springboard and to weave throughout discussions.

Another form which review might take could be a discussion based on the map which one student drew for the Cherokee banquet placemats. In creating that map, one student was remembering and reviewing the entire expedition. Having a whole class discussion around the map would create an opportunity for all participants to review the journey.

The process of expedition review should be the prelude for an atmosphere of productive final evaluation. *Cherokee Life* magazine would be an example of a culminating product that had its roots in assessment if its production included serious review followed by critique and revision of work. An honest assessment of a student report would therefore probe its connections to several different points and themes in the expedition, explore ideas for clarifying those ties, and include references to model work.

❖ External Assessment

External assessment processes consist of student presentations of their work to outside audiences, including members of a receiving community (for example, teachers in the students' next school), external review committees, and panels composed of community members. Presentations made to such groups allow students to hear the responses of a wider discourse community and think about the sorts of questions they raise. From the perspective of accountability to the entire school community, district, and state, such forms of external assessment can play a critical validating role.

❖ Continuing the Conversation

We recognize that each of the examples we shared provides only one window into this house we are building together. We will add to the corpus in subsequent issues of *The Web*. In closing, let us remind ourselves of the primary audiences and purposes of assessment: "to make students and teachers acute critics of the quality of work and able discussants of what should count as excellence (Wolf, 1990)."

Learning is not simply a matter of additively acquiring bits of information from external sources but rather of making sense of that information for oneself. From this perspective, the purpose of assessment is to help students understand the standards of quality performances, appreciate the many faces of excellence, and develop ways to improve their work.

No More Mysteries

by Mieko Kamii and Marie Keem

These are the voices of students confronting the mystery of standards: A second grader wonders aloud, "What should I do in the next draft of my story to make it better?" A cluster of sixth and seventh graders implores, "You want us to do this project as a group, but how do you expect us to contribute equally?" A tenth grader puzzles over why her latest biology lab report was marked "good" when the one before it was "excellent," and how she will explain to her best friend why his analytic essay in history was "good" while hers was "excellent."

These commonplace questions are the key to a grand mystery: What are the standards, expectations, and criteria by which work is judged, and what pathways lead to achieving high standards and one's personal best? Questions about "Why did I get ... ?" and "How can I do better ... ?" reveal the web of connections to larger issues of standards, assessment, and instruction: What makes work "good," "better," and "best"? How do we guide students toward achieving standards of excellence? Our goal is to transform the mysterious and inaccessible into everyday tools of teaching and learning.

◆ ◆ ◆

> Whereas assessment once took place in silent testing rooms, it now takes place in the midst of productive discussion.

◆ ◆ ◆

Let us begin with our second grade author who is poised to do another draft of her story but is uncertain about what she should do to improve it. Before answering her, we have a prior task, and that is to be clear about what our aspirations for her are. They may include the following:

- ◆ We want her to be able to write a story that is comprehensible and appealing to her peers, her parents, her teacher, and other interested people.
- ◆ We want her to develop the vocabulary and ideas that will help her understand and manipulate the elements of a story.
- ◆ We want her to be able to provide constructive criticism for the stories of her peers, and we want her to be able to receive and evaluate constructive criticism from them.
- ◆ We want her to try her hardest and to experience success. We want her to be proud of her finished work and the effort she has expended to produce it.

Considerations such as these are the foundation of standards: what we want our students to know and to be able and be disposed to do.

Once we articulate our goals and standards to ourselves, drawing on the work done at district, state, and national levels, we are in a position to discuss them very explicitly with students. The tenth grader's perplexity over why particular exercises are "good" or "excellent" should be removed when students become conversational partners in the discussion of standards, sharing their reactions, questions, suggestions, and even challenges to expectations. Whereas assessment once took place in silent testing rooms and at the teachers' desks, it now takes place in the midst of lively, productive discussion.

Invitations for conversation can take place in whole class, small group, and individual teacher-student conferences. The teacher might ask the entire class, "What else do you want to learn about or learn how to do? What else do you want to work on? Why is that important or useful?" In individual conferences the teacher might ask, "Why do you like this? What were you thinking of when you did it? Now that we've talked about this, is there anything you want to change?"

Through these discussions students can develop ownership of the standards: They come to understand as a class, and in terms of their own work, what makes student work "good," "better," and "best." Because the standards are explicit, subject to discussion, repeatedly referred to, and used, the shroud of mystery is finally removed.

Our next major task is to give the standards clear, demonstrable meaning by embodying them in classroom practice. We must think through the educational experiences we provide so that we can put success within students' reach. Standards are clear in classrooms where a "culture of revision" has been fostered. Creating the expectation that many, if not most, pieces of student work will undergo multiple drafts—because no one is able to do his or her best on the first try—leads to an ethic that supports the excellence which our standards envision: "In this class we work hard on developing interesting characters and plots for our stories," or "In this class we try hard to be polite to each other." These attitudes are the building blocks of a climate in which sustained work and high standards become the norm, and in which successive iterations of discussing, conferring, critiquing, and reflecting become standard practice. There is explicit emphasis on effort, perseverance, and doing one's personal best. There are multiple opportunities to place success within students' reach.

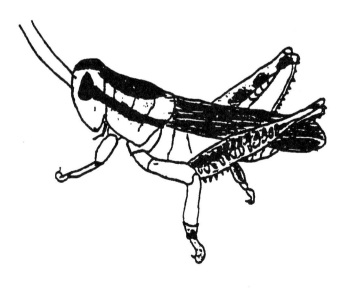

Spur-Throated Grasshopper, by Sara Horstmann, from the Heron Pond Field Guide made by Nancy Skaife's fifth-grade class at the Bryant Elementary School in Dubuque, Iowa.

◆ ◆ ◆

Just as students have to be taught how to use library resources, they must be taught how to critique each other's work.

◆ ◆ ◆

Creating such a culture poses new instructional challenges. We must provide multiple opportunities for children to learn from a variety of sources: through peer critique sessions; from models and exemplars; in one-on-one teacher-student conferences; through the use of library and community resources; and so forth. Here we highlight just one of these activities, the critique session. It is modeled on practices that have been used in the studio arts for a long time but are relatively rare in other classroom contexts.

Just as students have to be taught how to use library resources, they must be taught how to critique each other's work. Critique sessions are an important form of ongoing assessment, and teaching students how to participate in them is one of many instructional answers to the question of how we can guide our students toward the achievement of high standards. Ron Berger, a sixth-grade teacher in Shutesbury, Massachusetts, recently described the format he uses in teaching his students the structure and routine of critique sessions. First, students' work is pinned up for everyone to see (or the functional equivalent—stories are read aloud, science experiments are described). Each student explains her work—what she is trying to achieve, what she likes about it, or what she is having trouble with. Unlike some studios, however, Berger's sessions teach students a set of procedural rules.

◆ Students must begin their commentary with something positive ("I like ...," "I wish ...," "I noticed ...").
◆ In order for commentary to be constructive, it must be specific. Therefore statements must refer to particular aspects of the work under discussion ("I like the dialogue between Bob and the shopkeeper, after Bob returned from

his game," or "I noticed you got good balance by using a really bright color in the upper left. Otherwise that big thing on the lower right would sink the picture.").

- "Put-downs" are taboo. Students are instructed to use "I" phrases and not "you" phrases in offering criticism: "I wish you had ...," not "you didn't ..." The class also discusses and avoids nonverbal ways of putting people down, including using acceptable words but delivering them in a sneering or hostile tone of voice.

◆ ◆ ◆

> Students come to understand as a class, and in terms of their own work, what makes student work "good," "better," and "best."

◆ ◆ ◆

Berger teaches these routines through modeling. At the beginning of the year he creates a large piece of work in which he has deliberately included some good and some problematic features. He goes through the process of explaining what he is working on and what he is having trouble with, eliciting and commenting on students' positive and negative statements along the way. In the next day or two he appears in class with revision in hand, drafted on the basis of comments he had received from the students. He reports that his students are always amazed!

Berger encourages students to use technical terms appropriate to the particular subject in their critiques, words such as "dialogue," "humor," and "symbolism," when responding to a written story, and "control," "variable," and "data" in reacting to a lab report. Critique sessions are opportunities for students to use these terms in a richly embedded context. By using and hearing others use them, students clarify and deepen their understandings of the discipline-based ideas or concepts they signal. This is but one way in which assessment becomes "an episode of learning" (Wolf, 1990).

Ken Lindsay, a fourth-grade teacher in the same school, teaches techniques associated with critique—how to ask a question, what kinds of things to ask about, the words to use—through example. Sitting right alongside his students, he becomes a participant in whole-class critique sessions, raising his hand to be called on by a student reader and then using the same format of "I thought I heard you say ..." that he expects his students to use.

A drawing by a sixth grader at King Middle School in Portland, Maine, for a learning expedition that included children's books. Photograph by Scott Hartl/ Expeditionary Learning.

The use of this particular phrase points to an interesting difference between sixth and fourth graders, and Lindsay's solution to the problem it presents. Fourth graders are less adept at quickly focusing collectively on the same passage, issue, or detail than older children. To help focus the whole group's attention on the same feature, while leaving the child who is leading the session still in charge, Lindsay has instituted the practice of asking everyone to preface his or her commentary with "I thought I heard you say ..." to draw the group's attention to the same place. Thus during critique sessions, Lindsay prefaces his own responses with, "I thought I heard you say ..." In this there is an inherent message of care, respect, consideration, and conscious effort, attitudes which are valued in his classroom.

◆ ◆ ◆

Creating the expectation that most pieces of student work will undergo multiple drafts supports the excellence which our standards envision.

◆ ◆ ◆

These examples illustrate the connections among standards, assessment, and instruction. Standards without assessments are empty; standards divorced from instruction are superfluous; assessments separated from instruction and standards are invalid. A school that sets high standards and that commits itself to ensuring that all students will achieve them necessarily involves itself in challenging instructional and assessment issues. It takes time, effort, and enormous patience to open previously closed doors and to change habits.

❖ Conclusion

Questions of standards and what makes work "good," "better," and "best" should be a matter of classroom discourse and public discussion. By discussing work in small and large groups, observing models, analyzing examples, critiquing others' work, revising one's own work, and reflecting on the tools, processes, and products of learning, students and teachers gradually unravel the grand mystery. None of this is automatic. It involves reviewing and revising many instructional and assessment processes, teaching new vocabulary and conversational skills, and answering new questions. But these approaches hold great promise for teaching all students and for eliciting from them their very best work.

Opportunity Favors the Prepared Mind

Integrating Assessment and Curriculum

by Mieko Kamii

Traditionally, school systems have viewed the major elements of education—curriculum, instruction, and assessment—more or less as separate tasks. Curriculum specialists have been responsible for overseeing the content (scope and sequence) of instruction, reviewing textbooks and teaching materials, and helping teachers use those resources in their classrooms. Instruction has been framed as classroom delivery, as if teachers wearing familiar brown uniforms alighted daily from their UPS trucks bearing curriculum packages for their students' consumption. Textbooks and "teacher-proof" exercises left little room for imagination, for wonder, or for the excitement of constructing new knowledge and understanding. At the classroom level, assessment has been viewed primarily in terms of quizzes, tests, and other post-hoc activities designed to "measure" what students have learned but whose main function has been to rank students' performances against those of their classmates (grading). At the district and state levels, assessment has been the bailiwick of measurement experts, attending more to legislators' cries for accountability than matters of teaching and learning.

The justification for this division of labor is that it helped bring expertise to bear on each task. Yet it inevitably produces a fragmented view of each child. And frankly, it denies to teachers one of the more exciting adventures in our profession, the opportunity to spend time thinking about the mysteries and complexities of how children learn and what they ought to study. After all, college teachers design their own syllabi; why shouldn't classroom teachers be doing the same thing? And if we take seriously concepts such as "educating the whole child" and "valuing individual student progress," then we ought to reunite these tasks in earnest.

In Expeditionary Learning's design, teachers are assuming more and more of these critical responsibilities. Teachers are becoming curriculum designers by creating their own learning expeditions. Teachers are breaking from the mold of brown-suited, stand-in-front-of-the-class instructors by becoming expeditionary guides. And assessment is becoming an integral part of instruction.

> Once the unity between assessment and instruction is grasped, teachers no longer have to view one as taking time away from the other.

The starting point in all of this is the determination of appropriate standards. The impetus for NASDC's schools projects was a concern for elevating performance among all of our nation's students by elevating performance standards. At this juncture, talk about curriculum content and student performance standards is noisy and messy. It is messy because the standards—specifications of the kinds of knowledge and range of skills every child should acquire, and at what level of proficiency, by the time he or she leaves high school—are not self-evident, not constant and invariable, not easily composed or prescribed. We will return to the subject of standards in a future *Web* article. For the moment, we would call attention to the work on national curriculum standards and state curriculum frameworks being proposed by various professional associations (for example, *Curriculum and Evaluation Standards for School Mathematics,* by the National Council of Teachers of Mathematics, *Mathematics Framework for California Public Schools,* published by the California Department of Education, and *Benchmarks for Science Literacy, Project 2061* of the American Association for the Advancement of Science). These documents are valuable resources for developing learning expeditions, providing new perspectives on essential ideas and categories of knowledge and skills, and suggesting ways of approaching their study in real world contexts.

However messy and noisy the discourse on standards is at the moment, we know that whatever standards we settle on, students will approach them at different paces and along paths that will in some measure reflect their individual personalities, backgrounds, learning styles, and interests. No student is going to develop her capacities so effortlessly that she reaches high levels of performance rapidly. (Indeed, if a significant number of students do achieve success by our standards after only one try, we're obviously under-challenging them.) Consequently, successive stages of evaluation and revision will be part and parcel of learning for all students, and this perspective needs to underpin the curriculum.

As it turns out, the successive efforts at evaluation and revision are also what teachers will be using as a basis of their assessment of students. Hence, the business of building assessment into the curriculum is identical to building education into the curriculum. It is time to banish the old image of assessment—herding children into a room, having them spend an hour or two filling out sheets, as if the whole experience were divorced from the rest of their education. Assessment should and can be less stressful for students and teachers. Assessment should and can be "an episode of learning" (Wolf, 1990). But to make it so, teachers need to anticipate the assessment process and integrate it into their curriculum and instruction.

Consider as an example a hypothetical expedition to a small woodland pond. The fifth graders at the Table Mound and Bryant Elementary Schools in Dubuque undertook an expedition of this sort. Let's imagine, as in the Dubuque case, that one product of the expedition will be a field guide generated by the students, cataloguing the wildlife found there. Such an expedition already has the potential for integrating a variety of academic subjects, including science (plant and animal classification methods), art (illustrations for the field guide), and mathematics (observations about plant and animal species per square meter).

The question is, in thinking about such an expedition as part of a curriculum, what specific features might be folded in to anticipate and serve the process of assessment, to yield an integrated expedition? Let's consider just one aspect of the project, the students' artwork illustrations for a field guide.

A display from the Teaching Museum created by fifth graders at the Rafael Hernandez Bilingual School in Boston for a learning expedition on Native American cultures. Photograph by Harold Bingham/Expeditionary Learning.

Assessment presumes some standard of achievement appropriate for the age group. But not all teachers will be Cezannes. Therefore, when thinking about an expedition to a pond, teachers need to think in advance about "How am I, as teacher, going to assess my students' art work—are there things that I, the teacher, need to know about techniques of artistry?" Moreover, an important part of instruction will be to have students articulate, think about, and weigh these standards through discussions among themselves. So curriculum and instruction planning also needs to anticipate how these matters will be conveyed to students.

Provoked to thought about such things, a teacher might include a segment in the learning expedition that would expose the students to Audubon's sketchbooks or Roger Tory Peterson's guides to birds. These great works serve as exemplars or models of excellence and can help provoke conversations among students about which features make one drawing more successful than another. Or perhaps a segment would be included in which a local artist would visit the class and talk with students about how they would go about sketching and then elaborating their drawings: What do they think about? Where do they focus their attention? What sorts of techniques do they use? How do they go about assessing their works-in-progress, self-correcting, and revising the images on the page?

For older children, discussions of drawing might include consideration of the techniques of bringing perspective into an illustration, which naturally would draw in consideration of such math topics as geometric angles, ratios, fractional relationships, and scale.

◆ ◆ ◆

An important part of instruction will be to have students articulate, think about, and weigh standards through discussion among themselves.

◆ ◆ ◆

Producing a field guide means making certain that the distinctive characteristics of plants or animals are highlighted, which naturally leads the students into thinking about those features that are distinctive among plants that otherwise seem to have so much in common—that is, it draws them into the method of plant and animal classification in the natural sciences.

In sum, such an expedition is potentially rich in integrated instructional opportunities, as well as opportunities for assessment of student progress in a variety of academic areas. Hence Expeditionary Learning's encouragement to teachers, to envision and anticipate assessment as an integrated element of all that goes on in the classroom and beyond. Well-designed support for learning and occasions for assessment necessitate building into the curriculum time for discussions, critique sessions, and conferences, and very important, time for individual reflection in between these assessment activities. It is in the act of reflecting on others' comments about one's own work and revising it, and repeating this cycle as many times as it takes for students to feel they have done their very best work, that standards rise and all students' work becomes better. The attractiveness of this model is that once the unity between assessment and instruction is grasped, teachers no longer have to feel tensions between the two, or view one as taking time away from the other.

As in all things, opportunity favors the prepared mind. We must think as deeply as we can about the possibilities for integrated instruction which inhere in our learning expeditions. We must cross the disciplinary boundaries of our own schooling, and put aside the images of teaching so deeply embedded in our own experiences and memories. We must open our classroom doors and reach out to others who have expertise to share both with us and our students. We must anticipate as best we can how much time to allot for different kinds of learning activities, so that students will receive rich and ample feedback on their work and will be motivated to do multiple drafts. We must welcome review by community members outside the school building for the perspective they can provide on how well we and our students are doing in this enterprise called education, to which we are so deeply committed. We must prepare our minds well so that we can provide students with opportunities for achieving the measure of excellence and success they are capable of producing and experiencing. And we must take pride in the struggles we engage in to achieve these ends.

Outward Bound Resources

Expeditionary Learning Outward Bound
122 Mount Auburn Street
Cambridge, MA 02138
617-576-1260 (phone)
617-576-1340 (fax)
info@elob.ci.net (e-mail)

Harvard/Outward Bound Project in Experience-Based Education
Harvard Graduate School of Education
Gutman Library, 4th Floor
Cambridge, MA 02138
617-496-5220

Information about Outward Bound wilderness schools and urban centers may be obtained by contacting:

Outward Bound National Office
Route 9D, R2 Box 280
Garrison, NY 10524-9757
1-800-243-8520

For information about particular schools or regions, please call:

Colorado Outward Bound School
945 Pennsylvania Street
Denver, CO 80203-3198
1-800-477-2627

Hurricane Island Outward Bound School
P.O. Box 429
Rockland, ME 04841
1-800-341-1744

Hurricane Island Outward Bound School
Baltimore/Chesapeake Bay Program
1900 Eagle Drive
Baltimore, MD 21207
410-396-0813

Hurricane Island Outward Bound School
Portland Center
277 Cumberland Avenue
Portland, ME 04101
207-874-0417

New York City Outward Bound Center
140 West Street, Suite 2626
New York, NY 10007
1-212-608-8899

North Carolina Outward Bound School
121 North Sterling Street
Morganton, NC 28655-3443
1-800-841-0186

North Carolina Outward Bound School
Atlanta Center
320 North McDonough Street
Decatur, GA 30030
404-378-0494

Pacific Crest Outward Bound School
0110 SW Bancroft Street
Portland, OR 97201
1-800-547-3312

Thompson Island Outward Bound
    Education Center
P.O. Box 127
Boston, MA 02127-0002
617-328-3900

Voyageur Outward Bound School
111 Third Avenue South
Minneapolis, MN 55401-2551
1-800-328-2943